An Illustrated History of

SOUTHERN PULL-PUSH STOCK

Frontispiece Ex-LBSCR driving brake third No 3821 of set 726, seen at the rear of an Exeter–Salisbury local service at Axminster in 1959, wearing British Railways crimson lake livery. Its pull-push days are over and the coach ran for a year or two as a conventional locomotive-hauled vehicle, often coupled to a reframed LSWR third, as seen here. *R. C. Riley*

An Illustrated History of
SOUTHERN PULL-PUSH STOCK

Mike King

An imprint of
Ian Allan Publishing

Contents

Author's Notes and Acknowledgements		5
Bibliography		6
1.	General Introduction and Overview	7
2.	Routes and Operation	16
3.	Railmotors and Railcars	26
4.	LSWR Vestibule Stock	33
5.	LSWR Bogie 'Block' Sets	46
6.	LSWR Non-corridor Stock	55
7.	LSWR Corridor Stock	71
8.	LBSCR 'Balloon' Stock	81
9.	LBSCR Arc-roofed Stock	94
10.	SER and LCDR Stock	117
11.	SECR Railmotor Sets	126
12.	SECR Non-Corridor Stock	130
13.	SR Maunsell Stock	144
14.	Air-control Vans	149
Appendices		
1.	Memorandum of Meeting at Grosvenor Road, 22 November 1928	154
2.	Railmotor and Railcar Halts	157
3.	Summary of Southern Railway Pull-Push Sets	159

First published 2006

ISBN (10) 0 86093 596 5
ISBN (13) 978 0 86093 596 4

Published by Ian Allan Publishing

an imprint of Ian Allan Publishing Ltd, Hersham, Surrey KT12 4RG.
Printed in England by Ian Allan Printing Ltd, Hersham, Surrey KT12 4RG.

Code: 0611/A3

Visit the Ian Allan Publishing website at www.ianallanpublishing.com

Front cover: Pull-push set No 31 enters Medstead & Four Marks with a Winchester-Alton service on 8 May 1955. The leading coach is ex-SECR and replaced the original LSWR driving car in 1951. Class M7 0-4-4T No 30480 is at the rear. *R. C. Riley*

Back cover, top: Class M7 No 30328 stands between duties at Brockenhurst on 15 August 1959. The stock consists of an 'Ironclad' pull-push set with an SECR ten-compartment strengthener as the leading vehicle. *G. W. Powell, courtesy R. C. Riley*

Back cover, bottom: Following a brief station stop at Medstead & Four Marks, 'M7' No 30480 propels the train onwards towards Alton on 8 May 1955. *R. C. Riley*

Author's Notes and Acknowledgements

When the first electric trams and motor buses took to the roads over 100 years ago, few would have predicted the effect this might have on our railway network. However, within just a few years the trams in particular had siphoned off much town and inner city traffic and, before long, motor buses started to do the same in the suburbs and country districts. The railways had to fight back and, starting in 1903, the LSWR embarked on a programme of construction of steam railmotors, in an attempt to provide cheap and frequent competitive services. The other Southern constituent companies soon followed their lead, some experimenting as well with petrol railcars. Neither proved very successful and the eventual answer was the pull-push train — combining as it did a new idea with the reliability of the existing steam locomotive and this provision would continue for almost 60 years.

For those of us who remember the traditional steam-hauled pull-push trains (as opposed to the modern diesel or electric versions), thoughts are immediately conjured up of an idyllic country branch line, so beloved of railway modellers, with leisurely timetables, an elderly tank locomotive pulling and pushing a pair of equally ancient carriages through rural parts of Britain — oh, and very few passengers! But it was not always so. When pull-push was first developed this was seen as cutting-edge technology, designed to win back traffic in cities and urban areas, not some bucolic branch line or other backwater. It did so, for a while, but finally only heavy investment in electrification would be the answer for the suburban lines. Pull-push then retreated to the countryside, to become that quintessential picture of the rural railway, now vanished for ever.

As a child your author remembers watching a BBC television children's programme — a soap in today's language — entitled *The Old Pull and Push*, in the hope of seeing some likely railway footage. There was some, but not enough for his liking as the storyline followed the characters rather than the railway itself. Ramsay Street, 1959-style set in rural Kent instead of Australia, but there could be few railway subjects of this nature that actually became television entertainment — however brief.

The Southern Railway took over 80 pull-push units in 1923, continuing to develop such services until by 1935, the total reached a maximum of 96 units. In all, some 170 pull-push sets ran on Southern metals between 1905 and 1964 and in this book, I have tried to illustrate and describe all of them, with sufficient information to enable model construction of most examples. I have indeed been fortunate in that very many enthusiasts have pointed their cameras at pull-push trains over the years and photographic coverage of all but a few early types has proved possible, and I thank all the photographers, who are individually credited where possible, but where they are not, I apologise in advance, simply because I do not know who you are.

Individually, I would like to thank (in alphabetical order) Jim Aston, Terence Barry, Richard Casserley, Phil Coutanche, the late Denis Cullum, who incidentally awakened my interest in Southern coaches, David Gould, Roger Kidner, Roger Merry-Price, the late Dick Riley, Tony Sedgwick, the late John L. Smith (of Lens of Sutton) and the Lens of Sutton Association, Gordon Weddell, the late Ted (A. E.) West, and Glen Woods.

Readers may wish to know that many more photographs of pull-push (and other SR rolling stock) are being made available by the present-day Lens of Sutton Association and further information may be obtained from them at 46 Edenhurst Road, Longbridge, Birmingham B31 4PQ.

Mike King
Woking
March 2006

Title Page Oxted station at around 4pm on Thursday 15 June 1962. Passengers await the 3.8pm Victoria–East Grinstead service, while 'H' class 0-4-4T No 31518 and Maunsell pull-push set 605 stand in the bay, to follow with the 4.4pm to Tunbridge Wells West via Hever. This scene was soon to disappear for ever, as diesel operations commenced just three days later. *L. Sandler*

Bibliography

King, M.,	*An Illustrated History of Southern Coaches,*	OPC 2003
Gould, D.,	*Maunsell's SR Steam Carriage Stock,*	Oakwood Press 2000
Gould, D.,	*Southern Railway Passenger Vans,*	Oakwood Press 1992
Gould, D.,	*Bogie Carriages of the LBSCR,*	Oakwood Press 1995
Gould, D.,	*Bogie Carriages of the SECR,*	Oakwood Press 1993
Gould, D. ,	*Carriage Stock of the SECR,*	Oakwood Press 1976
Maycock, R, & Reed, M.,	*Isle of Wight Steam Passenger Rolling Stock,*	Oakwood Press 1997
Kidner, R.,	*Southern Railway Branch Line Trains,*	Oakwood Press 1984
Kidner, R.,	*Southern Railway Branch Lines in the Thirties,*	Oakwood Press 1976
Weddell, G.,	*LSWR Carriages Volumes 1 & 2,*	Wild Swan 1992 and OPC 2001
Jenkinson, D.,	*British Railway Carriages of the 20th Century,*	PSL 1988/90 and Volumes 1 & 2, Pendragon 1996
Jenkinson, D., & Lane, B.,	*British Railcars 1900-1950,*	Atlantic 1996
Dendy-Marshall, C.,	*A History of the Southern Railway,*	Ian Allan 1968 (revised edition)
Faulkner, J.,	*The LSWR in the 20th Century,*	David & Charles 1988
Gray, A.,	*The South Eastern & Chatham Railway,*	Middleton Press 1998
Marx, K.,	*Douglas Earle Marsh — His Life & Times,*	Oakwood Press 2004
Daniels, G. and Dench, L.,	*Passengers No More,*	Ian Allan 1964
Bradley, D.,	*LSWR Locomotives* (four volumes),	Wild Swan 1985-89
Bradley, D.,	*The Locomotives of the LBSCR* (three volumes),	RCTS 1969-74
Bradley, D.,	*The Locomotives of the London Chatham and Dover Railway; South Eastern and Chatham Railway; The South Eastern Railway* (three volumes)	RCTS 1979-85
Bradley, D.,	*The Locomotives of the Southern Railway* Volume 1,	RCTS 1975

Many other individual line histories have also been consulted in an effort to ascertain the dates on which pull-push operation started and finished, together with various official documents formerly part of British Transport Historical Records and now housed as part of the National Archive at the Public Record Office, Kew. These are now filed under references RAIL 411, 414, 633, 635, 645 and 649 categories.

Chapter 1.

General Introduction and Overview

At the beginning of the 20th century the railways began to face a serious challenge to their long-held virtual transport monopoly. This challenge was to come from the roads in the form of, firstly, the electric tramcar and, secondly, the internal combustion engine. Whilst the former was already using proven technology, the latter was as yet rather too unreliable to pose a real threat to that monopoly. However, given time and technical advancement this would change out of all recognition, resulting in the now almost universal reliance on road transport that we take for granted today and that has had such a devastating effect on our railway network.

But to return to the early 1900s, the problem facing the railways was two fold. In urban areas the new electric trams and motor buses would soon provide cheap, clean and frequent services with many conveniently located stops, while in rural areas the often sparse passenger traffic was unlikely to generate sufficient revenue to cover the steadily mounting operating costs. These facts, so often exacerbated by inconveniently located stations would eventually combine to give the new motor bus operators an unassailable advantage. At the time relatively few lines were operating at a considerable loss, but with the demands for higher wages, shorter working hours and increased costs of coal, this scenario could only become more widespread. The overriding need in both instances was seen to be greater economy, coupled hopefully with only a small capital outlay. Within the London suburbs, where passenger receipts were reasonably assured, electrification was to provide the ultimate answer, but there were many secondary routes and branch lines where the volume of traffic could never hope to support such levels of investment. Here, different economic answers would have to be found.

The development of the steam railmotor — a single lightweight combined locomotive and carriage arrangement — was seen as providing the initial answer to the problem and all three major pre-Grouping constituents of the Southern Railway,

together with one of the Isle of Wight companies, experimented with such formations between 1903 and 1920. In addition, two mainland and one of the Island companies also tried the internal combustion railcar option during the same period, but it soon became obvious that further development was needed before this mode of propulsion could be relied upon to any great extent. For a while at least, petrol and diesel railcar development retreated into the background. However, just like its road-mounted counterparts, this form of power source would eventually return with an all-conquering presence.

To be fair, the steam railmotor option was only marginally more successful, but it did contribute, initially at least, to reduced operating costs and increased levels of patronage, by allowing a more frequent and cheaper service to be provided. Once achieved, however, the railmotors almost invariably lacked the necessary power to cope with the increased demand as very few were capable of hauling a trailer car, and this required the substitution of conventional locomotives and carriage stock to deal with busy periods. Any economies were thus short-lived and the railway companies were forced to think again.

The last and ultimately most successful option was the push-pull train. This utilised a conventional steam locomotive and several carriages equipped with suitable operating gear to allow the locomotive to remain coupled at one end, pulling in one direction and propelling in the other. Alternatively, the locomotive could be sandwiched in the centre with the carriages coupled on either side. The driver would travel in the leading end in each instance, so some form of communication and control mechanisms were required between the locomotive and the front of the train. This mode of operation also allowed the locomotive and carriages to be separated for maintenance purposes, thereby removing another problem encountered with the railmotors: namely that the whole unit, including the passenger portion, had to be serviced within the smoky confines of locomotive sheds, with consequent cleaning difficulties. Equally, another

Plate 1 The opposition! West Norwood tram terminus in the early years of the 20th century. A London County Council tram waits to leave for Somerset House, while on the right, beside the Thurlow Arms, is a petrol motorbus service to Hammersmith. It was the growth of such services that provoked the railways into developing steam railmotors, petrol railcars and pull-push trains. Although described as West Norwood, the location is in fact Tulse Hill. *D. Cullum collection*

Plate 2 The rural branch line idyll. Petworth station on 28 May 1950, with the 1.56pm Pulborough–Midhurst service, consisting of former LSWR corridor set 737 and an 'M7' 0-4-4 tank. Located some 1½ miles south of the town, the station stood little chance of remaining open once the local bus operators got down to business. *D. Cullum*

Plate 3 In theory, trains of up to six coaches could be operated as a pull-push 'sandwich'. In practice, this seldom occurred, but during the Kent coast flood emergency of March-May 1953 such trains provided a shuttle service between Faversham and Herne Bay. Ex-SECR steel-panelled set 663, Seaton branch strengthening coach No 1050, ex-LCDR 'R' class 0-4-4 tank No 31671 and hybrid LBSCR/SECR set 714 provide an interesting combination at Herne Bay on 19 April 1953. *D. Cullum*

locomotive could be substituted with ease and additional coaches could be added when required, although it took some time for many of the companies to correctly predict the size of locomotive most suited to the duties involved. Initially the majority of locomotive superintendents of the period managed to under estimate these requirements considerably, probably placing economy before power output.

Push-pull operation removed the need for the locomotive to run round the train at each end of the journey, thereby simplifying operating procedures and this allowed more frequent short-distance services to be provided. If necessary and if the Railway Inspectorate would approve, the train could run without a guard (as was eventually sanctioned over certain sections of line), but if not the guard could be utilised to issue tickets on board the train, allowing the provision of small, unstaffed and thus inexpensive halts along the route.

In most instances, existing locomotives and stock were converted and there were relatively few companies that invested widely in new construction specifically for push-pull trains. The London & South Western Railway (LSWR) did this in 1906–10 and 1914 only, after which all provision was made by converting existing locomotives and stock. The London, Brighton & South Coast Railway (LBSCR) built new carriages but preferred to convert existing locomotives, while the South Eastern & Chatham Railway (SECR), apart from one class of locomotive, relied entirely on conversions. After the Grouping the Southern Railway continued the tradition of rebuilding existing vehicles, a policy that remained in place until the last push-pull stock entered service in 1960.

The lack of sophistication of the controls and couplings ensured that push-pull operation was always confined to relatively low speeds and restricted to not more than three coaches when being propelled. In theory, this could allow for trains of up to six coaches (three either side of the locomotive) but in practice, such a level of usage was rarely taken up. Until the 1960s in Britain, if not in other parts of the world, the Board of Trade and other regulatory bodies had always looked askance at the principle of propelling maybe eight to 12 coaches at high speed, but with the development of modern electrical controls combined with more positive coupling arrangements, this view has now completely reversed. These modern systems will be mentioned but briefly and will otherwise remain outside the scope of this study.

The Southern companies were, of course, not alone in their quest for these operating economies and before long railways the length and breadth of the country were investigating the possibilities of steam railmotors, petrol railcars and push-pull train operation. At this point it should perhaps be made clear that on the Southern (if not necessarily elsewhere) the official terminology was pull-push, rather than the other way around. Presumably, here one pulled before pushing, although reference to Carriage Working Notices (CWNs) shows that this was not always the case! In later years and after Nationalisation, they were less pedantic and either wording might appear. Alternative terminology, in the form of 'auto train' or 'motor train' could also be used and each company had its own preference. Hardly surprisingly, the terminology used by the locomotive running department might differ from that used by the traffic department and so on. All three terms will be used within this book, but from here onwards pull-push will be our preferred wording.

The mechanics of operation were also subject to some variation. The LSWR favoured an 'over-the-roof' three-wire and pulley system of dubious reliability, the SECR eventually standardised on a considerably more robust mechanical system of rodding beneath the carriage floors, while the LBSCR at first

Plate 4 Along the coastal plain from Brighton to Worthing and onwards to Portsmouth a number of small halts were opened by the LBSCR in 1905/06, to be served by the new pull-push trains. Traffic levels soon increased and from 1911 regularly warranted the provision of four-coach trains. In October 1930, sets 995/7 leave Lancing for Brighton, running either side of a 'D1' class 0-4-2 tank. *O. J. Morris*

also tried a mechanical system, later superseded by Westinghouse air control. Ultimately, time was to prove the superiority of the LBSCR 'air-control' system and this became universal throughout the Southern Railway after 1930 — one of very few occasions where former LBSCR policy was adopted as standard after 1923.

Although most enthusiasts might think that pull-push operation was always typical of country branch lines — and once the tentacles of electrification had spread this generalisation is largely true — it was far less so initially. The original intention was to provide cheap, rapid and frequent services within urban areas — to try to win back at least some of the traffic lost to the street tramways — or as a means of providing economical main-line stopping services. To compete with the trams, which could stop at every street corner, unstaffed halts were built at many urban locations to coincide with the introduction of the railmotors, railcars and pull-push trains. A list of these may be found in Appendix 2. Many of the routes that first saw railmotors would later see these replaced by pull-push services, only to be replaced in their turn by electric traction, modern diesel multiple-units or, the ultimate fate, to be closed entirely and the traffic lost to the roads altogether. Ironically, a couple of urban lines (Wimbledon–West Croydon and, in part, Selsdon Road–Woodside–Elmers End) have gone full circle. Having seen most of these methods of propulsion, they are now operating successfully as part of the Croydon Tramlink network! One would be hard pressed to think of many country branch lines being rejuvenated in such a fashion, but this is to digress . . .

The pre-Grouping scene
First in the field was the LSWR, with its railmotor-operated branch to East Southsea (jointly owned with the LBSCR),

commencing in 1903, while its first pull-push trains ran within the Plymouth suburbs in 1906, followed by Weymouth–Portland in 1910. However, it was not until during and after World War One that more extensive use was made of pull-push operation — once the initial failure of the company's 15 wholly owned railmotors was realised. Some of the services were urban, but others arose as a result of the electrification of the inner suburban area. In 1916 the company electrified the new Guildford line as far as Claygate, which left a 'stub-end' country branch line onwards to Guildford. During peak hours 'M7' class 0-4-4 tanks hauling eight-coach bogie 'block' trains provided the through London services, but for the local traffic a two-coach pull-push shuttle would suffice. A visitor to Claygate today, seeing its monotonous suburban electric service, would find it difficult to imagine the scene 90 years ago, when a three- or six-coach electric train from Waterloo connected with an Adams radial tank and bogie 'block' pull-push set for the onward journey to Guildford. Between 1916 and 1919 no fewer than four such sets were required to maintain the service.

The spread of electrification during Southern Railway days would give rise to other 'frontier' stations of this nature: Alton, Dorking, Maidstone West, Orpington and (later) Sevenoaks to name several where steam-hauled pull-push trains took over at the 'country' end of the line. Indeed, in some instances this actually increased the volume of auto train workings before the inevitable branch line closures of the 1950s began to seriously reduce their numbers.

At the other extreme there were of course the hopelessly unremunerative LSWR lines such as Alton–Basingstoke and Bishops Waltham, where any chance of operating profits, even in the 1900s, were slim. Here, minimum-cost provision was essential and it was on such lines that the railmotors stood the

best chances of success. However, this was not always so, for a variety of reasons that will be discussed in more detail in Chapter 3 — and pull-push was very often substituted within a short period of time.

On the neighbouring LBSCR the evaluation of alternative means of propulsion was carried out rather more comprehensively. By 1902/03 the financial situation on some of their routes was giving cause for concern, leading the Board to initiate research into more economical means of service provision. This involved visiting other railway companies and several rolling stock manufacturers, both at home and abroad, so it was not until January 1905 that they were in a position to recommend the purchase of two steam railmotors, two petrol railcars and the conversion of two 'Terrier' ('A1' class) locomotives to motor train operation. Two new trailer cars were constructed to run with the locomotives — nicknamed 'Balloons' on account of their large size, accentuated by the diminutive size of the engines.

The railmotors and railcars were tested between Eastbourne and St Leonards (the LBSCR wanted them to run through to Hastings, but this was blocked by the SECR, who later introduced their own railmotor service from here to Rye!) while the pull-push trains ran between Brighton and Worthing. Several new halts were opened on each route for the new trains to serve. The results of the trials, carried out between September and December 1905, were presented to the LBSCR Board in June 1906 and yielded some interesting figures, as below.

workings were quite complex, with each train serving a number of different routes in the course of a days' work. Only the Kemp Town branch, entirely within the Brighton conurbation, saw pull-push services initially (working alongside the railcars for a time), and it was not until later that branches such as Epsom Downs, Wimbledon–West Croydon and Seaford regularly saw pull-push operation, later using 'D1' class 0-4-2 tanks in place of the 'Terriers'. The Chichester–Portsmouth local service, serving the many halts along the coastal plain and known irreverently to the staff as the 'Muddy Bloater' was far more typical of LBSCR motor train operation.

On the South Eastern the same problem of reduced operating margins was worrying its directors. In June 1903, a sub-committee was formed, charged with investigating possible economies over any route then losing in excess of £1,000 per annum. The Sheppey Light Railway, between Queenborough and Leysdown, was a prime example and the first experiment involved the hire of two Dick, Kerr petrol railcars similar to those later purchased by the LBSCR. Some success was achieved — certainly more than on the Brighton — but a lack of local skilled fitters caused the idea to be abandoned and the railcars were returned to the makers.

It was then proposed to construct two steam railmotors at Ashford similar to the joint vehicles at East Southsea. However, before work commenced, news reached Harry Wainwright of the problems encountered and so the design and construction of a rather more powerful unit was entrusted to outside contractors.

Type of train	Initial cost	Cost per mile	Fuel consumption/mile	% availability
Steam railmotor	£2,145	3.41d	14.82lb coal	47.0
Petrol railcar	£2,175	3.19d	4.61 gallons	40.5
'A1' & P-P trailer	£895	2.88d	14.84lb coal	95.5

In addition, Douglas Earle Marsh was also able to report that a 37% increase in passenger loadings had been recorded between Brighton and Worthing. In terms of cost, and most certainly in terms of passenger comfort and reliability, the pull-push train won the day and was the preferred option for future development. Indeed, the LBSCR was to become the leading user of motor trains amongst the pre-Grouping Southern companies, opening in excess of 30 new halts on their system for the trains to serve. The railcars were soon relegated to the Kemp Town branch and were later converted for Engineer's Department use, but the two steam railmotors continued to work on until 1915, eventually being sold abroad in 1919.

Between 1906 and 1922 the company introduced many more motor trains. Most were employed on main-line stopping services rather than wholly on branch lines and many of the

That from Kitson & Company was deemed acceptable and two such vehicles were ordered and delivered early in 1906. Initial trials on the Sheppey line gave the following comparison with a conventional train of six-wheeled stock, seemingly without major problems.

Type of train	Initial cost	Cost per mile*	Fuel consumption per mile
Railmotor No. 1	£2,400	£1.25	15.2lb coal
2-4-0T & three coaches	Not recorded	£2.08	26.8lb coal

*Comparison of these figures with the LBSCR returns leads one to speculate on the relative methodologies involved.

Evaluation of the alternatives on the LBSCR

Plate 6 LBSCR steam railmotor No 2 at Bexhill, while working the Eastbourne–St Leonards service, between 1905 and 1912. *IAP*

Plate 7 LBSCR petrol railcar No 3 at Kemp Town circa 1906. The two petrol railcars had a number of differences – No 4 is illustrated in Plate 33. *IAP*

Plate 8 LBSCR pull-push train. 'Terrier' tank No 82 *Boxhill* and original 'Balloon' driving trailer No 1327 at Worthing in 1905/06. Only the first two 'A1' class conversions were modified as 2-4-0 tanks by Marsh, but this refinement was soon considered unnecessary and both reverted to orthodox 0-6-0 tanks by 1913. Note the gangway connection at the locomotive end of the coach – removed later. *F. Moore*

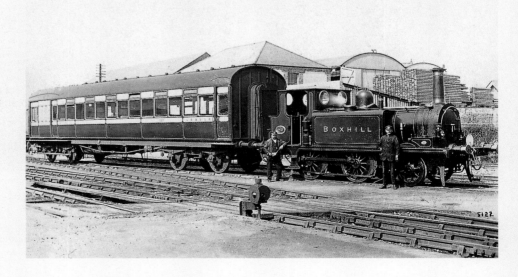

With such figures before them, it is perhaps not surprising that the SECR Board readily agreed to the purchase of six more almost identical railmotors. However, the usual lack of flexibility rapidly became apparent. Increased levels of traffic soon brought about the need for trailer cars and half a dozen six-wheeled coaches were equipped to run with them. These often had to be run round at the end of each journey and this inconvenience could sometimes guarantee a late departure for the next service — never mind whether the railmotor could actually haul a fully-laden trailer! A further review of performance in October 1907 wisely recommended against further railmotor purchases and the decision was made to investigate pull-push operation instead.

Over the next few years the eight 'P' class 0-6-0 tanks were constructed especially for pull-push operation, while one former LBSCR 'Terrier' and eight LCDR 0-4-4 tanks were also converted, together with at least ten sets of carriages. These were tried over a number of (mostly) inner city suburban services and

considerably greater success was achieved, although widespread use of pull-push trains on former SECR lines did not occur until after the Grouping.

The eight railmotors continued to serve, but by 1920 all were in store with no further plans for their return to traffic. The Southern Railway subsequently rebuilt the carriage portions and four were later equipped for pull-push operation. As such they will be described in Chapter 11.

On the Isle of Wight, urban tramway competition was hardly a problem, but economical operation undoubtedly was, especially in winter. The Isle of Wight Central Railway purchased one steam railmotor from Hurst Nelson & Company in 1906, for the Merstone-Ventnor West branch. They were most impressed with its economy, far less so with its reliability. As an alternative they produced a 'home-grown' railmotor-cum-pull-push train using a second-hand Midland Railway carriage and an 0-4-2 shunting tank engine. Predictably it was not a success and both this and

Plate 10 In 1912, two SECR 'P' class 0-6-0T locomotives were allocated to the Nunhead–Greenwich Park branch service, operating with two pairs of LCDR bogie pull-push vehicles. Brake composite No 2713 is leading and brake third No 3396 trails locomotive No 325 at Greenwich Park terminus in June 1912. The pair were later allocated SECR set number 271 and lasted until 1936 as SR set number 732, latterly running between Ash and Aldershot. Further views of this formation will be found in Chapter 10. *F. Moore*

Plate 11 The Isle of Wight Central Railway's steam railmotor No 1. Built in 1906 by R. & W. Hawthorne (locomotive) and Hurst Nelson (carriage), it certainly looked the part, finished in metallic crimson lake with cream upper panels to the carriage portion. Although economical, its reliability was poor and it ran in this form only until 1913.
Hurst Nelson & Co

the Hurst Nelson product were separated into their component parts within a few years. Further pull-push operation on the Island would wait until after 1923.

The final pre-Grouping development took place in 1913, when the tiny Freshwater, Yarmouth & Newport Railway took delivery of a 12/15-seat Drewry petrol railcar. With just one line, only 12 miles long, this probably made economic sense, but the vehicle was hardly of robust construction and passenger protection from the elements was basic, to say the least. The Southern Railway was not impressed and relegated the vehicle to departmental service. It was withdrawn from even that duty by mid-1927.

At this point it is worth recording that the Somerset & Dorset Joint Railway possessed six pull-push equipped carriages in 1930, when the line's stock was divided between the Southern and LMS railways. Most had been used on the Wells branch, although there was a short-lived auto train service between Templecombe and Bournemouth West in 1928-30. All six vehicles passed to the LMS, along with the locomotives and few, if any Southern Railway pull-push services subsequently ventured onto the line.

A summary of development prior to the Grouping is as follows:

Post-1923 development

The Southern continued to expand the pull-push fleet and the number in service at any one time reached a peak of 96 sets during 1935, although by this date all the six-wheelers had been withdrawn and replaced by newly converted bogie vehicles and a modest programme of replacement continued into British Railways' days. Standardisation of the operating systems took place from 1929 onwards with most vehicles receiving the LBSCR air-control apparatus soon after this date. Ex-LBSCR pull-push stock was, of course, equipped with vacuum brakes at the same time.

On the South Western section many of the existing 'O2' and 'M7' locomotives were re-equipped but the 'T1s', Adams radials (Class 0415) and the solitary ex-LBSCR 'A1X' locomotive were not and these classes did not feature in pull-push operation after 1931 at the latest. Two other 'Terriers' (Nos B655/661) were actually fitted with LSWR three-wire gear in 1926, in lieu of Westinghouse equipment! On the Brighton, the 'A1'/'A1X' classes were gradually stripped of their motor gear, this being refitted to more 'D1' class 0-4-2 tanks, all of which received vacuum ejectors and combination valves to enable them to work with any pull-push stock thereafter. From 1933 some 30 'D3'

Company	Steam railmotors	Petrol railcars	P-P locomotives	P-P stock
LSWR	16*-all converted to coaches	-	72 (of five classes)**	25 sets
LBSCR	3* — one scrapped and two sold	2 in ED use+	80 (of two classes)	46 sets
SECR	8 — all in store	-	17 (of three classes)#	10 sets#
IWCR	2 — converted to ordinary coaches	-	-	-
FYNR	-	1 later transferred to ED use	-	-

By no means all of the locomotives were employed for pull-push working at any one time.

*One jointly owned vehicle in each instance.

** There had also been 12 unsuccessful 2-2-0 and 0-4-0 tanks built between 1906 and 1910. All were later rebuilt or sold by the LSWR.

+There were other petrol railcars that were always in Engineers Department use.

One locomotive and at least two sets of carriages had P-P gear removed prior to 1923.

The number of pull-push sets quoted equates to the number of driving trailers (ie. those with driver's controls) — some were single units, most were 2-coach sets but there were a few three-coach sets of six-wheelers. There were also a number of loose coaches (mostly full thirds) equipped to run as strengthening vehicles that are not included in the totals.

bogie tanks gradually replaced them and many saw service on former SECR lines. On the Isle of Wight three 'A1X' locomotives were equipped with pull-push fittings, working the Ventnor West branch along with a pair of ex-LCDR four-wheeled sets until these were replaced by LBSCR arc-roofed stock. The Island 'Terriers' were replaced in their turn by two motor fitted 'O2s' sent over in 1949. On the South Eastern their solitary secondhand 'Terrier' had been stripped of pull-push gear as early as 1917 while further ex-LCDR 'R' and 'R1' class 0-4-4 tanks received the necessary fittings. The 'P' class tanks were not re-equipped with air-control gear and were relegated to shunting duties after 1930. After Nationalisation, a number of H class tanks were used as replacements — these and the LSWR 'M7s' alone surviving to the end of pull-push operation in 1963/64.

Despite the obvious success of the pull-push system, Maunsell continued to investigate alternative means of propulsion,

Plate 12 Photographs of LSWR Adams radial tanks (Class 0415) working auto trains are rare. Here, LSWR No 058 propels a Wimbledon–Tooting–Ludgate Hill service over Dundonald Road level crossing, between Wimbledon and Merton Park on 21 June 1924. The stock is a bogie 'block' set. *H. C. Casserley*

Plate 13 An LBSCR motor train at Ford. 'D1' class 0-4-2T No B605 stands in the loop platform with arc-roofed set 988 in 1932. This station saw many pull-push services to and from Littlehampton, Arundel, Barnham, Bognor and Portsmouth – connecting with main line trains on the mid-Sussex or coast lines. *O. J. Morris*

purchasing one petrol railcar and one Sentinel steam railmotor, as well as trying out a 'Michelin' diesel unit for a short period during the early 1930s. None proved sufficiently reliable to challenge the traditional steam locomotive and it would fall to British Railways to look for more modern replacements during the 1950s and 1960s.

Electrification of the inner suburban area was largely completed by 1930 and had extended to the Kent, Surrey and Berkshire commuter belt by 1939, resulting in the gradual banishment of pull-push to the country areas by these dates. No 'modern' pull-push rolling stock existed until the conversion of five LSWR 'Ironclad' corridor sets in 1948-52 and the final development in traditional stock took place in 1959/60, when 20 Maunsell sets were converted to replace the remaining pre-Grouping vehicles that were approaching the end of their working lives, and it was these sets which saw out the end of traditional pull-push working during 1964, ending an era that had started almost 60 years previously. But not quite — in 1963 all former LSWR lines west of Salisbury had been transferred to Western Region control and this included the pull-push workings at Seaton and Yeovil. For a short period the Western Region replaced these with their own auto trailers worked by either '1400' 0-4-2 '5400' or '6400' pannier tanks. Until about February 1965 a few duties remained, covering shortages or failures of WR diesel multiple-units.

By this time, thoughts of a very different method of pull-push operation were in mind for the forthcoming Bournemouth line electrification scheme. One 'Crompton' diesel locomotive (No D6580) and a six-coach pull-push unit (No 601), formed using redundant 4-COR and 6-PUL electric stock was tested on the Oxted line from mid-1965. Further trials into 1966, including high-speed evaluation followed, leading finally to Ministerial approval for up to 90mph pull-push diesel and electric services to commence between Waterloo, Bournemouth and Weymouth in July 1967. This mode of operation has since been mirrored elsewhere in the country with complete success, but it is a far cry indeed from the traditional steam-hauled pull-push trains that will concern us here.

In the following chapters, we shall look first at the routes and methods of operation and then move on to deal with the various types of stock used on pull-push services, as well as briefly discussing the alternatives, namely railmotors and railcars. The pull-push stock has been divided by origin and type, rather than chronologically, so where vehicles of mixed origin constituted a set, these have been dealt with by placement according to the origin of the driving trailer. Thus, for example, set 37 (originally one SECR and one LSWR coach) appears with other SECR non-corridor stock, and 1931-formed sets 649/50 are classed along with ex-LBSCR arc-roofed vehicles, despite originally being formed with one LSWR and one LBSCR vehicle. Where sets changed formation subsequently, most remain under their original heading, regardless of the origin of the later carriages. The exceptions here are sets 714/5, which ended their days in the late 1950s including ex-SECR vehicles, despite previously being wholly of LBSCR origin.

Loose coaches are a little more difficult to place, as these tended to wander around the system, sometimes being coupled to pull-push sets of different origin. In general these have been listed alongside either the stock that they most commonly worked with or in the chapter relevant to that type of stock. In the tables the dimensions given are the nominal body length and width, odd fractions being ignored. Bodyside and end mouldings in particular, could add ¾in to the figures quoted.

Plate 14 All but two of the SECR pull-push sets were formed of six-wheeled stock. 'P' class 0-6-0T No 323 propels the Sevenoaks auto train out of Otford in May 1926. The set is believed to be SR 649 or 650 – both it and the locomotive retain pre-Grouping livery. *Rev. A. W. V. Mace*

Plate 15 Almost at the end of SR pull-push operations, 'M7' No 30052 approaches Lymington Junction with a Brockenhurst-Lymington service on 1 May 1964. By this time just eight 'M7s' remained at Bournemouth and all were withdrawn before the end of the month. The stock is a Maunsell pull-push set, augmented by a loose open second.
R. A. Panting

Chapter 2.
Routes and Operation

As stated in Chapter 1, the original intention was to provide pull-push trains largely over urban lines and on main-line stopping services rather than wholly on rural branch lines, so from inception until around 1929 it would be possible to see motor trains throughout almost the whole of the Southern system. Retreat to the country began even before 1925, as the first phases of suburban electrification were completed. Indeed, a glance through the list of lines worked by pull-push trains (pages 17 to 19) will show a number of inner city routes ceasing to be operated during or just after World War One and relatively few of these were reinstated subsequently, at least not as steam-hauled services.

Probably the last inner city route to retain pull-push operation was that between Wimbledon and Ludgate Hill via either Haydons Road or Merton Abbey, Streatham and Tulse Hill. This was a joint LSWR/LBSCR service that had been suspended in 1916 and reinstated following pressure from the Underground companies in 1923, which finally ceased running on 3 March 1929. By then, the service comprised just four through trips daily, so was hardly a money-spinner! Just over a year later, in June 1930, the last outer London pull-push service succumbed to electrification, this being the former LBSCR line between Wimbledon and West Croydon.

The *Southern Railway Magazine* for November 1930 carried an article on pull-push trains — coincident with the adoption of the LBSCR's air-control system throughout the Southern, and this listed 29 routes where the trains would operate in the future. Whilst not a full list, it is significant to note that not a single route remained within the London area.

Certain lines did not see regular auto train operation at all, including, perhaps surprisingly, several in the west of England for which this mode of operation would have seemed eminently suitable. Perhaps the variation between summer and winter traffic levels was the reason, or possibly the existence of so many through trains or portions from Waterloo? West of Salisbury, only the Yeovil Town, Seaton and Turnchapel branches enjoyed prolonged periods of pull-push operation, yet such lines as Bodmin–Wadebridge–Padstow, Sidmouth, Lyme Regis and Torrington–Halwill did so only occasionally, or in some instances not at all. The Exmouth branch did so only rarely after about 1920 and these later workings might have been a case of the relief set normally stabled at Exeter Central being pressed into service to cover a shortage of other stock.

It was, of course, not unknown for a pull-push set to be included in a conventionally hauled train from time to time. Instances of such workings into Victoria were not unknown up to 1960, and this was the usual method of delivering a set to workshops for overhaul when convenient. Similarly, shortages of pull-push fitted locomotives arose from time to time, resulting in some odd combinations being seen. Even a Bulleid Pacific coupled to a pull-push set was not unknown on the Eastbourne–Hailsham or Brockenhurst–Wimborne–Bournemouth services during the early 1960s. A 'Crompton'-hauled LBSCR set was recorded at Allhallows in 1960, so for modellers there could be a prototype for everything!

Other lines might see pull-push operation only occasionally, but still on a regular basis and not necessarily every train over a particular route would be so worked. Some lines might see just one or two workings per day, or even per week. For example, the set based at Yeovil Town made one early morning trip to Templecombe (possibly for the benefit of railway employees) as well as a couple of trips to Pen Mill later in the day. After electrification of the Seaford branch in 1935, just one pull-push service continued to traverse the line for many years during the late afternoon, presumably because it was a convenient fill-in duty between other services radiating from Lewes, while a Tonbridge-based set made one round trip to Wadhurst daily in the 1940s and 1950s. One of the Guildford-based 'gate' sets did a Wednesday lunchtime journey to Witley in the 1930s, presumably for the benefit of shoppers going home after half-day closing hours, so there was plenty of scope for odd workings.

Branch lines with through London services, such as Seaton, Lymington and Swanage, posed an interesting operational problem, as the through portion would not be piped for air-

Plate 16 Wareham station on 14 July 1960. The Weymouth portion of the 'Royal Wessex' has departed and 'M7' No 30108, coupled to set 31, has left the down bay and set back onto the Swanage portion of the train (Mk1 brake second and composite) left in the down main platform. It is now leaving for the branch, sandwiched between the two portions. This sort of manoeuvre would occur at any location where the branch train was formed of a pull-push set and the through coaches, or parcels van, horsebox, etc. were required to be conveyed by the same service.
H. C. Casserley

Plate 17 In the reverse direction, on 1 June 1950, an 'M7' hauls the 1.33pm Swanage–Wareham train past Pike's siding and narrow-gauge system, north of Corfe Castle. The branch train is formed of an LSWR non-corridor pull-push set (one of 34/5/6), while the through coaches for Waterloo at the rear are formed of Bulleid two-coach-set R from the series numbered 63-75. At Wareham, the locomotive and pull-push set would run round the through coaches before attaching them to the rear of the London train from Weymouth. *J. C. Flemons*

control working. In these circumstances (or if other stock such as a luggage van or a horsebox needed to be conveyed) it was perfectly permissible for these to be coupled at the rear of the train if the locomotive was pulling, but if the pull-push unit was being propelled, then these vehicles would have to be coupled behind the locomotive and hauled, sandwich-fashion, in the normal manner. Such procedures could give rise to interesting shunting manoeuvres at the end of the journey, particularly when the through portion had to be attached to the London service. Stations such as Brockenhurst, Wareham and Seaton Junction would certainly make interesting models from the operational point of view.

There now follows a summary of lines over which regular pull-push operation has been recorded, together with known dates. Inevitably, there may be omissions, especially from the pre-Grouping period or when operation was limited to short periods of time. In a number of instances these routes had also

previously seen railmotor operation and further details of these appear in Chapter 3. Comparison of commencement dates with original construction/conversion dates of stock may yield some clues to original allocations, by no means all of which were recorded at the time.

As time progressed and especially once air control became universal, transfers became widespread and it was not at all unusual to find, for example, a South Western bogie 'block' set or an arc-roofed LBSCR set on an Eastern section duty. More uncommon was the sight of a Brighton or South Eastern set on a West Country branch and only Seaton and Yeovil managed this with any regularity. This flexibility did not extend to the LSWR 'gate' stock or the LBSCR 'Balloon' vehicles and these were always confined to their respective pre-Grouping lines.

Throughout the list, closure indicates the end of passenger services as in many instances goods traffic continued for a further period.

South Western Section

Most duties were fairly self-contained, with the same set running to and fro over the same section of line in the course of a day's work. Details of the pre-1923 period are sometimes conflicting and throughout the pull-push era some lines saw this mode of operation only for short periods. For example, the Netley line saw auto trains perhaps twice — first when Woolston station received bomb damage in 1941 and a shuttle service was provided from Fareham and secondly in 1957, when there was an initial shortage of diesel multiple-units after the Hampshire dieselisation scheme was introduced. In both instances, the duration of these services was brief.

Line	Dates	Notes*
Plymouth Friary–St Budeaux/Bere Alston/Callington	1906-1961	2, 3
Plymouth Friary–Turnchapel	1906-closure	1
Exeter–Honiton	1914-c1920	
Exeter–Exmouth	1914-c1920	
Seaton–Seaton Junction	1914-1963	12
Yeovil Town–Yeovil Junction (incl. Templecombe and Pen Mill)	1919-1963	1,12
Weymouth–Portland–Easton	1910-1931	11, 14
Swanage–Wareham (incl Bournemouth and Dorchester)	1922-1964	1, 4
Hamworthy Junction–Broadstone	1926-closure	11
Bournemouth–Christchurch–Ringwood	1922-closure	
Bournemouth–Wimborne–Ringwood–Brockenhurst	1926-closure	4
Lymington Pier–Brockenhurst	c1920 & 1926-1964	1, 4

Line	Dates	Notes*
Gosport–Fareham (incl Stokes Bay branch)	1914-closure	1
Lee-on-the-Solent–Fort Brockhurst	1914-closure	
Bishops Waltham–Botley	1920-closure	14
Alton–Fareham (often onward to Gosport)	1926-closure	
Alton–Winchester–Eastleigh (and onward to Southampton T)	1937-1957	2
Andover Junction–Romsey–Eastleigh	1937-1959	2, 11
Bordon–Bentley (and onward to Guildford)	1919-closure	14
Midhurst–Petersfield (later Pulborough–Petersfield)	1926-closure	
Guildford–Tongham–Farnham	1919-closure	
Farnham–Aldershot–Ascot	1919-electrification	2
Claygate–Guildford (also possibly Leatherhead–Guildford)	1916-1919	
Bisley–Brookwood (special service only)	1918-closure	13
Windsor–Woking	1915-1916	
Ascot–Woking via Sturt Lane curve	1919-electrification	11
Virginia Water–Weybridge (and onward to Surbiton/Egham)	1916-electrification	1
Virginia Water–Woking–Guildford	1916-electrification	2
Wimbledon–Merton Abbey–Tooting–Ludgate Hill	1915/16/23-closure	5
Clapham Junction–Kensington–Hammersmith–Richmond	1915-1928	6
Hounslow–Feltham	1916-1917	

* For explanation of references see page 19.

Isle Of Wight

Line	Dates	Notes*
Ventnor West–Merstone Junction	1926-closure	1
Bembridge–Brading (often not in pull-push mode)	1947-closure	

Central Section

Workings here were often complicated and many motor trains ran on a number of different routes in the course of a day's work. Indeed, it is probably fair to state that almost every LBSCR line outside London saw pull-push trains at some time. Centres of operation were Portsmouth, Bognor, Littlehampton, Brighton, Horsham, Eastbourne, Tunbridge Wells and West Croydon.

Line	Dates	Notes*
Chichester–Portsmouth (and onward to Barnham/Bognor)	1906-electrification	2
Bognor–Barnham–Ford–Littlehampton/Arundel	1909-electrification	1, 2
Hayling Island–Havant	1907-1916	7, 11
Brighton–Worthing (later onward to Littlehampton)	1905-electrification	
Kemp Town–Brighton	1905-closure	
The Dyke–Brighton	1906-closure	8
Horsham–Brighton	1906-1961	
Horsham–Cranleigh–Guildford	1906-1961	2
Horsham–Dorking (some trips ran to/from Pulborough)	1925-electrification	
Horsham–Three Bridges–Horley/Redhill	1907-electrification	2
Chichester–Midhurst–Pulborough (later Petersfield-Pulborough)	1921-closure	2
Brighton–Haywards Heath–Horsted Keynes	1906-electrification	2
Brighton–Lewes–Seaford	1906-electrification	2, 9
Brighton–Uckfield–Crowborough–Tunbridge Wells	1907-c1950	2
Brighton–Lewes–East Grinstead	1906-closure	2, 10, 11
Brighton–Lewes–Eastbourne	1930-electrification	2
Lewes–Haywards Heath	1906-electrification	
Eastbourne–Hailsham	1912-1962	
Eastbourne–Heathfield–Tunbridge Wells	1924-1962	
Eastbourne–St Leonards–Hastings (from 1924 on to Rye)	1912-electrification	2
Three Bridges–East Grinstead–Tunbridge Wells	1907-1964	2
Oxted–Tunbridge Wells via Hever or East Grinstead	1907-1963	15
Wimbledon–Mitcham Junction–West Croydon	1909-electrification	11
Epsom Downs/Belmont–Sutton–West Croydon	1906-electrification	2
Wimbledon–Tooting–Streatham via Haydons Road	1907-17/23-electrification	
Streatham–East and West Croydon	1916-electrification	
West Croydon–Crystal Palace–Coulsdon North	1907-electrification	2
Norwood Junction–Beckenham Junction (joint with SECR)	1912-1915	

* For explanation of references, see page 19.

South Eastern Section
A considerable number of changes took place during World War One and several inner-city routes saw brief periods of pull-push operation during this period.

Line	Dates	Notes
Otford–Sevenoaks (Tubs Hill)	1909-electrification	1, 11
Gravesend West Street–Swanley Junction	1914-closure	
Port Victoria/Grain–Gravesend Central/Dartford	1914-closure	2
Allhallows/Grain–Gravesend Central	1932-closure	
Beckenham Junction–Norwood Junction (joint with LBSCR)	1910-1915	
Beckenham Junction–New Beckenham	1915-1916	
Greenwich Park–Nunhead (and onward to Victoria)	1912-closure	
Sheppey Light Railway (Leysdown–Queenborough)	1910-1924	11
Gravesend Central–Gillingham–Strood–Maidstone West	1930-electrification	2
Chatham Central–Strood	1910-closure	
Crystal Palace (High Level)–Nunhead–Snow Hill	1914-electrification	2, 11
Moorgate Street–Brixton	1914-1916	
Victoria–St Pauls	1914-1916	
Elmers End–Hayes	1915-1916	
Bromley South–Chatham	1925-electrification	
Maidstone West–Paddock Wood–Tonbridge–Sevenoaks	1930-electrification	2
Westerham–Dunton Green (and onward to Tonbridge)	1912-closure	1, 8, 11
Orpington–Sevenoaks–Tonbridge	1925-electrification	2
Hawkhurst–Paddock Wood (and onward to Tonbridge)	1930-closure	1
Sandgate/Hythe–Sandling Junction	1910/15-17/31-closure	1, 11
Dover Priory–Canterbury East	1912-17	11
Bexhill West–Crowhurst Junction	1915/16/38-1958	
Hastings–Rye (later Eastbourne–Rye or Appledore)	1920-1961	
New Romney/Dungeness–Appledore (and onward to Ashford)	1910-1961	11, 16
Ramsgate–Birchington	1916-1921	
Margate Sands–Minster (incl Ramsgate and Canterbury West)	1917-closure	
Ash–Aldershot (and onward to Reading)	1909-electrification	17
Kent Coast flooding emergency (Herne Bay–Faversham)	March-May 1953	

Notes
1. Listed in 1934 SR Working Appendices as being able to operate without a guard.
2. Not all journeys traversed the full length of the line.
3. Not in pull-push mode when travelling over the Callington branch. Occasional trips also as far as Tavistock.
4. Maunsell pull-push sets continued in use after May 1964, but not in pull-push mode.
5. Service cut back to Wimbledon–Merton Abbey–Tooting in 1916, but full route reinstated in 1923. Joint LSWR/LBSCR services with running powers over SECR.
6. Service cut back to Clapham Junction–Kensington (Addison Road) in 1916.
7. Pull-push operation listed but not confirmed. In 1937-39 pull-push sets 727/8 were allocated to the line but doubtful if any 'A1X' locomotives remained so fitted by then.
8. Maunsell/Sentinel steam railmotor also used during 1933-38 period.
9. One steam worked pull-push service remained after electrification.
10. Original closure in 1955, reopened with statutory minimum service 1956-58. Pull-push stock often used in this period but not always in pull-push mode.
11. Not continuously operated by pull-push trains.
12. Replacement GWR auto trains provided until February 1965 at the latest.
13. In connection with National Rifle Association meetings only.
14. Possibly the last locations to use the LSWR three-wire control system.
15. Some services extended to Tonbridge during British Railways ownership.
16. Drewry petrol railcar also used during 1929-34 period.
17. LSWR line but operated using SECR stock.

The number of trips made by each individual train could vary considerably. For example, the duty between Yeovil Town and Yeovil Junction involved no less than 24 round trips between 6am and 10pm, along with the early morning run to Templecombe and two visits to Pen Mill later in the day. Admittedly, the individual journey times were in the order of four minutes each! The set allocated to the Westerham branch was similarly heavily utilised, with 14 round trips per day. In comparison, one set based at Brighton made just two round journeys to Horsham, with a further trip to Guildford in between — a total of six individual journeys per day. Locations with very low levels of traffic might allow for the two coaches to be uncoupled, with just the driving trailer (the coach with driving controls) being used, the other coach standing spare. Locations where this instruction was issued included Lee-on-the-Solent,

Bishops Waltham and the Petersfield–Midhurst service.

Some of the LBSCR pull-push sets had little space for luggage accommodation and to overcome this problem up to ten six-wheeled Brighton passenger brake vans were equipped with through air pipes around 1924. Known as air-control vans, these were mainly used on former LBSCR branches in Sussex. After 1939 they were replaced by five ex-SECR utility vans. It was by no means unusual, however, for a non-air-piped van to trail the set or locomotive, depending on the direction of travel.

The direction of pull (or push) could vary — where it was critical this was stipulated in the locomotive or carriage working notices, but where it was not, the direction faced was, presumably, left either to custom and practice or to the enginemen's preference. Various factors could influence the decision, such as convenience of shunting, availability of coaling and watering facilities or gradients along the route. Wherever possible, duties were arranged such that the locomotive was at the downhill end of the train, to minimise the effects in the event of a breakaway. For this reason, the Alton service 'over the Alps' normally ran with the locomotive pushing from Eastleigh. On lines that could be served from either end, eg. Bournemouth–Wimborne–Brockenhurst, Three Bridges–Tunbridge Wells, Maidstone West–Paddock Wood, the direction faced seemed less important and trains might run 'either way round'. However, on most lines there appeared to be a preferred way of working and a few examples are listed below:

Locomotive facing junction, noted at: Seaton, Swanage*, Gosport*, Lymington (during BR period), Bisley (post-war period), Kemp Town, The Dyke, Epsom Downs, Allhallows, Hawkhurst*, Bexhill West, Gravesend West Street*, Hythe and New Romney*.

Locomotive facing terminus, noted at: Turnchapel, Yeovil Town, Bordon, Ventnor West, Lymington (during SR period), Bishops Waltham and Bisley (pre-war period).

Those marked * have occasionally been noted facing in the other direction.

At Westerham and Bognor trains facing either direction were noted fairly regularly.

Wherever possible, the locomotive was coupled to the pull-push set at the bunker end, allowing normal forward running when both driver and fireman were on the footplate. However, this was not always possible and coupling 'chimney to train' sometimes occurred. With air-control this did not pose a problem as all locomotives were equipped with the necessary hose connections at each end, but this was not always so easy in the

days of mechanical control, especially with the LSWR system. It may therefore be significant that coupling 'chimney to train' was always more common on the South Eastern section.

We now come to the actual mechanics of operation. On the earliest railmotors, the control systems between the remote driver's cab and the locomotive portion appear crude in the extreme — often being limited to just a brake valve, whistle control cable and a bell communication cord with which the driver conveyed his instructions to the fireman using a pre-arranged series of codes. The control arrangements in the first pull-push vehicles may have been only a little less rudimentary, placing great reliance on the fireman, who remained alone on the engine when the driver occupied the leading carriage.

The LSWR adopted a three-wire and pulley system on their pull-push sets. The two outer wires ran from the locomotive regulator over pulleys located on the cab roof and thence along the carriage roofs, down into the driving cab of the leading vehicle and around a wheel attached to a dummy regulator handle. Operation of this caused the movement to be replicated in the locomotive cab. The centre wire was connected directly to the locomotive whistle. In addition, there was a vacuum brake release valve and a hand brake wheel provided in the driving cab of the pull-push unit. All this is illustrated in **Figure 1**, originally published in *The South Western Magazine* for 1 March 1916. No further advances were made with this system and new conversions for the South Western section continued to be so equipped until 1927 at least.

The South Eastern eventually adopted a similar control method but with the improvement that the control cables were replaced by rodding enclosed within 1½in diameter steel tubing

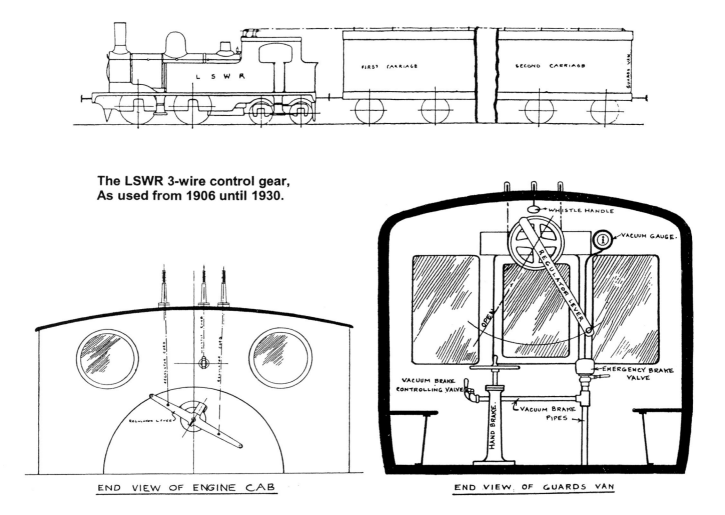

The LSWR 3-wire control gear, As used from 1906 until 1930.

END VIEW OF ENGINE CAB

END VIEW OF GUARDS VAN

Figure 1 Originally published in the *South Western Magazine* in March 1916, the LSWR three-wire pull-push control apparatus could only be described as basic. Just how ineffective it was took more than 10 years to become apparent.

Plate 18 In July 1912, 'M7' No 481 (the last locomotive of the class) was equipped with three-wire gear and ran trials with up to six coaches – presumably bogie 'block' set 2B seen here, with one of the 1906 or 1909 vestibule pairs coupled ahead of the engine. Close examination of the equipment reveals double pulleys on the cab roof, with adjustment turnbuckles fore and aft of the cab. The 'production' gear had only single pulleys facing aft and no provision for adjustment, so presumably attachment at the chimney end proved difficult and no more than three coaches were ever propelled using this arrangement. *Norman Collection/ South Western Circle*

beneath the carriage floors, connected between carriages by universal joints and to the locomotive regulator by bell cranks. The whistle control cord ran over the roof, enclosed within ⅛in diameter steel tubing. These fittings were denoted in the carriage registers by the entry 'Through driving rod' — but this description only seems to have been used from 1912 onwards, yet SECR pull-push vehicles had been running since 1909 at least (and 1906 if the railmotor trailers are counted as such), leading to some speculation about the original control method employed. From the evidence of **Plate 136** there was also another communication cord, probably for the bell control, at least on the ex-LCDR bogie vehicles converted in 1912.

On the LBSCR, the original 'Balloon plus Terrier' conversions utilised just a mechanical linkage between locomotive and carriage, however by 1909, a rather more sophisticated system was in use, employing Westinghouse air pressure to operate the regulator. At this time a mechanical linkage was retained to indicate the position of the regulator handle to the driver in the leading carriage, this arrangement being described in *The Engineer* for 17 December 1909, together with **Plate 19**. By 1914 this had been refined somewhat and an electrical indicator replaced the mechanical linkage and sector plate. This system is illustrated in **Figure 2** and the earlier vehicles were soon altered to conform. All subsequent Brighton pull-push sets were so equipped, as were the two ex-LCDR four-wheeled sets transferred to the Isle of Wight in 1924, despite the fact that none of the Island 'Terriers' was equipped to operate with them until early in 1926.

Plate 19 'D1' class No 627 at Brighton in July 1909, together with driving brake composites Nos 632/3 (later SR Nos 6929/30 to diagram 434). These were the first LBSCR pull-push coaches to be equipped with air control. Although the coaches carry the then standard livery of umber and white, the locomotive livery, with the 'Liver & Bacon' lettering, was confined to just four engines, Nos 284, 290, 605 and 627, during 1909 only. *LBSCR*

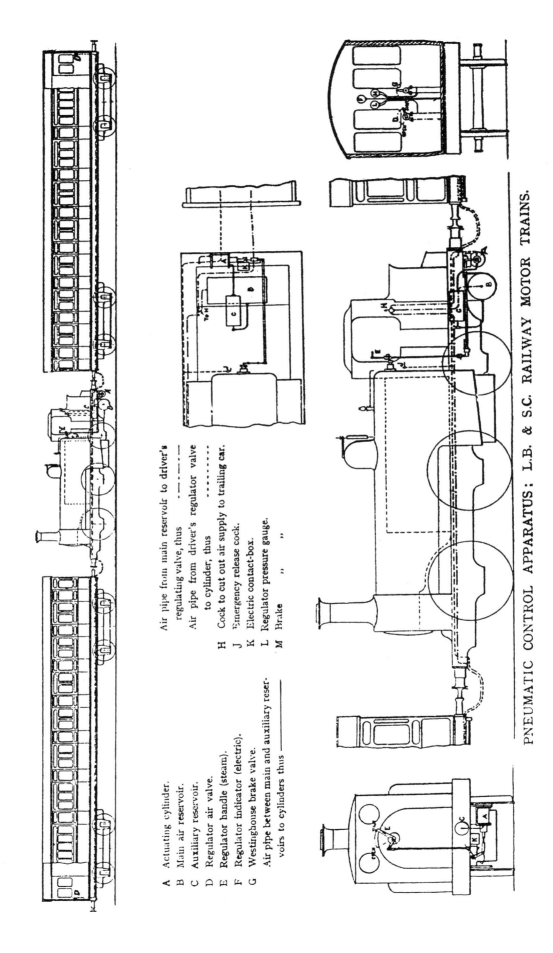

The LBSCR air-control gear as used from 1909 onwards. This shows the later version with electronic indicator.

A   Actuating cylinder.
B   Main air reservoir.
C   Auxiliary reservoir.
D   Regulator air valve.
E   Regulator handle (steam).
F   Regulator indicator (electric).
G   Westinghouse brake valve.
    Air pipe between main and auxiliary reservoirs to cylinders thus ———

Air pipe from main reservoir to driver's regulating valve, thus — · — · —
Air pipe from driver's regulator valve to cylinder, thus · · · · · ·
H   Cock to cut out air supply to trailing car.
J   Emergency release cock.
K   Electric contact-box.
L   Regulator pressure gauge.
M   Brake   „   „

PNEUMATIC CONTROL APPARATUS: L.B. & S.C. RAILWAY MOTOR TRAINS.

Figure 2 Diagrammatic arrangements of the final LBSCR air-control apparatus, taken from *The Model Engineer & Electrician* for December 1914. The 1909 apparatus differed in that the position of the regulator was shown in the driving cabs by a mechanical sector plate instead of an electrical indicator.

Plate 20 In August 1928, 'D1' tank No B234 was equipped with vacuum brakes and combination valves and, together with LBSCR set 754, toured a number of SE and SW section branches to demonstrate the operation of the air-control equipment. This is the official portrait of the locomotive – seemingly, that for the pull-push set has not survived. Note the various pipe work connections on the buffer beam – scope for getting these wrongly connected was minimised by colour and size coding. *O. J. Morris*

The Southern Railway therefore inherited three different methods of control with, at first, no plans to standardise the arrangements. Initially, ten more LSWR bogie block sets were converted in 1926/27 using the three-wire apparatus, together with 12 'M7' class engines, as well as two LBSCR 'Terriers' (for the Lee-on-the-Solent branch). However, after several overruns on the Bournemouth–Wimborne–Ringwood–Brockenhurst service and a more serious incident at Virginia Water in 1927, the SR Board requested a report. This was presented in October of that year and concluded that the LSWR system was extremely unreliable — often the apparatus was not connected at all and the crews relied entirely on an exchange of whistle signals — while the SECR system worked better but suffered from springing and backlash between the front and rear of the train. The LBSCR system was easily the most effective and therefore less likely to be ignored by footplate crews.

Accordingly, LBSCR set 754 (coaches Nos 6930 and 2038) was equipped with vacuum brakes, under order L359, dated 1 August 1928, together with 'D1' class 0-4-2T No 234 which was fitted with vacuum ejectors and brake combination valves, to enable it to work the brakes and pull-push gear separately. This combination then toured a number of South Eastern and South Western branches between November 1928 and February 1929, including Gravesend West Street, Port Victoria, Ash–Aldershot, Farnham–Guildford, Bordon, Yeovil and Seaton. No difficulties were experienced and in a report to the SR Rolling Stock Committee on 25 March 1929, Maunsell recommended that the air-control system be adopted as standard. This was subsequently approved and the following orders were issued to enable this to be implemented without delay (see Appendix 1 for further details of the original works and stock involved):

Plate 21 The somewhat spartan interior of a pull-push unit cab – in this instance one of the LBSCR vehicles with a sliding door on each side of the compartment, photographed in the 1950s. Visible are the air regulator valve (the removable control handle is not present), brake release valve, windscreen wiper control and hand brake standard, six light switches for the headcode lamps, vacuum gauge and air pressure gauge. Out of view above these two gauges is the electric indicator showing the degree of regulator opening. *The Lens of Sutton Association*

Order No	Date	Works	Completed by
B452	19/4/29	Equip 69 (later amended to 67) Central section pull-push fitted engines with vacuum ejectors and brake combination valves (including engine No 234 already modified).	5/29-5/30
L456	6/5/29	Conversion of 97 Central section pull-push coaches from Westinghouse to vacuum brakes.	11/29-6/30
A545A & B	20/5/30 (amended 5/7/30)	Equip 16 'R' and 'R1' class engines (fitted with 'H' class boilers) with air-controlled regulator gear for P-P working. (Eight each on sub-orders A and B.)	8/30
E546	20/5/30	Equip 31 (later amended to 37) 'M7' class engines with air-controlled regulator gear for P-P working.	2/31
L547	20/5/30	91 coaches to be equipped with air-control regulators for P-P working (90 actually done).	3/31

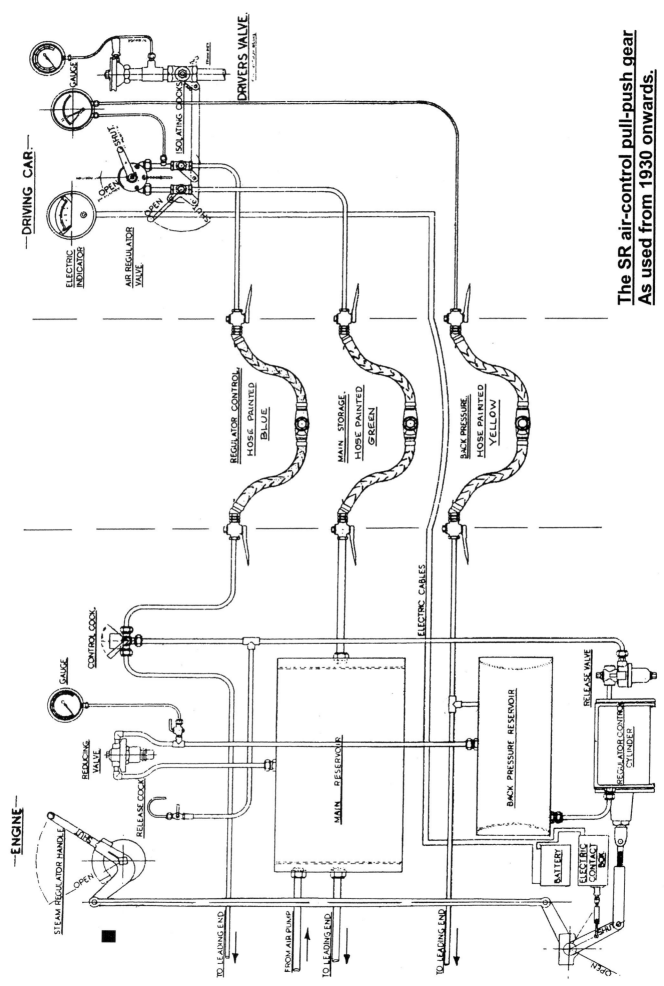

Figure 3 Taken from SR internal publication *Practical Hints for Enginemen*, this shows the air-control pull-push equipment in detail. Following two incidents on the LBSCR (at Edenbridge Town in March 1912 and a more serious affray at Littlehampton in August 1920) when inexperienced staff wrongly connected the gear, the connecting hoses were made smaller than the vacuum/Westinghouse pipes and were colour coded. This overcame mistakes of this nature and the features were retained through to British Railways days.

Soon after, order L670 was issued for the conversion of 28 more carriages for pull-push operation, while order E692 was issued for the conversion of five 'O2' class engines for the Seaton and Turnchapel branches and A776 was issued to cover the fitting of 30 'D3' class engines with P-P gear, mostly recovered from older 'A1X' and 'D1' classes. Other orders followed from time to time as additional or replacement locomotives and stock were needed, including more of classes 'R1', 'O2' and 'M7', plus (after 1948), the 'H' class.

The last LCDR six-wheeled sets were withdrawn from the Otford–Sevenoaks service in November 1929, while the LSWR three-wire equipment probably saw its final duties either at Portland, Bishops Waltham or Bordon in 1931, although some of the 'gate' stock carried the roof fittings for another couple of years. During the changeover period a number of 'D1' class locomotives were transferred to Eastern and Western section routes and these remained in the area until about 1939. For further details of the locomotives, the reader is referred to the many works by the late Don Bradley, published either by Wild Swan or the RCTS (see bibliography).

In order to familiarise the enginemen with the new equipment, the Southern Railway issued various operating instructions, including the schematic diagram reproduced as **Figure 3**, taken from internal publication *Practical Hints for Enginemen*, issued at intervals between 1930 and 1948. This gave the following instructions:

Pull and Push Engines

These engines are fitted with a regulator control cylinder, to operate the regulator by compressed air. A steam pump on the engine pumps air into a main reservoir, from which there is a connection through a reducing valve to a back-pressure reservoir. Low pressure is continuously applied to one end of the regulator control cylinder to keep the regulator normally in the shut position. The driver, by means of a valve fitted in the driving car, applies higher pressure air from the main reservoir to the other end of the control cylinder to open the regulator. If the fireman requires to close the regulator in an emergency, he does so by means of a release cock on the engine, which exhausts the pressure being supplied to the control cylinder from the main reservoir, and the back pressure returns the regulator operating gear to the closed position. Adjacent to the release cock is a two-way cock to be set according to the relation of the engine to the driving car.

The driver is enabled to see the amount of regulator opening by the indicator in the car, operated electrically from a contact box, attached to the regulator mechanism on the engine. Bells are also provided for communication between driver and fireman, and before the driver opens or closes the regulator from the car end, he must ring the bell on the engine and receive acknowledgement from his fireman.

The only exception to this rule is in case of emergency; otherwise it is most important that bell signals are properly exchanged, to avoid misunderstandings between driver and fireman.

The driver is responsible for coupling and uncoupling the regulator control gear on the engine regulator; the fireman is only permitted to do this if an emergency occurs while running. On leaving the car at the end of the journey, the driver must remove the handle from the air regulator valve, secure it with the safety pin, and, with the same handle, close the isolating cocks.

The following connections are made between engine and coaches:

> *Main storage (green).*
> *Regulator control (blue).*
> *Back pressure (yellow).*
> *Three-pin electric coupling.*
> *Earth wire.*

When the driver is at the car end, the fireman operates the reversing screw or lever, the cylinders and sand when necessary.

Care must be taken not to open the sand valves until the regulator has been closed, and the driver must be on the alert for slipping under unfavourable rail conditions. The fireman must take care not to carry the water level at such a height as to give rise to priming, especially in view of the fact that the driver is unable to detect this from the car end.

Any defects in the operation of the apparatus must be promptly reported, such as excessive back pressure, failure of the bell system, etc. If defects develop during service, the engine must run round the train, and under no circumstances may the fireman operate the regulator from the footplate, with car end leading.

Bell Codes

The following bell codes were used on the Southern Railway (some modifications were made after Nationalisation):

Normal working

CODE	RINGS
About to open or close regulator from driving compartment	1 short
Take brake off	2 short
Driver leaving driving compartment to carry out rules, etc.	5 short

Emergency working

Sound locomotive whistle	3 short
Reverse	4 short
Shut main regulator	2 long
Open main regulator	3 long
Driver leaving driving compartment to carry out rules, etc.	5 short

Despite all these careful instructions, it was by no means unknown for the regulator coupling in the locomotive cab not to be connected and the opening and closing of the regulator was performed by the fireman, using a combination of his own route knowledge and the bell codes or other (perhaps unofficial!) signals from the driver. In those rather more carefree days and safe in the knowledge that many of the routes traversed were often fairly quiet, few problems were experienced. Were the system in operation today, things would certainly be different!

Plate 22 Once air control became universal, in theory locomotives and stock could run anywhere on the system. Ex-LBSCR 'D3' class 0-4-4T No 2365 and pull-push set 722 arrive at Sandling Junction with the 4.20pm from Hythe on Saturday, 2 July 1938. This locomotive achieved fame in November 1942; while working the New Romney branch it caught the attention of a German fighter aircraft, but the pilot misjudged his attack and came in too low. The locomotive boiler exploded when raked with cannon-fire and the sudden up-rush of steam brought the aircraft down. The 'D3' survived the incident while the Focke-Wulf 190 did not. *R. F. Roberts*

Chapter 3.

Railmotors and Railcars

We will start by looking briefly at the alternative forms of propulsion, namely the railmotors and railcars, before moving on to tackle the true pull-push vehicles. It will soon become obvious why the mainland railmotors in particular deserve attention, for most reappeared later minus their locomotive portions as pull-push coaches, while many of the routes over which they were employed would later see regular auto train operation. The lessons learnt with the railmotors also had a direct effect on the development of pull-push trains.

The idea of a combined steam locomotive and carriage as a single unit has its origins in the very early days of our railways. As far back as the 1840s the engineer William Bridges Adams (not to be confused with William Adams, LSWR Locomotive Superintendent from 1878 until 1895) attempted such a concept but the necessary technical expertise was not then developed and the idea foundered. By 1902 the production of small steam-powered units had become technically possible and Dugald Drummond, then LSWR Locomotive Superintendent, proposed the construction of two such vehicles for use on the short, easily graded East Southsea branch from Fratton, which was jointly operated with the LBSCR. This line, entirely urban in character, was losing traffic rapidly to the new street tramways then opening within the city of Portsmouth. This otherwise insignificant branch may therefore claim its place in railway history as the birthplace of the British railmotor.

The first unit, lettered as 'SW & LB&SC Joint railmotor No. 1' (and classified 'K11' in LSWR parlance), was ready for traffic in April 1903. Much interest was aroused within railway circles and the new vehicle was immediately dispatched to the Great Western for trials in the Stroud (Gloucestershire) area. The company was sufficiently impressed to embark on its own designs — albeit very much more powerful than the Drummond prototype, and no fewer than 99 such units were eventually at work on GWR metals until the 1930s. It must be admitted that the GWR vehicles were very much more successful than any other British railmotor, as demonstrated by their longer lifespan.

The first joint vehicle, in its original form and complete with small vertical boiler, is illustrated in **Plate 23**. Despite the apparent success of the GWR trials, in service at Fratton the unit soon displayed its feeble power output, so Joint No 2 was equipped with a much larger vertical boiler before entering service in May 1903, as seen in **Plate 24**. Success remained elusive, so Drummond reconstructed both vehicles within a year of introduction with high-pitched horizontal boilers — undoubtedly more effective but aesthetically disastrous, as may be judged from **Plate 25**. In their modified form both units provided the East Southsea service, with varying degrees of success, until the outbreak of war in August 1914. This gave a good excuse to suspend the service, which was destined never to resume, despite being readvertised briefly in 1918.

A 20-minute frequency was offered and this soon won back some of the traffic already lost to the trams. However, the initial success was not sustained and would quickly prove the undoing of these and practically all subsequent railmotors — in that the extra traffic generated soon outstripped the capacity of the unit, both in terms of accommodation and, more importantly, steam-raising capabilities. Another difficulty which became apparent after a fairly short time was that maintenance of the locomotive portion had to be completed alongside other locomotives and in smoky atmospheres, with the inevitable adverse effect on the cleanliness of the carriage portion. Compensation claims from passengers who had experienced soiled clothing followed (as it did for most railways that operated railmotors) and this problem was never really overcome, despite extra attention from the cleaning staff.

Both railmotors were stored at Eastleigh from August 1914 until 1919, when because of the joint ownership, one was dispatched to Brighton Works, where it was subsequently broken up. The South Western retained the other and it was later rebuilt

Plate 23 LSWR & LBSCR joint railmotor No 1, as first completed in April 1903, with small vertical boiler. This proved hopelessly inadequate and was soon replaced. The livery is LSWR green for the locomotive portion and LBSCR umber and white for the carriage section. Note also the poorly protected second driving position, which resulted in the driver staying put in the locomotive cab when travelling in reverse, relying on the guard to stand at the leading end, even when the Board of Trade inspector was present. Not surprisingly, he made some adverse comments, but despite this, enclosure does not appear to have taken place until 1908. *Norman Collection/South Western Circle*

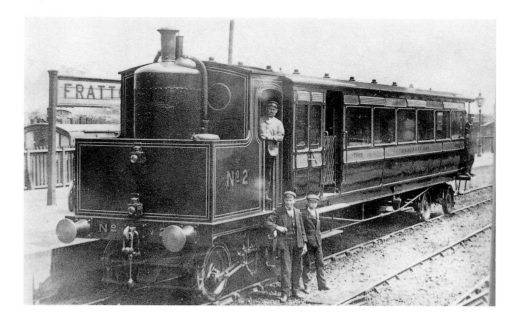

Plate 24 Joint No 2 at Fratton with enlarged vertical boiler, as completed in May 1903. The larger boiler was only marginally better and recourse was often made to a 'Terrier' tank to either haul or give the unit a good shove! The livery in this instance was LSWR throughout, with salmon pink and brown carriage bodywork. *Author's collection*

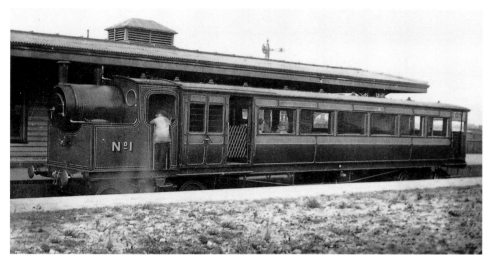

Plate 25 Joint No 1 again, after rebuilding in September 1903 with a more conventional horizontal boiler, although aesthetically it was a disaster. This proved sufficiently effective for both railmotors to remain on the East Southsea branch until suspension of the service in August 1914. Note the already grimy state of the paintwork compared with Plate 23. *Norman Collection/South Western Circle*

Plate 26 LSWR 'H12' railmotor No 1, as completed for the Basingstoke–Alton line in 1904. Slightly smaller than the joint cars, it had eight first and 32 third class seats – (the earlier vehicles had 14 first and 32 thirds) – but the gradients on the line proved too much for them and both were moved elsewhere within a few weeks of introduction. The steel sheeting hides the locomotive portion. *Norman Collection/South Western Circle*

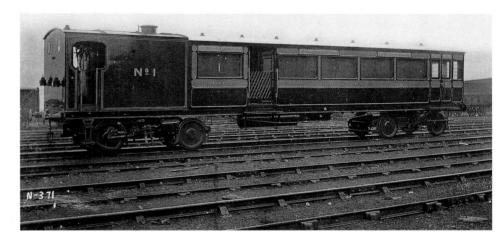

as a slightly more conventional carriage and features again in Chapter 4. Opinion varies as to which railmotor suffered which fate, as official records disagree.

Despite the apparent lack of success with the joint railmotors, Drummond was not a man to be beaten and in 1903 he ordered two more vehicles. Described as Class H12 and, rather confusingly also numbered 1 and 2, but this time wholly LSWR-owned, they were superficially similar to joint Nos 1 and 2. These were slightly shorter (perhaps as a concession to weight-saving?) but the locomotive portions were enclosed within slab-sided steel sheeting. More importantly, the boiler was turned through 180 degrees and this allowed both driving positions to face outwards, although this made the task of smokebox cleaning particularly unpleasant for the fireman. They were destined for the Basingstoke–Alton line — a charming rural backwater built under the auspices of the Light Railways Act of 1896, partly as a means of blocking any Great Western aspirations of reaching Portsmouth and partly to unlock the agricultural potential of this area of Hampshire. However, passenger traffic potential was meagre in the extreme, so economic operation was paramount.

The pair entered service in May/June 1904 but again problems were soon encountered. Overcrowding was hardly an issue, but the severe gradients in the region of Cliddesden caused the railmotors to stall even when lightly loaded and conventional

Plate 27 The interior of an 'H12' class railmotor, showing the three-ply birchwood seating. One can only presume that the perforations were to prevent the passengers from sliding about! This feature was typical of all LSWR steam railmotors and vestibule cars – cloth upholstery being provided only during the 1920s. *LSWR*

trains had to be substituted within three months of their introduction. The railmotors were then reallocated to more easily graded lines — No 1 went to Bishops Waltham and No 2 to Plymouth for the Turnchapel branch, where they remained for a number of years. Their final duties were more urban, in the Gunnersbury/Hounslow/Twickenham area before withdrawal in 1914-16, although No 1 was recorded at Fratton some time before final withdrawal, suggesting that it might have been used at East Southsea or on the Cosham–Havant duty. Both were converted to pull-push trailers in 1922 and reappear in Chapter 4.

Drummond held his faith in the railmotor principle and late in 1904 requested permission to build seven more vehicles of an improved design. These were to be used on the following services:

Whitchurch–Fullerton Junction	Two units
Poole–Bournemouth–Christchurch	Two units
Bodmin–Wadebridge–Padstow	Two units
Plymouth–Turnchapel (relief)	One unit

The LSWR Board was not convinced until Nos 1 and 2 had proven themselves at Bishops Waltham and Turnchapel, so permission was not granted until May 1905. Construction of Nos 3-9 to Class H13 then went ahead between October 1905 and February 1906. In this instance Drummond felt confident that he could design a power unit capable of hauling a trailer car, a requirement never put to the test, although at least two of the final batch (Nos 10 and 11, intended for Exeter–Honiton services) were equipped with a gangway connection at the 'carriage' end.

As **Plate 28** shows, these were much more handsome vehicles, having the locomotive portion completely enclosed within the carriage body and the whole resembling the then current South Western body styling. The encasing of the locomotive portion required the provision of a large hatch in the roof, to enable the power unit to be lifted out for major servicing. Slightly greater success was achieved with these vehicles and six more were authorised late in 1905, being completed in March–June 1906. The last batch had double doors and removable sections of floor and headstocks in place of the roof hatch, allowing the power unit to be run out through the end of the bodywork without the use of lifting equipment (see **Plate 29**).

The final six units eventually allowed the following additional services to be operated, the original allocations being shown in brackets:

Exeter–Honiton and Exeter–Topsham (Nos 10/11 and 12/13)
Plymouth–St Budeaux
Bentley–Bordon (Nos 14/15)
Lee-on-the-Solent–Fort Brockhurst
Cosham–Havant
Guildford–Aldershot–Farnham
Southampton Royal Pier tramway

The South Western was to become the greatest user of railmotors amongst the pre-Grouping Southern companies and most of its stock of 15 units 'did the rounds' of these and the duties listed earlier over the period 1906-1916. Several other routes were also tried, including Weymouth-Portland, the Callington branch and possibly a number of Southampton area local services, but with rather less success. Experience showed that considerable economies could be obtained, provided the capacity of the unit was not exceeded. However, when this occurred neither of the two alternatives — that of increased service frequency or the substitution of conventional trains — proved economically viable, while the ever-present problem of cleanliness of the passenger accommodation remained unsolved and by 1916 their shortcomings were finally admitted by the Board. All except Nos 3, 4 and 10 at Wadebridge were taken out

Plate 28 The final design of LSWR railmotor was very much more modern and in keeping with the then current carriage styling. The locomotive portion was also encased within the bodywork, necessitating the provision of a roof hatch – just visible in the photograph. The LSWR livery of salmon pink and brown extended around the ends. No 5 is seen when new in 1905. *F. Moore*

Plate 29 A Whitchurch–Fullerton Junction railmotor calls at Hurstbourne about 1908. No 12 was one of the final batch with removable headstock and opening end doors in place of the roof hatch, hence the changed window layout. *Author's collection*

Plate 30 SECR steam railmotor No 2, one of the original pair with longer side tanks and few opening windows, is seen in crimson lake livery at Chatham Central station around 1910. The window arrangements were later altered, as seen in Plate 9. It is likely that the train and station staff outnumbered the passengers. *Author's collection*

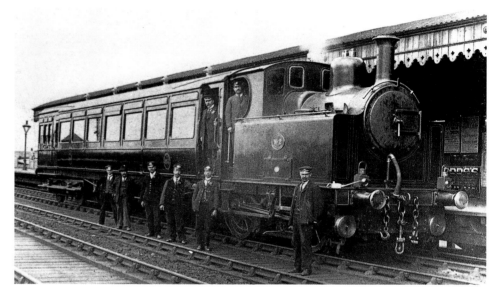

of traffic and authority was given for their rebuilding into pull-push carriages. The date at which this rebuilding took place is, however, a matter of conjecture. The final three ceased operation as railmotors in 1919, soon joining the others as more conventional rolling stock and as such will be dealt with in the next chapter.

Next came the turn of the South Eastern. Harry Wainwright had closely followed the developments at East Southsea and proposed the construction of a rather similar vehicle for use on the Sheppey Light Railway. However, Ashford Works were fully committed with other tasks, which proved rather fortunate, as the company was able to benefit from the failure in traffic of the joint vehicles. Ashford's designs were set aside and more powerful alternatives were sought from various rolling stock manufacturers. After some modifications, the design submitted by Kitson & Company was considered acceptable and two railmotors were ordered in June 1904, with delivery promised before the end of the year. Kitson sub-contracted the carriage body construction to the Metropolitan Carriage & Wagon Company and this delayed delivery until early 1905.

The two vehicles were finished in the SECR crimson lake carriage livery and were numbered 1 and 2 in their own separate series. The locomotive sections looked fairly conventional and could be separated from the carriage portion for major repairs, but not for routine maintenance. No 1 took up the intended duties at Sheppey, while No 2 was employed on the Chatham Central branch — a lightly patronised urban route whose original

raison d'être was to give the South Eastern a share of Rochester and Chatham traffic in the days before amalgamation. After 1899 its importance declined considerably and final closure came as early as 1911.

Initial results were promising, so Wainwright was able to order six more railmotors (Nos 3-8), delivery taking place between March and May 1906. These differed slightly from the original pair in that the locomotive side tanks were slightly shorter and the carriage windows were altered to give improved ventilation. This allowed deployment on the following additional services:

Dunton Green–Westerham
Sevenoaks–Otford
West Wickham–Hayes
Selsdon Road–Woodside (operated alternately with the LBSCR)
Hundred of Hoo branch
Appledore–Lydd–New Romney

Along with Sheppey and Chatham Central this gave employment for all eight railmotors, until the LBSCR took its turn on the Woodside route (every alternate 1st July for 12 months — 1 July 1907 LBSCR provided the service, 1 July 1908 SECR provided the service, etc), which released one unit to cover overhauls and other maintenance requirements. On some routes the railmotors met with modest success while at others they failed dismally. The Westerham branch passengers took such a dislike to the vehicle that ordinary locomotives and

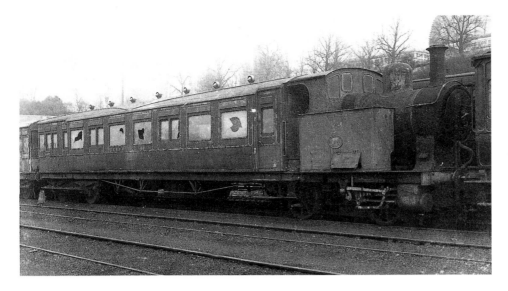

Plate 31 SECR No 5 in store at Crystal Palace about 1920, in company with Nos 1 and 6, plus several of the trailer cars (just visible at right). This is one of the later batch with increased ventilation and shorter side tanks. The condition is typical of all eight when passed to the Southern Railway in 1923. *T. A. Barry collection*

rolling stock had to be substituted by March 1907! A further series of changes led to the introduction of a Hastings–Rye service, as well as between Beckenham Junction–Crystal Palace and Dover Town–Sandling Junction (reverse)–Sandgate.

Several six-wheeled ex-SER trailer coaches were equipped to run with the railmotors — alone of the vehicles described, these appear to have had sufficient power (just!) to handle an additional coach, although no specific details of control methods have come to light and it therefore seems likely that some at least had to be run round at the end of each journey. This process would clearly negate some of the claimed advantages of railmotor operation, so it is hardly surprising that the trailers saw little use, several of which being subsequently adapted for use with pull-push fitted locomotives.

In due course, the railmotors were tried out on Dartford–Gravesend services and also between Folkestone Junction and Elham, but even before this in October 1907 the SECR Board was questioning their reliability, leading them to suggest to Wainwright that pull-push might be a better alternative for future branch line operation. However, they were prepared to accept that where the railmotors were performing adequately, they should be allowed to continue until major repairs became necessary.

Various modifications were made over the years, all of which combined to improve reliability, and several of the class achieved fairly respectable mileages between 1909 and 1914, taking into account the short journeys over which they were usually employed. Withdrawal commenced in June 1914 and only Nos 2, 4, 7 and 8 remained operational until the end of World War 1, Nos 4 and 8 latterly serving a War Department depot at Crayford Ness. Nos 1, 5 and 6 were stored at Crystal Palace High Level (**Plate 31**) and these were cannibalised to

keep the others running. Nos 2 and 7 were the last in traffic, being withdrawn from the Hastings–Rye service in February 1920 — the last railmotors to remain in service on Southern constituent company lines. All eight became Southern Railway stock in 1923, but with no plans for their return to traffic. The Southern, always adept at finding a use for otherwise redundant vehicles, gave authority for the rebuilding of the carriage portions into rather extraordinary passenger coaches and their further history will be recounted in Chapter 11.

On the LBSCR, Robert Billinton had delayed the construction of similar vehicles until the results of trials on the Great Northern and North Eastern railways had been completed. This did not occur until early 1905, shortly after Douglas Earle Marsh had taken over, but were somewhat inconclusive, so the Brighton Board decided, after some deliberation, to conduct its own series of trials. Beyer Peacock had just completed two railmotors for the North Staffordshire Railway, so two vehicles of basically the same design were ordered for service on the LBSCR. Numbered 1 and 2 in a separate railmotor series, these commenced work between Eastbourne and St Leonards in September 1905.

In similar vein, two petrol railcars were ordered from Dick, Kerr & Company of Preston, to work alongside the steam railmotors. Numbered 3 and 4, these were delivered to New Cross Gate workshops in August 1905, where the engines, gearboxes and other mechanical equipment were fitted by the Daimler Car Company. After brief trials and crew familiarisation with what at that time must have been revolutionary technology, the cars entered service in late August 1905. At the same time, two 'A1' class locomotives and 'Balloon' auto-trailers commenced work between Brighton and Worthing for comparative tests, as recounted in Chapter 1.

Plate 32 LBSCR steam railmotor No 1 in service between Eastbourne and St Leonards, probably approaching Stone Cross Junction. This shows the untypical carriage body styling – the product of the builder rather than Brighton. There were slight differences between the two railmotors; compare this with Plate 6. *T. A. Barry collection*

Some success was achieved with the steam railmotors, but the railcars proved unreliable and unpopular in service. At first, failures in traffic were commonplace and passengers soon complained of excessive vibration and petrol fumes. Both types of propulsion suffered from the usual problem of being incapable of coping with extra traffic, although there appears to have been some plan to provide trailer cars for the railmotors and to run the two railcars coupled together. In the event, a couple of six-wheeled coaches were equipped as trailer cars but did not run as such for very long, if at all. By January 1906 the railcars were relegated to the Kemp Town branch, where they continued to run intermittently until Daimler undertook major repairs to the engines. After this a modicum of success was achieved and the cars returned to main line service between Eastbourne and St Leonards as reliefs to the steam railmotors, as well as running between Lewes and Seaford. However, a further series of failures eventually led to both vehicles being relegated to the Engineer's Department and reallocation to Peckham Rye depot, for maintenance of the AC overhead electrical equipment, a task fulfilled from 1911/12 until Southern Railway days.

The steam railmotors continued to operate the Eastbourne–St Leonards service until replaced by pull-push trains in May 1912, in preparation for the summer services as the railmotors could not cope with the additional traffic. No 2 was retained as a spare vehicle for a time while No 1 went to Tunbridge Wells to cover certain off-peak pull-push duties. From July 1913 both were employed on the Woodside-Selsdon Road service until the SECR again took over the duty in July 1914. After brief service between Lewes and Seaford, both vehicles were stored at Brighton until 1918, when they were dispatched to Slades Green to serve the Army Depot at Crayford Ness. By May 1919 both had been returned to Brighton and were subsequently advertised for sale. Remarkably, a buyer in the shape of the Trinidad Government Railway appeared and both units left Britain in February 1920. No 1 served its new owners intermittently until 1936.

The limited development of steam railmotors and petrol railcars in the Isle of Wight found little favour with the newly formed Southern Railway, but it is perhaps significant to note that the first pull-push service initiated there after Grouping was destined for the Ventnor West branch — the same location as

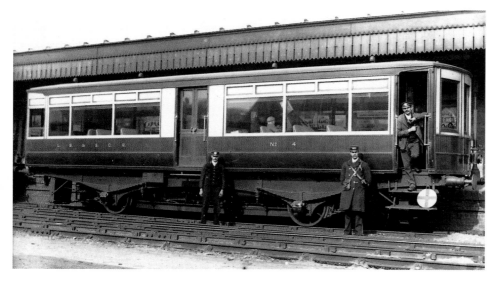

Plate 33 LBSCR petrol railcar No 4 at Kemp Town circa 1906. Of a rather different style to No 3, seen in Plate 7, it nevertheless exhibits a functional yet pleasing appearance. Unfortunately, its performance failed to match. Note the conductor/guard. *IAP*

used for the IWCR railmotor experiments of 20 years earlier. In 1925 a similar auto service was advertised for the Bembridge branch, but although four of the former SECR railmotor coaches (albeit rebuilt) were sent there, they were not, in fact fully pull-push fitted until their return to the mainland a few years later. Of this, more in Chapter 11.

By the mid-1920s pull-push operation was clearly the favoured option for most SR branch lines that fell outside the suburban network. However, there were still a few locations where even a pull-push train might prove expensive and in June 1927 Maunsell was given authorisation to purchase a 26-seat Drewry petrol railcar for evaluation on the most sparsely trafficked lines. Numbered 5 in a separate railcar series (Nos 1-4 were Ryde pier tramcars), this entered service during March 1928 on the Andover Junction–Romsey line. At first, the reliability of the vehicle was poor, but once the idiosyncrasies of the gearbox had been mastered most off-peak services could be worked without difficulty. As usual, traffic soon developed as a result of this initiative and eventually exceeded capacity, requiring the substitution of conventional trains. The unit was then briefly tried between Reading and Blackwater and in April 1929 was transferred to Ashford for working the New Romney branch — a location at that time unlikely to generate much passenger traffic, except at summer weekends.

A serious breakdown followed in February 1930, resulting in the up-rating of the engine from 50 to 64 horsepower and the reduction of the seating capacity to 22 persons. The railcar continued to operate the line, mainly during the quiet winter,

spring and autumn periods until sold to Colonel Stephens' Weston, Clevedon & Portishead Light Railway in July 1934. There, it was equipped with a small trailer vehicle to increase capacity, as seen in **Plate 34**. It continued to serve that concern until the line closed entirely in 1940.

Some economies were obtained but clearly the seating capacity was too small for most duties, so in October 1932 Maunsell ordered a Sentinel steam railbus from that company. From 1923 the Sentinel Waggon Works, in association with Cammell Laird & Company had developed a new design of steam railmotor that allowed a slight renaissance for this mode of propulsion. Now described as a railcar or railbus, rather than a railmotor, the first of these was completed for the narrow gauge Jersey Railway. Further development in conjunction with the LNER led to the production of no fewer than 96 such vehicles, together with 15 for the LMS and four more for the CLC between 1925 and 1930 by either Sentinel or Clayton of Lincoln.

The SR directors evidently felt that the idea warranted investigation, and an order for just one vehicle was placed, although an option to purchase another five was reserved. Numbered 6 in the railcar list, delivery took place on 19 March 1933, with the vehicle running under its own power from Birmingham to Brighton via Willesden Junction. According to *The Railway Gazette*, the 109-mile journey was completed using 315 gallons of water and just 4¾cwt of coal — a mere 4.88lb per mile, while a speed of 60mph had been maintained for much of the trip. With reports of such economical working, much was expected of the vehicle.

Plate 35 Sentinel railbus SR No 6 at The Dyke terminus on 11 October 1933. The roof board states 'Brighton and The Dyke', indicating a small measure of publicity. On this occasion at least, there appears to be a good head of steam. *H. C. Casserley*

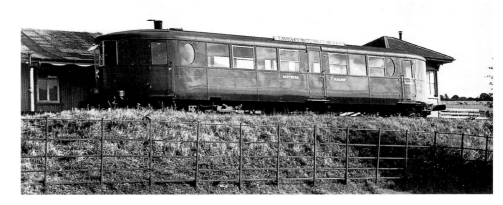

The lightweight, 44-seat bodywork was completed by Metro-Cammell Ltd and was quite remarkable in its styling. At the time, streamlining was very much in vogue and the unit was undoubtedly eye-catching, as may be judged from **Plate 35**, although not to everyone's taste and looking strangely dated by today's standards. The unit was equipped with a standard Sentinel vertical boiler working at 325lb/sq in and this was fed mechanically with coal and incorporated a crusher. This obviated the need to carry a fireman under normal circumstances, allowing even greater economy. The 100hp engine was of two-cylinder compound form, having a high-pressure cylinder of 4½in diameter and a low-pressure cylinder of 7in diameter, both having a stroke of 6in.

The railbus was tested between Brighton and Worthing and entered regular service on The Dyke branch on 1 May 1933. This 3½-mile line left the main line just west of Hove and climbed into the South Downs through a series of reverse curves and gradients as steep as 1 in 40. It had always been a difficult line to work and was poorly patronised except on Saturday afternoons and Sundays, when it was expected that a two-coach pull-push train would be needed. The vehicle proved popular and soon a halt was opened at Rowan Drive, to serve a new housing estate. The weekend substitution did, however, allow No 6 to be tried elsewhere on these days, either between Horsham and Three Bridges or on the Westerham branch, although this entailed rather a lot of empty running to effect the transfers. It also enabled rather better evaluation of the performance, which was judged satisfactory enough by February 1934 to persuade Maunsell to recommend the purchase of the other five units: two for use on the Staines, Ascot, Camberley and Aldershot services and one each for the Westerham branch and the Three Bridges–Horsham line with a spare to cover overhauls and maintenance requirements.

However, the General Manager requested that the capacity be increased to 65 seats, perhaps by using two-coach units if this were feasible. Trials then took place with a slightly larger Sentinel vehicle, a Clayton steam railbus and an Armstrong-Whitworth diesel-electric vehicle, the latter failing dismally by catching fire while on test! It proved impossible to meet the General Manager's requirements using any of these methods of propulsion and in April 1935 Sir Herbert Walker recommended that most of the proposed routes be electrified instead, using two-car electric trains to provide the basic service. This would enable extra traffic to be catered for without difficulty. The order for the additional five Sentinels was finally cancelled in March 1936.

By early 1936, the traffic on The Dyke branch was regularly exceeding the capacity of the railbus and it was transferred permanently to Tonbridge for service on the Westerham branch — the only one of the lines previously considered that had failed to make a case for electrification. Here, it was rather less well received than at The Dyke (a repeat of the experience with the SECR railmotors, 30 years earlier!), especially as it had the rather unfortunate habit of stalling on the climb from Tonbridge to Hildenborough on the early morning outward trip. Over this section, it was found necessary either to employ a fireman or utilise the hauling power of the Sevenoaks shunter as pilot. Once on the branch itself, the somewhat lightweight bodywork took rather a buffeting on windy days. Occasional trips were made over the Hawkhurst branch or to Edenbridge, but the final straw came on a round trip to Tunbridge Wells West on the evening of 22 April 1937. The vehicle failed completely on Colebrooke Viaduct on the return journey and had to be towed back to Tonbridge shed in disgrace, having caused complete havoc to other services in the meantime.

The unit remained there for several months before eventual removal to Ashford Works for repairs and a return to work, expected to be on the Gravesend West Street branch. However, the boiler failed to pass examination and the vehicle was instead consigned to a corner of the works yard, for use as a messroom for Home Guard staff. It remained there until finally broken up in 1949, despite having been officially withdrawn in January 1942.

Any further development of alternative means of propulsion now ceased and it was not until 1953, when the Southern Region of British Railways undertook trials of an ACV railbus on the Allhallows branch, that the idea of internal combustion power for branch lines was revived, leaving the steam-hauled pull-push train as the undisputed mode of propulsion for rural branch lines for the remainder of the Southern Railway's existence.

Chapter 4.

LSWR Vestibule Stock

The first true pull-push stock to be described are these highly distinctive vehicles. They later became referred to amongst enthusiasts as 'gate' stock, on account of their rather unusual entrance arrangements, but in LSWR and early Southern working notices they are described as vestibule cars and, prior to the 1912 carriage stock renumbering scheme, were numbered from 1 upwards in their own separate series.

They were not quite the first pull-push vehicles to run in southern England — that distinction going to the prototype LBSCR 'Balloon' trailers — but they came a very close second. In appearance and general design they are contemporary with the final batches of LSWR railmotors; indeed, this is the form in which they were first conceived. In February 1906 three steam railmotors and three vestibule trailers capable of being driven from either end were ordered for Plymouth district local services. However, Drummond was probably well aware that the railmotors might have difficulty in hauling a trailer car so only a month later this order was replaced by another for ten four-coupled motor tank locomotives and six vestibule trailer cars of types A and B — three of each type. Drummond was also insistent that the cars be lit by gas rather than by electricity, perhaps because the weight of the dynamos and battery boxes and/or the frictional drag of the dynamo belts might tax the capacity of the diminutive locomotives. With the benefit of hindsight, we can suggest that he was right to have these concerns.

The six vestibule cars were built as intended, each being 48ft long and 8ft 6in wide over body, very much in the style of the 'H13' class railmotors that preceded them. Accommodation for 113 third class passengers was provided in each two-coach set of brake third and full third. This lack of first class seating ensured that the three sets remained on the duties for which they had been designed (Plymouth–Turnchapel and Plymouth–St Budeaux–Tavistock), only rarely being seen elsewhere before withdrawal in 1939/40. One set may have been tried out on the Weymouth-Portland-Easton service or in the Bournemouth area in 1907, but this has not been confirmed. The sets did traverse

the Callington branch fairly regularly, but not in pull-push mode owing to the combination of sharp curves, steep gradients and the existence of several ungated level crossings. The regular operation of mixed trains also rendered pull-push operation somewhat inconvenient. One set was noted at Yeovil Town in May 1935, but this might have been en route to or from overhaul at Eastleigh Works.

The most obvious unusual feature of the vehicles was the collapsible metal 'trellis' gates (known to many by their trade name of Bostwick), but less obvious was the provision of narrow, LSWR-pattern gangway connections between the two coaches instead of the British standard type then being fitted to other LSWR corridor vehicles and, internally, the perforated three-ply birchwood seating. This might have been lightweight and easy to keep clean, but was unlikely to be comfortable for the passengers. The only saving grace here was the fact that most passenger journeys would be of short duration. Later, the seats were covered with upholstery, possibly during the 1920s when several of the ex-railmotor brake composites were similarly treated. Electric lighting was also provided between 1916 and 1920, by which time the rather more powerful 'O2' class tanks were providing the motive power.

The four-coupled motor tanks appeared as somewhat unconventional 2-2-0 tanks of Class C14 and, despite being optimistically described in *The Railway Magazine* for January 1907, soon proved themselves almost as powerless as the railmotors. Two slightly larger 0-4-0 tanks of Class S14 were completed later — perhaps to work with the larger 1909 vestibule stock, but when these proved equally ineffective the entire group of 12 locomotives were replaced from 1912 onwards with complete success, by 0-4-4 and 4-4-2 tanks. Of course, by this time Robert Urie had replaced Drummond as Locomotive Superintendent and he would have become well aware of the shortcomings of the original designs!

The original concept is illustrated in **Plate 36**. These were the first vehicles to be equipped with the three-wire control

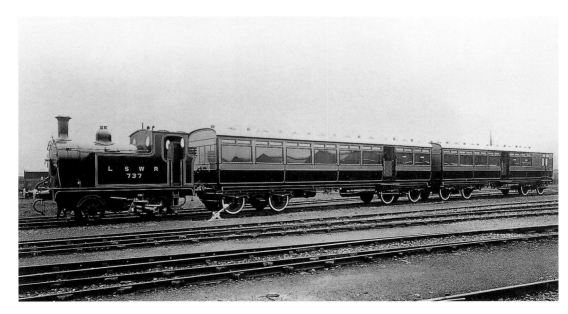

Plate 36 'C14' class 2-2-0T No 737 and vestibule cars Nos 1 and 2 at Eastleigh Works in 1906. The similarity with the 'H13' railmotors is apparent. Note the three-wire pulleys on the cab roof – facing rearward only. These small motor tanks were soon replaced in the Plymouth area by the 'O2' class 0-4-4Ts. *LSWR*

apparatus, as described in Chapter 2. No LSWR set numbers were allocated to these three sets (or to the 1909 and 1914 vestibule cars) and it was not until after 1923 that permanent SR set numbers (367-9) were applied. By this time two of the driving trailer cars had been swapped, hence the out-of-sequence SR numbering of these vehicles. In 1930, the sets received the ex-LBSCR air-control apparatus as well as standard SR pull-push driving ends, with four tall windows overlooking the track, each being 1ft 4in wide and 3ft high.

No further pull-push stock was ordered until July 1909. The South Western was due to take over the operation of the Weymouth–Portland–Easton branch (jointly owned with the Great Western) from January 1910, for a five-year period and after brief, unsuccessful trials with a steam railmotor it was proposed to use the same method of operation here. Three 56ft long vestibule cars were ordered — two brake composites and a full third, these closely resembling the 1906 stock in general details. However, just whether it was intended to run the trains as a three-car set or separately as a two-car and single unit, or as 2 + 1 either side of a locomotive, is not entirely clear. Whatever the intention, just how the three-wire apparatus would be arranged is equally uncertain and some modification (or ingenuity on the part of the locomotive crew) would have been needed to make the system work if all three vehicles ran as a single train. Coupling at the bunker end would not have given a problem, but just how to couple at the chimney end was another matter entirely.

Evidence that all three did run together comes from **Plate 39** — a very distant panoramic view of Portland, but as with the 1906 cars no permanent set numbers were allocated. The situation becomes clearer after 1919, when the former joint line railmotor from Southsea was rebuilt into a more conventional

Plate 37 Once air control was introduced, several LBSCR 'D1' class 0-4-2 tanks were sent to South Western lines, remaining there until 1939. Here, No B259 with sets 367 and 368 pass adjacent to Plymouth Friary loco shed while working the Turnchapel branch around 1931. Note the different positions for the lettering and carriage numbers – either on waist or cantrail panels. *Author's collection*

Plate 38 A close-up view of 'O2' No 207 and diagram 25 coach 735 of set 369 at Turnchapel on 22 May 1935. The coach is fully lined out and cloth upholstery is just visible through the windows. *H. C. Casserley*

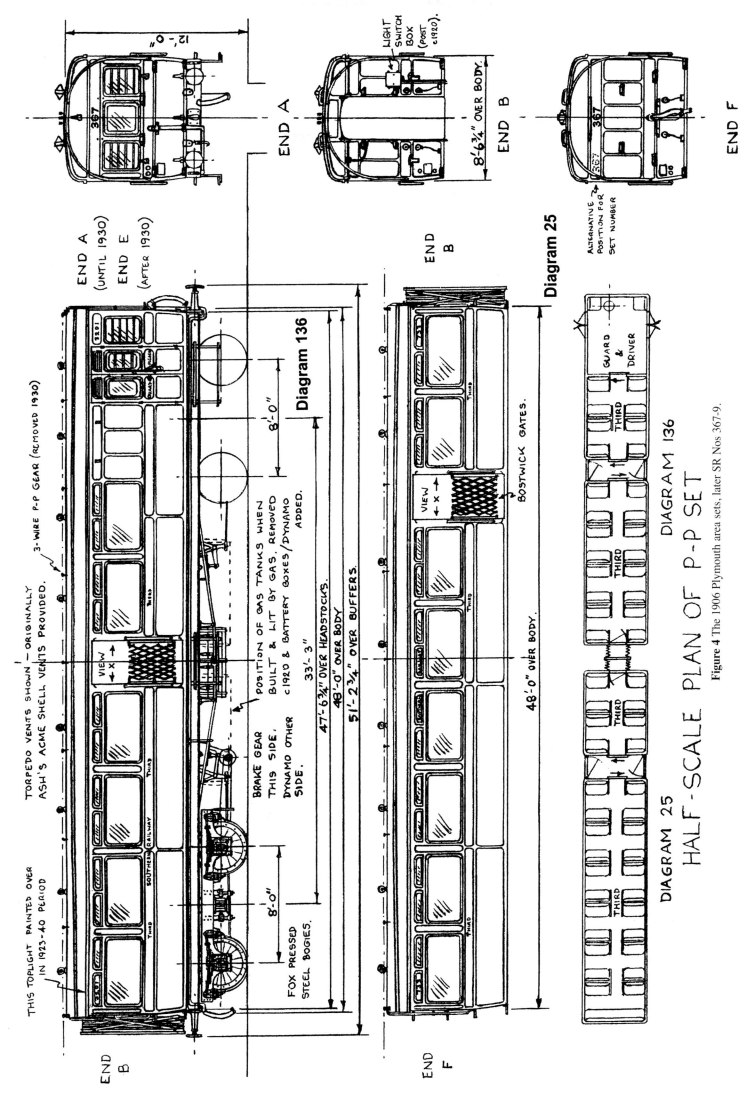

END A
(UNTIL 1930)
END E
(AFTER 1930)

END A

END B

END F

12'-0"

LIGHT SWITCH BOX (POST c.1920).

8'-6¾" OVER BODY.

367

367

ALTERNATIVE POSITION FOR SET NUMBER

TORPEDO VENTS SHOWN — ORIGINALLY ASH'S ACME SHELL VENTS PROVIDED.

3-WIRE P-P GEAR (REMOVED 1930)

Diagram 136

8'-0"

Diagram 25

THIS TOPLIGHT PAINTED OVER IN 1923-40 PERIOD.

POSITION OF GAS TANKS WHEN BUILT & LIT BY GAS. REMOVED c.1920 & BATTERY BOXES/DYNAMO ADDED.

BRAKE GEAR THIS SIDE. DYNAMO OTHER SIDE.

33'-3"

47'-6¾" OVER HEADSTOCKS.

48'-0" OVER BODY.

51'-2¾" OVER BUFFERS.

8'-0"

FOX PRESSED STEEL BOGIES.

END B

VIEW →x←

SOUTHERN RAILWAY

THIRD

BOSTWICK GATES.

VIEW →x←

THIRD

THIRD

48'-0" OVER BODY.

END F

Diagram 25

GUARD & DRIVER

THIRD

THIRD

THIRD

THIRD

DIAGRAM 25
HALF-SCALE PLAN OF P-P SET

DIAGRAM 136

Figure 4 The 1906 Plymouth area sets, later SR Nos 367-9.

Plate 39 All three 1909 vestibule cars (Nos 7, 8 and 9) appear in this view of Portland, coupled to an 'O2' tank, circa 1910. In the distance, in front of the oil storage tanks, is an arc-roofed two-coach local set. *B. L. Jackson collection*

trailer third and equipped with three-wire gear, allowing two two-coach sets to be permanently formed — each having similar seating capacities if not similar appearance. (Although the GWR should have resumed operations at Portland in 1915, this had not occurred owing to wartime conditions.) These two later became SR sets 370/1 and remained on the line until World War Two; however, the set formations began to change once the three-wire apparatus was stripped after 1931. Quite possibly, these two sets were amongst the last to retain the gear and were still so recorded in the SR carriage working notices dated September 1931. However, by this date some (possibly all) Portland line duties were provided by both sets coupled together and not in pull-push mode.

It was presumably expected that the GWR would take over operations again from 1930, as the list prepared to accompany the air-control planning meeting held at Grosvenor Road offices in November 1928 (see Appendix 1) indicates that both sets would be fitted with air-control equipment and be moved to the Midhurst branch from that date. Neither event took place and the stock remained at Weymouth for the Portland line. Formations then changed with great regularity, with ex-railmotor thirds being added to make four-coach trains, as well as ex-railmotor brake composites replacing the 1909 vehicles. However, this period does not form part of the pull-push story. Both sets, in whatever form, remained on the line until 1941, when on the night of 4 May a German air raid destroyed or badly damaged all eight cars while stabled in Weymouth sidings. Withdrawal followed and the Portland line services were then entrusted to standard LSWR corridor stock. **Plates 39** and **40**, together with **Figures 5** and **6**, illustrate these 'gate' vehicles.

Three more two-coach pull-push sets of 56ft stock were ordered in June 1913, for Seaton, Lee-on-the-Solent and Exeter–Honiton and Exeter–Exmouth services. These duties are confirmed by a paragraph in *Railway News* dated 13 June 1914, the date of delivery of the sets. However, a posed official photograph exists showing one set coupled to 'S14' 0-4-0 tank No 147 at Christchurch, so there may have been a trial over the Hurn branch or on the previously railmotor-operated service between Bournemouth West and New Milton. At Lee-on-the-Solent, the motive power was supplied using one of the ex-LBSCR 'Terrier' tanks purchased second-hand by the LSWR. The only other known LSWR allocation for these sets comes in November 1918, when one was recorded as being at Fratton instead of Seaton, perhaps for a Havant–Cosham service. It might have been intended to use it on the East Southsea line, but it is not believed that the service was actually reinstated after the war, although resumption was advertised briefly. Quite possibly, the set never left the Seaton branch, as the same set was allocated here both in 1914 and after 1923.

The set allocated to Seaton also required an additional coach around 1916, provided in the form of ex-'Eagle Express' corridor saloon third No 72. The corridor would have facilitated ticket issue and collection by the guard, and it seems to have been the only one of this type so equipped. It was later allocated SR number 648, but no mention of the pull-push gear appears in SR registers. In 1925, the coach was upgraded to first class and sent to the Hastings line, so clearly was not in pull-push use by then. Just whether it was used at any other location as a pull-push strengthening coach is unknown.

The 1914 coaches were essentially similar to the 1909 vehicles; indeed, the brake composites were almost identical

Plate 40 'O2' No E189 and sets 370/1 at Melcombe Regis (Weymouth) probably after the three-wire control apparatus had ceased to be used in 1931. Photographs of the 1909 stock are uncommon. The conductor/guard is in attendance. *Author's collection*

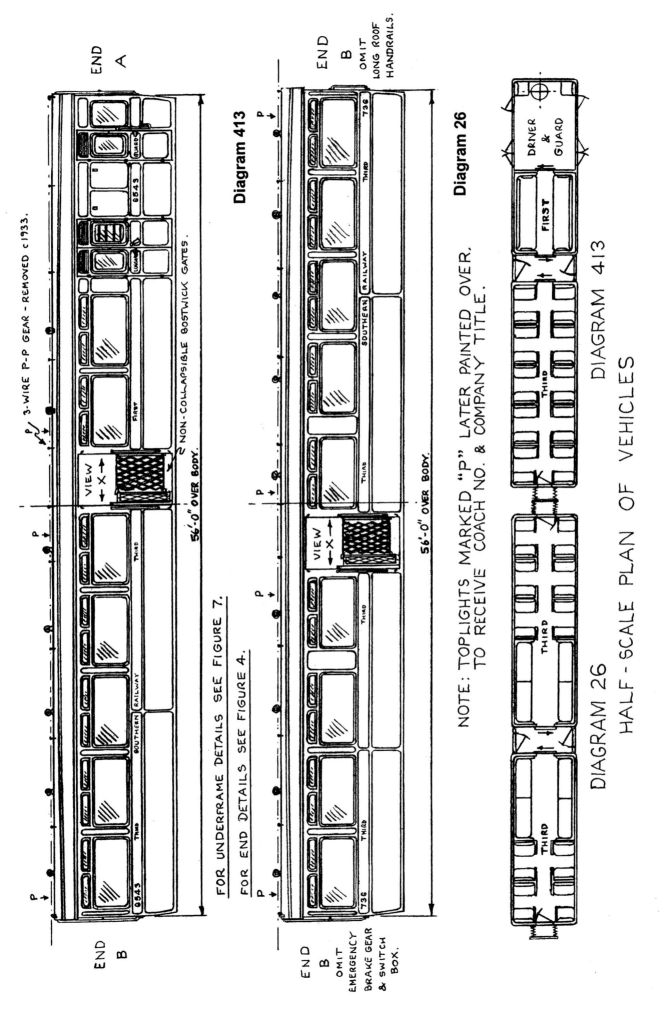

END A

3-WIRE P-P GEAR - REMOVED c 1933.

GUARD

6543

First

VIEW X

2 NON-COLLAPSIBLE BOSTWICK GATES.

Third

SOUTHERN RAILWAY

56'-0" OVER BODY.

6543

Third

END B

Diagram 413

FOR UNDERFRAME DETAILS SEE FIGURE 7.

FOR END DETAILS SEE FIGURE 4.

END B

OMIT LONG ROOF HANDRAILS.

736

Third

SOUTHERN RAILWAY

VIEW X

Third

56'-0" OVER BODY.

736

Third

END B

OMIT EMERGENCY BRAKE GEAR & SWITCH BOX.

Diagram 26

NOTE: TOPLIGHTS MARKED "P" LATER PAINTED OVER. TO RECEIVE COACH NO. & COMPANY TITLE.

DRIVER & GUARD

FIRST

THIRD

DIAGRAM 413

THIRD

THIRD

DIAGRAM 26

HALF - SCALE PLAN OF VEHICLES

Figure 5 The 1909 Portland line stock.

37

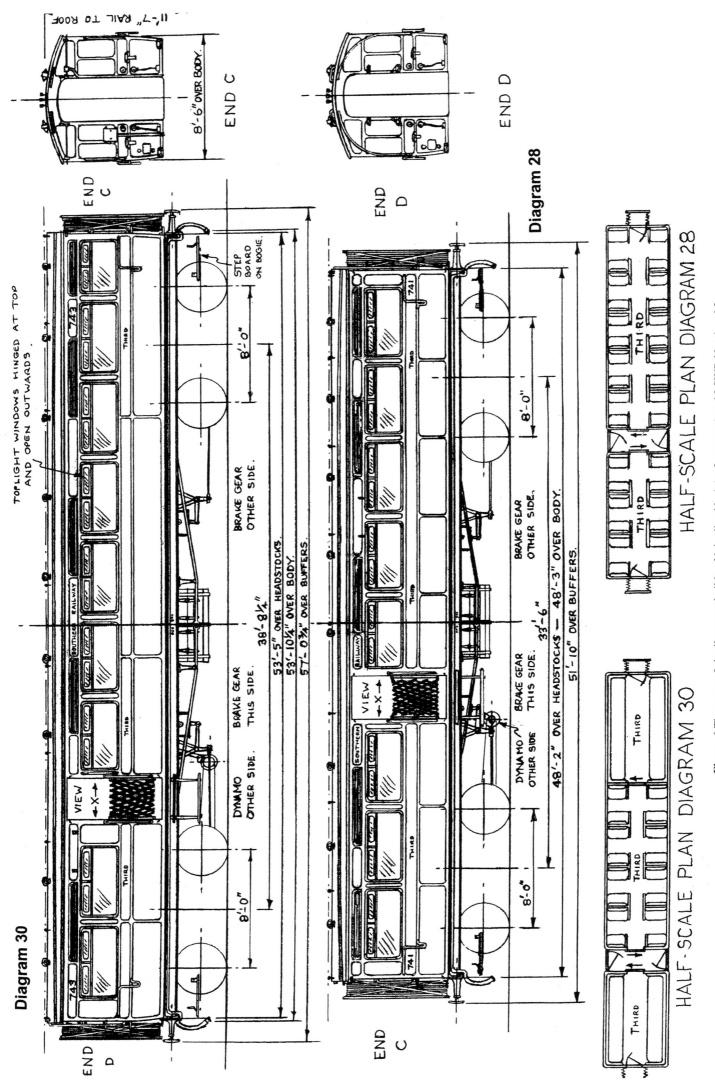

Figure 6 The arc-roofed railmotor rebuilds of joint line No 1 (or 2, see text) and LSWR Nos 1 and 2.

Plate 41 The final day of passenger services at Lee-on-the-Solent. 'D1' class tank No B239 and 1914 'gate' set 374 at the windswept terminus on 31 December 1930. The local press reported that the last train carried six passengers and a dog, who sang songs as they journeyed along. How the dog joined in wasn't recorded! *Portsmouth Evening News*

save for taller driving end windows, but the trailer thirds had the vestibule moved nearer to one end of the coach, to accord with the proportions of smoking to non-smoking accommodation. One obvious difference, most noticeable to the passengers, was the provision of elaborate wrought iron entrance gates instead of the previous trellis pattern. Gas lighting was again provided, probably the last time that this was supplied to new LSWR stock. Conversion to electricity followed in 1919/20, at the same time as the 1909 vehicles were converted.

These sets became SR numbers 372-4 and all received air-control apparatus in 1929/30, together with standard SR pull-push driving ends. By this time set 372 had been permanently split up and the brake composite (coach No 6546) was allocated to the Bishops Waltham branch, working singly. Its companion (coach No 737) was not allocated to any working between 1929 and 1933. Sets 373 at Seaton and 374 at Lee-on-the-Solent could also be split up as required and the brake composite alone used for off-peak duties on their respective branches. If indeed, there could ever be a 'peak hour' at Lee-on-the-Solent! Set 372 was reformed following the cessation of the Bishops Waltham passenger service in 1933, but was for some reason, allocated the now vacant set number 363 and retained this identity for the remainder of its life. It then took over the Yeovil Junction–Yeovil Town service — a duty with which the last 'gate' sets would always be associated.

Set 374 provided the final service at Lee-on-the-Solent in 1930 (**Plate 41**), moving on to Guildford and could then be regularly seen at Ascot, Farnham and Bordon until 1937. The three sets were downgraded to all-third in 1939 and sent to

Plymouth as replacements for the 1906 sets, which were being withdrawn. Their regular duties became Plymouth–Turnchapel and Plymouth–St Budeaux–Tavistock, as well as journeys over the Callington branch — the latter not using pull-push operation. These three sets were to become the most well known of the 'gate' stock and were employed on a number of rail tours during the 1950s, as well as being seen and photographed at locations as diverse as Plymouth, Callington, Exeter, Yeovil, Salisbury, Bisley, Bournemouth, Poole and Swanage between 1952 and 1960. Set 373 was the final survivor of the genre and latterly ran with one driver's door steel-sheeted, as well as losing most of the wooden panelling to the same finish. Preservation was contemplated, but following water damage while stored in a siding at Crediton, the vehicles were scrapped instead in November 1960. If any railway vehicles had come close to mirroring the competing tramcars then surely these must be considered the front-runners.

By 1916, the LSWR Board was ready to accept that the railmotors were no longer proving economical to operate. In October of that year, the decision was taken to withdraw 12 out of the remaining 15 vehicles and to convert these into slightly more conventional brake composite carriages. 'H13' railmotors Nos 3, 4 and 10 (by now numbered 4203/4/10) were retained at Wadebridge, for Bodmin and Padstow services until mid-1919, when they too were withdrawn for conversion. However, there seemed no rush to convert any of the vehicles immediately, as none appeared in their new guise before March 1919, while the others reappeared at intervals up to December 1919, formed into two-coach pull-push sets 11P-16P, plus loose trailer third

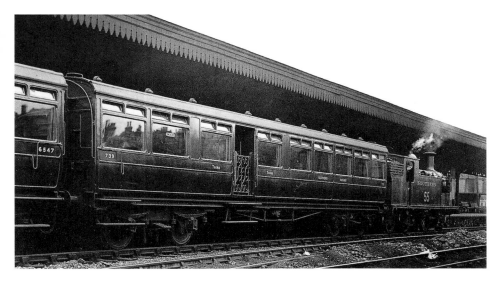

Plate 42 Diagram 27 trailer third of set 374, on a Farnham service in Platform 8 at Guildford on 10 June 1933, with 'M7' No 55. Both carry full Maunsell livery. Note the wrought-iron gates, unique to the 1914 sets. *H. C. Casserley*

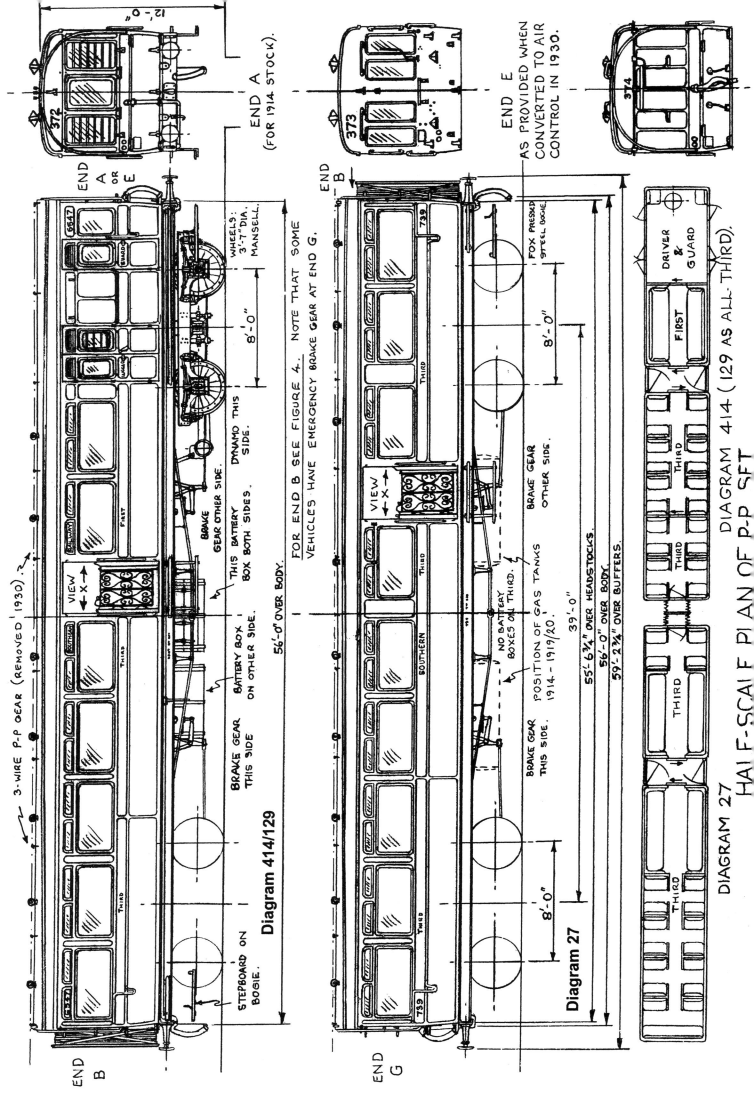

12'-0"

372

END A OR E

END A (FOR 1914 STOCK).

END B

WHEELS: 3'-7" DIA. MANSELL.

8'-0"

DYNAMO THIS SIDE.

THIS BATTERY BOX BOTH SIDES.

BRAKE GEAR OTHER SIDE.

56'-0" OVER BODY.

FOR END B SEE FIGURE 4. NOTE THAT SOME VEHICLES HAVE EMERGENCY BRAKE GEAR AT END G.

3-WIRE P-P GEAR (REMOVED 1930).

BRAKE GEAR THIS SIDE

BATTERY BOX ON OTHER SIDE.

VIEW X

GUARD

RAILWAY

FIRST

SOUTHERN

THIRD

THIRD

STEPBOARD ON BOGIE.

6647

Diagram 414/129

373

END E AS PROVIDED WHEN CONVERTED TO AIR CONTROL IN 1930.

374

FOX PRESS'D STEEL BOGIE.

8'-0"

BRAKE GEAR OTHER SIDE.

NO BATTERY BOXES ON THIRD.

POSITION OF GAS TANKS 1914 - 1919/20.

39'-0"

BRAKE GEAR THIS SIDE

VIEW X

THIRD

SOUTHERN

THIRD

739

8'-0"

739

END G

Diagram 27

55'-6¾" OVER HEADSTOCKS.

56'-0" OVER BODY.

59'-2¾" OVER BUFFERS.

DRIVER & GUARD

FIRST

THIRD

THIRD

THIRD

THIRD

DIAGRAM 414 (129 AS ALL-THIRD).

DIAGRAM 27

HALF-SCALE PLAN OF P-P SET

Plate 43 Diagram 129 (ex-414) brake third No 2624 of set 374 in malachite green livery at Bere Alston on 6 July 1948.
J. H. Aston

Plate 44 'Gate' set 373 of 1914 on an RCTS rail tour at Plymstock on 2 May 1959. By now this was the last survivor and much of the bodyside mouldings and the nearest door had been covered with steel sheeting. Livery was Southern Region green. *J. H. Aston*

Figure 7 The 1914 vestibule sets, later SR Nos 372-4.

No 4260, equipped to run as a strengthening vehicle. The two former 'H12' railmotors, also out of use since 1916, were similarly rebuilt at trailer thirds Nos 4258/9 in 1922, leading to the suggestion that trailer third No 4260 did not appear until 1922 either. LSWR records and committee minutes of the period are not entirely consistent.

The 12 vehicles formed into two-coach sets 11P-16P were equipped with British standard gangways at the non-driving ends and both coaches in each set retained a driving position, allowing a locomotive to be coupled at either end and still operate in pull-push mode. In this feature they became almost unique amongst SR pull-push stock. The LSWR set numbers followed on from the bogie 'block' sets 1P-10P (described in the next chapter), so the set numbers may not have been allocated originally, as block sets 9P and 10P were not converted until 1922. They became familiar sights at such locations as Bodmin, Callington, Torrington–Halwill, Guildford–Farnham and the Bordon branch during the 1920s. Set 362, normally used on the Bordon branch, was recorded at Bisley in July 1927, providing the National Rifle Association special service in connection with that year's shooting competitions. By September 1931 none remained in pull-push service and only coach No 6556 was ever equipped with SR air-control apparatus — running as a loose vehicle until withdrawn in December 1939. Its duties in this period are not recorded and just whether it received a standard SR pull-push driving end is also unknown.

Once the three-wire gear had been stripped there remained little need to keep the vehicles in permanent sets and individual coaches began to wander around the South Western section. Set 361 was reformed using one of the 'H12' trailer thirds and was variously allocated to Portland, Torrington–Halwill, Barnstaple,

Plate 45 Interior view of set 373 at Poole on 5 September 1960. Livery is recorded as pale cream and reddish brown, with reddish brown floral pattern upholstery. The curtains were probably similar. The set was withdrawn from service less than a month later. *A. E. West*

Plate 46 Ex-railmotor set 362 (coach Nos 6550/2) at Bisley on 16 July 1927, with the NRA special service, together with 'O2' No 232. The set number is just visible on the coach end and it seems the 'gate' stock often carried their set numbers at both ends, in marked contrast to most other pull-push stock, which was only branded at the driving (green) end. Quite possibly, the green livery was carried around both outer ends, and maybe on the inner ends as well. Standard procedure was to paint all carriage ends, apart from the driving end, black. *H. C. Casserley*

Plate 47 Loose trailer brake composites Nos 6557/8 at Bere Alston on 28 June 1949. Both vehicles were then running on the Callington branch, sometimes singly and sometimes together. They were the last surviving former railmotors and were withdrawn in April 1956. *J. H. Aston*

Plate 48 Former 'H12' railmotor No 2, now running as third No 741 (in set 361 with coach No 6548) at Wadebridge on 29 August 1945, in unlined Maunsell green livery. For a drawing of this vehicle see Figure 6. *H. C. Casserley*

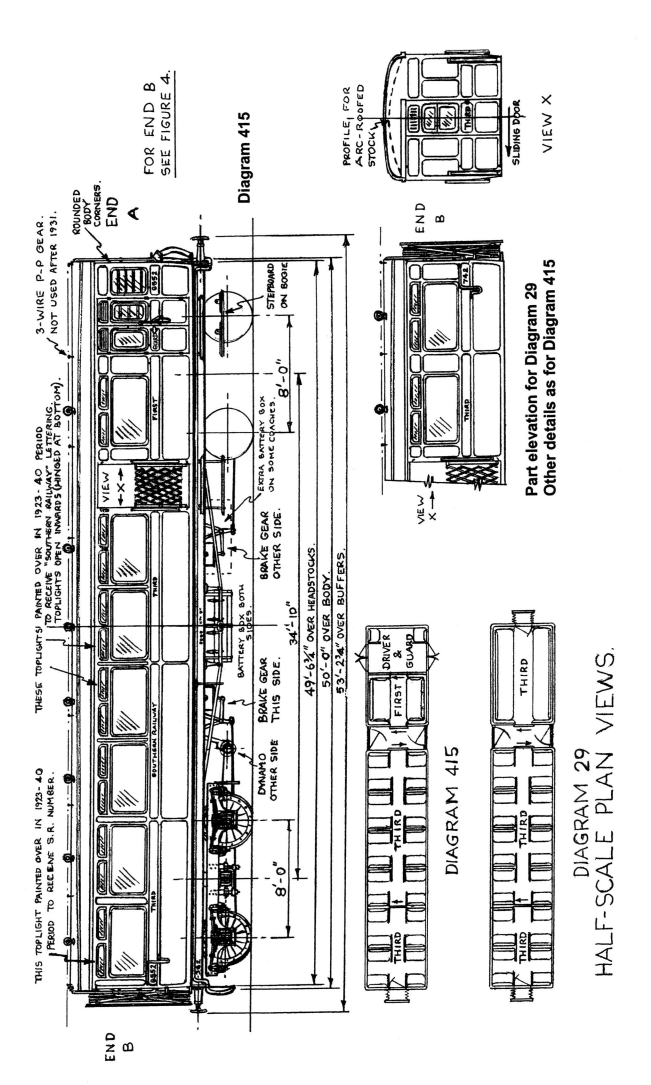

Figure 8 The 'H13' railmotor rebuilds, to diagrams 29 and 415.

Wadebridge and Callington before withdrawal in March 1956 — the last 'numbered' former railmotor set in service. Set 362 alone retained its original formation on the Callington branch until 1942, but none of the others kept permanent formations after 1933. From this time onwards the vehicles were described in carriage working notices as 'loose trailer brake composites' and vehicles No 6557/8 alone remained on Plymouth–Bere Alston–Callington line services until withdrawn in April 1956, sometimes working together and other times singly. Other locations that saw the vehicles include Lyme Regis in 1935 (No 6559), Bordon in 1941 (No 6551), the Exmouth branch in 1935/6 (Nos 6549/53/7/8), Okehampton for the Meldon quarrymen's working in 1945-7 (No 6551) and at Barnstaple

Junction for an early morning service to South Molton Road during the same period (No 6549). As recorded above, sets 370/1 at Portland included at least three ex-railmotor brake composites and four trailer thirds during the 1933-41 period. Although the three-wire gear had been disused since 1931, several coaches retained the fittings for a number of years afterwards.

Table 1 gives full numbering of all the pull-push sets formed of these vehicles, plus individual carriage details. It should be noted that the set formations presented here are slightly different to all earlier published accounts, including those attributed to the present author, but it is now believed that the details given below are a correct record of the sets during their pull-push days.

Table 1
Ex-LSWR Vestibule Stock Sets

SR Set No *	Running Dates	SR Coach Nos		Allocation 9/31	Remarks
361 (14P)	10/19-c1933	6549	6551	Weymouth (1/35 at Torrington)	Not P-P after mid-1931. By 1935 set formed of 6548 741 (until 3/56)
362 (11P)	3/19-c1942	6550	6552	Callington	Not P-P after mid-1931
363 (13P)	5/19-1931	6554	6555	Callington	Not P-P after mid-1931. Coaches later to set 371
364 (12P)	3/19-c1933	6548	6553	Callington	Not P-P after mid-1931. Coaches later to sets 361/70
365 (15P)	11/19-c1933	6558	6559	Bodmin	Not P-P after mid-1931
366 (16P)	5/20-1931	6556	6557	Torrington	Not P-P after mid-1931. Coach 6556 later equipped with air control and ran as a loose vehicle until 12/39
367	1906-6/39	3201	733	Turnchapel	Brakes 3200/1 transposed prior to 1923
368	1906-12/39	3200	734	Plymouth	Brakes 3200/1 transposed prior to 1923
369	1906-4/40	3202	735	Plymouth	
370	1909-c1933	6543	736	Weymouth	Not P-P after late 1931. Set later augmented to 4 coaches for Portland line (until 5/41)
371	c9/19-c1933	6544	743	Weymouth	Not P-P after late 1931. Set later augmented to 4 coaches for Portland line (until 5/41)
372	1914-1929	6546	737	Bishops Waltham (coach 6546 only)	Coaches separated in 1929, reformed in 1933 as 'new' set 363 (see next entry)
363	1933-11/58	6546	737		Coach 6546 downgraded to third class as 2623 in 10/39
373	1914-10/60	6545	738	Seaton	Coach 6545 downgraded to third class as 2622 in 8/39
374	1914-10/56	6547	739	Guildford	Coach 6547 downgraded to third class as 2624 in 11/39

* LSWR set numbers in brackets — only the six rebuilt railmotor sets carried LSWR set numbers. After 1930 only sets 367-9 and 372-4 (set 372 reformed as 363) plus loose coach No 6556 were equipped for air-control operation. Loose thirds 740-2 were also equipped for three-wire operation until 1931, after which they ran in sets 361/70/1. Loose 'Eagle Express' saloon third LSWR No 72 (SR No 648) was equipped with three-wire apparatus in 1916 for strengthening the Seaton branch set.

Table 1.1
Carriage Summary

SR Diagram	SR Nos	LSWR Post-1912 Nos	LSWR Pre-1912 Nos	Date built	Dimensions L x W	Seats 1st	Seats 3rd	Remarks
25	733-5	4251-3	1, 3, 5	10-11/06	48ft x 8ft 6in		65	For Plymouth area
26	736	4254	8	12/09	56ft x 8ft 6in		72	For Portland
27	737-9	4255-7		6/14	56ft x 8ft 6in		73	
28	740-1	4258-9	Railmotors 1&2	Reb 6-10/22	48ft 3in x 8ft 6in		64	Arc-roof profile. 'Strengthening cars'
29	742	4260	Railmotor 10	Reb 11/22	50ft x 8ft 6in		66	'Strengthening car'
30	743	4261	Joint railmotor 2	Reb c9/19	53ft 10in x 8ft 6in		70	Arc-roof profile. 'Strengthening car'
129	2622-4			Ex-D414	56ft x 8ft 6in		54	Downgraded from diag. 414, in 8-11/39
136	3200-2	4276-8	2, 4, 6	10-11/06	48ft x 8ft 6in		48	For Plymouth area
413	6543-4	4301-2	7, 9	12/09	56ft x 8ft 6in	10	40	For Portland
414	6545-7	4303-5		6/14	56ft x 8ft 6in	10	40	Downgraded to diag. 129, 8-11/39
415	6548-59	4306-17	Railmotors 3-9/11-15 (not in same order)	Reb 3/19-5/20	50ft x 8ft 6in	6	48	Originally 49 third class seats (if no gangway fitted)
19	648	72		P-P fitted 1916	47ft 6in x 8ft		35	Strengthening coach for Seaton branch. Ex-'Eagle Express' saloon

Note: Some records state that Joint railmotor No 1 was retained by the LSWR, with no 2 being scrapped at Brighton instead. All vehicles except diagram 19 were to SR route restriction 6– to be confined to former LSWR lines only.

Chapter 5.

LSWR Bogie 'Block' Sets

Between 1902 and 1912 the LSWR had practically re-equipped its entire suburban network with no fewer than 145 four-coach bogie 'block' sets — so named because the intermediate couplings within each set were formed of a cast-iron circular spacer block, through which passed a jointed steel drawbar, secured at each end to the stretchers carrying the bogie centre castings. Some cushioning was provided by India rubber shock absorbers but this stock was always noted for its harsh riding and snatching action as the train accelerated or decelerated. LSWR working notices drew attention to the fact that the sets were not to be used on services timed in excess of 40mph, or run for more than 30 miles without a stop — the latter presumably because no lavatories were provided.

The blocks ensured that the vehicles could be closely coupled together (1ft 2in between coaches), thereby maximising the number of compartments that could be crammed into a given train length. On suburban services trains of one, two or even three blocks could operate, with loose coaches added at the front, rear or between the blocks as necessary. By 1912, therefore, LSWR

commuter trains presented a very uniform and tidy appearance. At this time it was decided to electrify the inner suburban area using the third rail 600-volt direct current principle. Because so much of the stock was relatively new and could not really be used elsewhere, it made sense to rebuild and equip many of these vehicles as electric units and this task commenced in 1914 — continuing into Southern Railway ownership until the last bogie 'block' sets were converted in 1931.

There were, however, a few inner suburban lines that would remain steam-hauled where trains of, perhaps, just two coaches might be required. In the interests of uniformity it was therefore logical to split a number of the sets in half and equip these 'half bogie blocks' with three-wire pull-push apparatus and normal buffing gear at the 'locomotive' end. Two four-coach sets were split to form four pull-push trains (later becoming LSWR sets 1P-4P) for Clapham Junction–Kensington–Hammersmith (Grove Road)–Richmond and Wimbledon–Merton Abbey–Tooting–Ludgate Hill services — at least this is how LSWR minutes of the period record the intention. However, an article in the *South*

Plate 49 LSWR bogie 'block' set 5P leaving Weybridge for Virginia Water circa 1923, propelled by an 'O2'. Notice the position of the home signal, surrounded by the trackside allotments – so placed to be visible to trains coming round the curve from Addlestone Junction. *D. Cullum collection*

Figure 9 The three versions of bogie 'block' driving brake third.

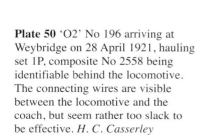

Plate 50 'O2' No 196 arriving at Weybridge on 28 April 1921, hauling set 1P, composite No 2558 being identifiable behind the locomotive. The connecting wires are visible between the locomotive and the coach, but seem rather too slack to be effective. *H. C. Casserley*

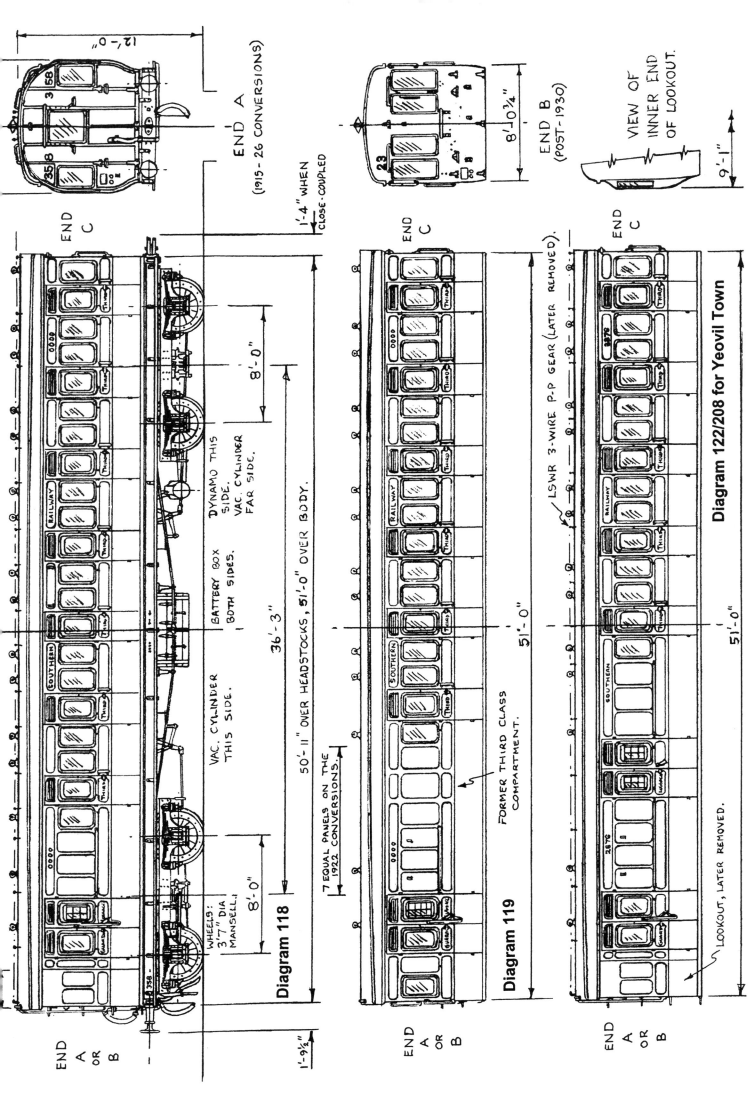

END A
(1915 - 26 CONVERSIONS)

12'-0"
3 58
35 8

1'-4" WHEN
CLOSE-COUPLED

END B
(POST-1930)

8'-0¾"
23

VIEW OF
INNER END
OF LOOKOUT.

9'-1"

END
C

END
A
OR
B

WHEELS:
3'-7" DIA
MANSELL.

VAC. CYLINDER
THIS SIDE.

BATTERY BOX
BOTH SIDES.

DYNAMO THIS
SIDE.
VAC. CYLINDER
FAR SIDE.

8'-0"

8'-0"

36'-3"

50'-11" OVER HEADSTOCKS, 51'-0" OVER BODY.

7 EQUAL PANELS ON THE
1922 CONVERSIONS.

1'-9½"

358

Diagram 118

END
C

END
A
OR
B

FORMER THIRD CLASS
COMPARTMENT.

51'-0"

Diagram 119

END
C

END
A
OR
B

LSWR 3-WIRE P-P GEAR (LATER REMOVED).

2876

51'-0"

LOOKOUT, LATER REMOVED.

Diagram 122/208 for Yeovil Town

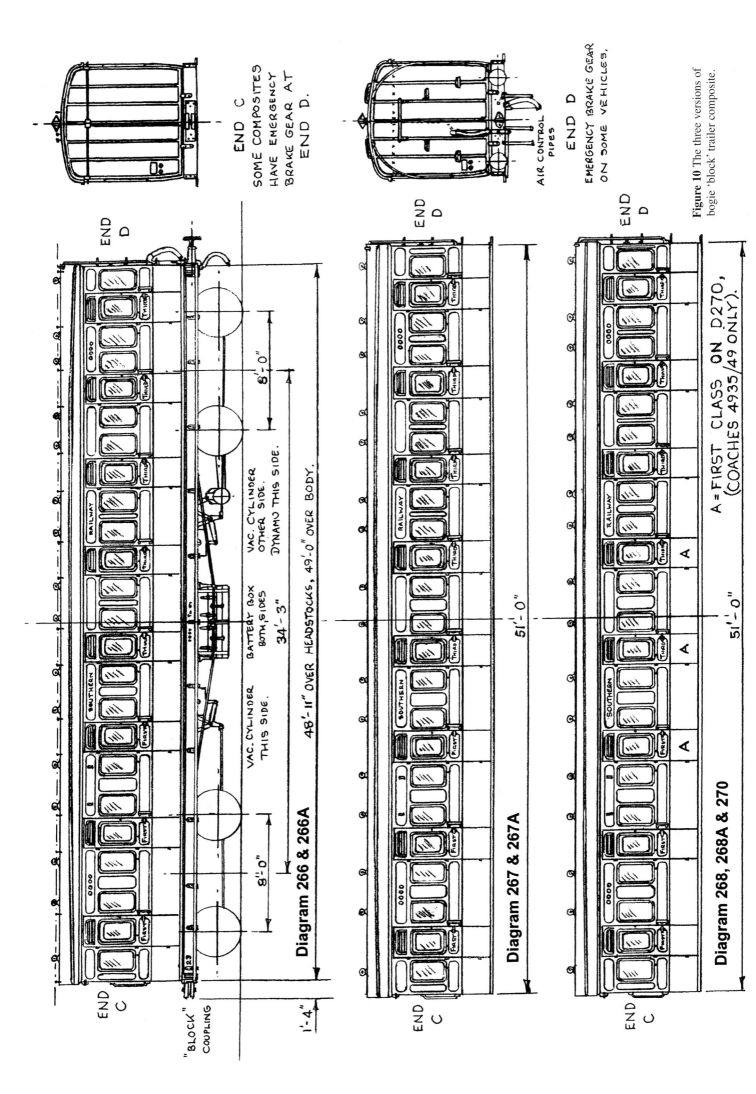

END C
SOME COMPOSITES HAVE EMERGENCY BRAKE GEAR AT END D.

END D

AIR CONTROL PIPES

EMERGENCY BRAKE GEAR ON SOME VEHICLES.

END D

Figure 10 The three versions of bogie 'block' trailer composite.

END D

THIRD | OOOO | THIRD | RAILWAY | THIRD | SOUTHERN | FIRST | D

VAC. CYLINDER OTHER SIDE.
DYNAMO THIS SIDE.

VAC. CYLINDER THIS SIDE.

BATTERY BOX BOTH SIDES.

8'-0"

8'-0"

34'-3"

48'-11" OVER HEADSTOCKS, 49'-0" OVER BODY.

END C

"BLOCK" COUPLING

1'-4"

Diagram 266 & 266A

END D

THIRD | OOOO | THIRD | RAILWAY | SOUTHERN | FIRST | D

51'-0"

END C

Diagram 267 & 267A

END D

THIRD | OOOO | THIRD | A | THIRD | RAILWAY | A | A | SOUTHERN | A | FIRST | D

A = FIRST CLASS ON D270, (COACHES 4935/49 ONLY).

51'-0"

END C

Diagram 268, 268A & 270

Western Magazine for February 1916 reports that pull-push services had commenced two months earlier on the Clapham Junction–Richmond service, but also on Windsor–Woking and Gosport–Fareham lines. It is known that a two-coach local set of non-corridors was converted for the latter duty (described at the beginning of the next chapter) and the 'gate' set at Lee-on-the-Solent would also have been available for some services, but it is not entirely clear which vehicles were provided for the Windsor–Woking duty — although 'half bogie blocks' could, at that time, have been almost the only other candidates.

In any event, this service lasted but a year, while the Clapham Junction–Richmond route was truncated at Addison Road and that to Ludgate Hill was cut back to Wimbledon and Tooting only during 1916. This released at least two of the sets which were then put to good use on the Weybridge–Virginia Water shuttle — although a couple of early morning and late evening trips were extended to Surbiton in one direction and to Egham in the other, initially using Adams radial tanks, later with 'T1' or 'O2' tanks as motive power. Another short-lived service provided at this time was between Hounslow and Feltham — replacing one of the withdrawn steam railmotors.

Electrified services over the new Guildford line as far as Claygate commenced in November 1916 and two more 'block' sets were split to provide the necessary four pull-push sets (LSWR numbers 5P-8P) for the onward services to Guildford. Claygate then became the 'frontier' station between the electrified suburban services and the steam-hauled country area — the first of many such locations as recounted in Chapter 1. In this instance, the Adams radial tanks could not keep to the scheduled times and were soon replaced by the more powerful 'M7' tanks. This service provision was to last only until June 1919, as the consequent increase in traffic on all the newly electrified lines resulted in a shortage of stock, so the Claygate electrics were withdrawn and the units deployed to augment the services on the other electrified lines — steam returning to the new Guildford line services until after the Grouping. The pull-push stock was diverted to Yeovil and the Guildford-Aldershot-Farnham and Ascot group of services.

Two more 'half bogie blocks' were formed in 1922 (LSWR sets 9P and 10P) for the Swanage branch. To cater for the greater volume of luggage expected at a seaside resort, the brake thirds in these sets had their passenger accommodation reduced from seven to six compartments, increasing the guard's van by the width of one compartment. The van section was completely rebuilt to give seven equal panels, unlike later conversions of this type. All ten LSWR sets later became SR set numbers 351-60 in the same order and the brake thirds retained their ogee lookouts and had a large centrally positioned window added at the driving end. The composites were of no fewer than three types — depending on the sets chosen for conversion — while various later changes in the amount of first class accommodation resulted in several more different diagrams being allocated after 1923.

It was soon found that the set allocated to the Yeovil Town–Junction duty also had insufficient van space to deal with the volume of luggage and parcels traffic being carried, and in June 1924 SR order E35 was issued for the conversion of LSWR brake third No 1836 in set 1P (SR No 2876/set 351) into a five compartment vehicle — losing two third class compartments and gaining a second set of double doors to the luggage van. This work was completed in October 1924 and the set returned to Yeovil, now repainted and renumbered in SR livery. It was unique amongst the 'block' sets and remained at Yeovil until withdrawn in 1940. Incidentally, its replacement was ex-SECR set 659, which also had additional luggage van space provided.

In 1926, it was decided to extend pull-push operations in the Bournemouth area, the Meon Valley line and the Lymington branch. Order E218, issued in November 1926, called for bogie 'block' sets 238-41 (and LSWR set 19B, earmarked for conversion by the LSWR but not yet done), to be turned into pull-push sets 23-30 and 376/7, while order E219 was issued for the conversion of 12 more 'M7' tanks to three-wire operation. These were the last conversions to this method of control before its reliability was

Plate 51 Set 351 runs into Yeovil Junction, some time between 1924 and 1929. The reconstructed five-compartment brake third (SR No 2876) can be seen. *D. Cullum collection*

Plate 52 Most of the 'block' sets converted between 1922 and 1927 had one compartment in the brake third added to the luggage van. Set 24 was one of these, seen at Ash Vale on an Aldershot–Ascot working in December 1938, shortly before electrification of the route. The former door, droplight and compartment window positions are clearly visible in the panelling. *F. E. Box*

called into question. They generally resembled the earlier sets, apart from the removal of the side lookouts and the provision of what would become the standard SR pull-push driving end, with four tall windows overlooking the track. Sets 23-30 (but not 376/7, ex-LSWR set 19B) also had the luggage van enlarged by the width of one compartment, but unlike the 1922 conversions the van side was not repanelled, but instead the droplight and window openings were simply sheeted in. **Plate 52** makes this clear.

From time to time it became necessary to augment these sets to three coaches and a small number of LSWR 48ft eight-compartment thirds, later to SR diagram 12, were fitted with three-wire apparatus so that they could be coupled between the set and the locomotive. This seemed to be most essential on the Claygate–Guildford and Weybridge–Virginia Water services. However, at Yeovil, 42ft brake third No 1649 (later SR No 2631 to diagram 109) was equipped instead. This was of course before set 1P was altered to provide additional van space. The coach was also noted at Lymington *c*1920, again a location often requiring extra luggage accommodation, so it may have moved around somewhat. These loose coaches are detailed along with other LSWR non-corridor stock in Table 3 at the end of the next chapter.

Following an overrun at Virginia Water in 1927 when, after investigation, it transpired that the three-wire apparatus was not in a fit state to be capable of connection, officialdom suddenly awoke to the fact that this was the norm rather than the exception and that urgent remedial action would be necessary. The procedure that followed is recounted in Chapter 2 and Appendix 1 and all 20 'half bogie blocks' were converted to air control between April and September 1930, as well as having the bogie springing altered from fixed to swing link — this modification partially overcoming the restriction to 40mph from applying in future — not that many pull-push trains were ever likely to be travelling at great speed. Apart from set 351, which returned to

Yeovil after conversion, there was a general change around in allocation as a result and some sets then found themselves on the South Eastern section, mostly being based at Gillingham or Strood and appearing on North Kent area duties.

Apart from the provision of ex-LBSCR air control, the LSWR lookouts were removed from the original ten conversions and standard SR driving ends were fitted. A droplight was also added on each side of the driving compartment. These alterations would allow complete interchangeability with almost any other type of pull-push set, irrespective of origin, and this became a general feature of SR motor train working from 1930 onwards. Only the LBSCR 'Balloon' sets and the LSWR 'gate' stock remained, confined to their respective sections of the Southern Railway after this time.

This matter of interchangeability also brought about the conversion of the final bogie 'block' pull-push sets. It had originally been proposed to convert eight more LSWR vestibule sets to air control (see Appendix 1), but it was soon realised that because of their rather unusual constructional features it would be better to restrict these to former LSWR lines. Instead, eight additional bogie 'blocks' were substituted and sets 22, 350/78-80, 731, 977/8 were converted in 1930 in lieu of 'gate' sets 361-6/70/1, which were never equipped with air control and remained on South Western section duties. By the time that sets 977/8 were converted in November 1930, the accompanying 'block' composites had already been taken for electric stock conversion, so two 50ft non-corridor composites to SR diagram 272 were substituted. In order to couple to these, the brake thirds had to have normal buffers and conventional couplings fitted at the non-driving end. Strictly speaking, they were not therefore 'half block sets' at all and could have been described in the next chapter, but following our convention stated earlier, have been included here.

Sets 22, 379/80, 731 and earlier conversions 354/8/78 were all initially allocated to the South Eastern section. Indeed, set 731

Plate 53 A Wimbledon–Ludgate Hill via Tooting service calls at Merton Abbey on 23 August 1927, formed of an 'M7' and set 358 – the latter still in original LSWR condition and livery, with ogee lookouts and three end windows. The regulator handle may be seen through the centre window. The LSWR set number (8P) is just visible beneath the more recently applied SR set number. *H. C. Casserley*

Plate 54 Set 376, converted to pull-push in December 1927 (and incidentally, the last three-wire conversion), forms a Swanage branch train with 'M7' No 108, photographed soon after leaving the main line at Worgret Junction, in 1935. Air control is now fitted, together with a standard SR pull-push driving end. *Real Photographs*

Plate 55 Between 1922 and 1937 the Bournemouth area saw a number of bogie 'block' pull-push workings. 'M7' No 47 takes water between duties at Bournemouth West, coupled to set 29. Notice that the headcode disc has been reversed to indicate the train is not in service. *D. Cullum collection*

Plate 56 The Guildford area also had a number of bogie 'block' sets allocated until 1939. 'M7' No 481 shunts past Bordon loco shed, with an unidentified set that includes a seven-compartment brake third (diagram 119), some time during the 1930s. *A. B. Macleod*

Plate 57 The final two bogie 'block' conversions (sets 977/8) were not really bogie 'blocks' at all and could have been classed as ordinary non-corridor stock. These had 50ft diagram 272 composites instead, but no photographs of these are known, so the composite has been illustrated by camping coach No 22 (ex-4989), seen at Corfe Castle on 12 June 1948. *J. H. Aston*

was tested between Maidstone West and Snodland on 4 July 1930 and even got a mention (and photographs) in the *Kent Messenger* newspaper! This set may also have been unique in having the set number painted on the driving end twice, above the left- and right-hand windows, rather in the manner applied to corridor stock. That said, however, it should be noted that the last two conversions (sets 977/8) seem to have eluded the photographers, so might have been treated similarly. In 1932, set 359 also acquired a diagram 272 composite and the brake coach required

normal buffing gear to be fitted so it was no longer considered a 'block' set. It then joined the above seven sets on the South Eastern section, being based at Strood. At least two more of the sets (Nos 28 and 350) also later ran on this section.

These sets seem to have only rarely appeared on Central section workings and the author can find only three photographs of such an event. One was noted on a Guildford-Horsham working (**Plate 58**) in 1937, which might have been the result of a failure at Guildford of the usual LBSCR set, the second was at

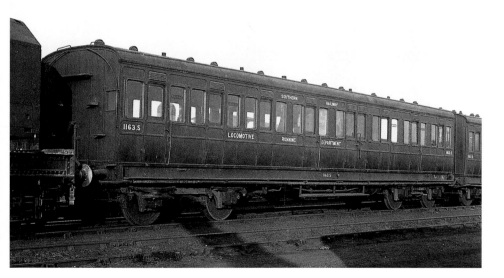

Three Bridges on a Horsham service (possibly the same set), while the third was on a Bognor-Barnham duty around 1935. This might have been a case of using a set either en route to or from Lancing Works for repairs.

Withdrawal of the stock commenced in 1936, along with general withdrawal of most short LSWR non-corridor vehicles. Many had timber underframes (flitched with steel plate, so this design change was not readily apparent) and the decision to commence withdrawal of these vehicles dated from the previous

year. All were out of traffic by mid-1940, set 351, by then the relief set at Yeovil, being the last survivor. Several coaches, including both from sets 25, 350/1/78 then entered departmental service and lasted into the 1950s. This was relatively unusual and few other pull-push coaches were granted a further lease of life in this manner. Table 2 lists the set formations and details of the individual vehicles.

Table 2
Ex-LSWR Bogie 'Block' Sets

SR Set No.*	Running dates	SR coach Nos* BT	C	Allocation 9/31	Remarks
22	7/30-12/39	2847	4904	Port Victoria/Gillingham	
23	12/26-11/39	2871	4868	Chertsey	6 compt brake third
24	12/26-9/39	2809	4976	SW Section, later Guildford	6 compt brake third
25	12/26-11/39	2819	4865	Bordon	6 compt brake third
26	12/26-11/37	2818	4984	Chertsey	6 compt brake third
27	12/26-12/39	2821	4862	SW Section, later Gillingham	6 compt brake third
28	12/26-8/39	2820	4985	Gosport, later Gillingham	6 compt brake third
29	12/26-12/39	2823	4863	Gosport	6 compt brake third
30	12/26-11/39	2822	4986	SW relief set	6 compt brake third
350	7/30-3/38	2888	4968	Swanage, later SE relief set	
351 (1P)	1915-4/40	2876(1836)	4917(2558)	Yeovil Town	Altered to 5 compt brake third, 10/24
352 (2P)	1915-2/39	2870(1800)	4916(2611)	Bournemouth area	
353 (3P)	1915-12/39	2807(1360)	4915(2526)	Bournemouth area	
354 (4P)	1915-8/39	2806(1359)	4918(3042)	Gillingham	
355 (5P)	11/16-6/37	2775(1274)	4920(2957)	Bournemouth area	
356 (6P)	11/16-8/39	2774(1273)	4914(2958)	Bournemouth area	
357 (7P)	11/16-2/37	2839(1611)	4913(2271)	Bournemouth area	
358 (8P)	11/16-3/38	2830(1573)	4919(2395)	SE relief set	
359 (9P)	1922-4/32	2893(1258)	4884(2942)	SE relief set	6 compt brake third
	8/32-6/36	2893	5004	Strood (in 1935)	6 compt brake third. Not close-coupled
360 (10P)	1922-5/36	2892(1257)	4949(2941)	SW relief set	6 compt brake third
376	12/27-11/39	2772	4891	SW relief set, later Guildford	
377	7/27-9/38	2773	4956	Reading	
378	7/30-10/37	2860	4905	SE relief set, later Gillingham	
379	7/30-11/39	2817	4969	Port Victoria/Gillingham, later Guildford	
380	7/30-12/39	2867	4935	Maidstone West	
731	7/30-7/39	2865	4870	SE relief set	Accident damage at Hoo Jcn, 7/39
977	11/30-10/36	2853	4988	Guildford	Not close-coupled
978	11/30-11/37	2846	5010	SW Section	Not close-coupled
	12/37-12/38	2846	4835	SW Section	Not close-coupled

* LSWR set and coach numbers in brackets. All sets fitted with air-control gear in 1930.

Table 2.2
Carriage Summary

SR Diagram	SR Nos	Relevant LSWR Nos	Date of P-P conversion	Dimensions L x W	Seats 1st	3rd	Remarks
119	2772-5, 2806/7/17/30/39/46/7/53/60/5/7/70/88	1273/4, 1359/60, 1573, 1611, 1800	1915/6 & 1926/7/30	51ft x 8ft (9ft 1in over lookouts)		70	Nos 2774/5, 2806/7/30/9/70 converted by LSWR and retained lookouts until 1930. Also included LSWR 1836/SR 2876 until 10/24.
120	2809/18-23/71/92/3	1257/8	1922/6	51ft x 8ft (9ft 1in over lookouts)		60	Nos 2892/3 converted by LSWR and retained lookouts until 1930.
122/208?	2876	1836	1915 (reb 10/24)	51ft x 8ft (9ft 1in over lookouts)		50	Rebuilt from diagram 119 in 10/24 for Yeovil. Originally converted by LSWR and retained lookouts until 1930.
264	4835		12/37	48ft x 8ft	10	50	Compartment layout 3331L133 Not close-coupled. See note below.
266	4862/3/5/8/70/84/91, 4904/5/13-16	2271, 2526, 2611, 2942/58	1915/6/22 & 1926/7/30	49ft x 8ft	18/24	50	Compartment layout 11133333 Nos 4913/4 always had 24 first class seats, rest altered to diagram 266A in 1935-7.
267	4917/8/76/84-6	2558, 3042	1915/26	51ft x 8ft	18/24	50	Compartment layout 11133333 Nos 4917/8 altered to diagram 267A in 1935.
268	4919/20/56/68/9	2395, 2957	1916 & 1927/30	51ft x 8ft	18/24	50	Compartment layout 11133333. All except No 4920 altered to diagram 268A in 1935/6.
270	4935/49	2941	1922/30	51ft x 8ft	18/24	50	Compartment layout 33111333. Both altered to diagram 268 in 12/30, later diagram 268A.
272	4988, 5004/10		1930/2	50ft x 8ft	12/16	60	Compartment layout 33311333. No 4988 to diagram 272Ain 7/35. Not close-coupled.

Both diagram numbers shown against coach No 2876 may be incorrect, as they were officially allocated to other vehicles as well.
The seating alterations of 1935-7, with 'A' suffix to diagram numbers involved removal of armrests in first class compartments with an increase from six to eight seats in each compartment.
The diagram 264 composite formed in set 978 from 12/37 was the only coach to this diagram to be fitted for pull-push working.
Vehicles with lookouts were to SR route restriction 3, all others were restriction 0.

Chapter 6.

LSWR Non-corridor Stock

Perhaps surprisingly, very few ordinary LSWR non-corridor coaches (excluding the 'block' sets) were pull-push fitted until the mid-1930s — indeed, only one such set received three-wire apparatus — and so this chapter deals primarily with the post-1935 period. However, as noted in the last chapter, the *South Western Magazine* for February 1916 records that pull-push operation had recently commenced between Gosport and Fareham. The 'gate' set at Lee-on-the-Solent entered service in June 1914, but the same LSWR minute, dated June 1913, authorising the construction of the three 1914 vestibule sets, also called for one of the existing two-coach bogie set trains to be converted to pull-push operation, specifically for Fareham-Gosport and Stokes Bay services. The exact date of conversion is not clear, but it must have been some time between late 1913 and December 1915. Quite possibly it was in June 1914, to coincide with the introduction of the Lee-on-the-Solent auto train service, despite what was stated by the *South Western Magazine*!

Most of these two-coach bogie set trains were formed during 1910 for branch line services and comprised a 42ft brake third coupled with a 45ft brake composite. Each coach originally had seven compartments and the 1910 rebuilding involved stripping two third class compartments at one end of each vehicle and their replacement by a guard's van. There were at least three versions of sets, with either arc or semi-elliptical roof profiles, as well as two versions of guard's van layout — one with the lookouts at the carriage end and one where the lookouts were adjacent to the passenger compartments. True to form, LSWR minutes do not tell the full story about these conversions, since 20 sets were to be formed during the period March-December 1910, yet a total of 27 such sets became SR property in 1923. So exactly when the other seven conversions took place is debatable, but from photographic evidence some of the arc-roofed sets could have been in traffic by 1907.

Plate 61 Arc-roofed pull-push set 375 from Gosport has eluded the photographers, so may only be illustrated by a non-pull-push fitted example. An identical combination of 45ft brake composite and 42ft brake third is seen at Braunton on 10 August 1929, strengthened with a diagram 12 third. On set 375 the nearest end of the brake composite received an additional centrally placed driver's window and control gear, as seen in Figure 11. Just prior to publication, a photograph of the set surfaced, taken about 1924 at Broadstone Junction, on a service from Hamworthy. *R. W. Kidner*

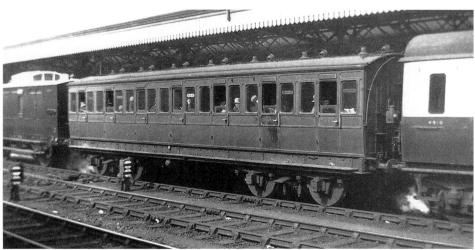

Plate 62 Set 375 might not have been photographed, but arc-roofed strengthening third No 163 (to diagram 10) certainly was! Clearly not running pull-push, it is seen at an unknown GWR station, in the company of rather mixed stock, circa 1925-30. The three-wire gear may be seen along the roof. *P. Coutanche*

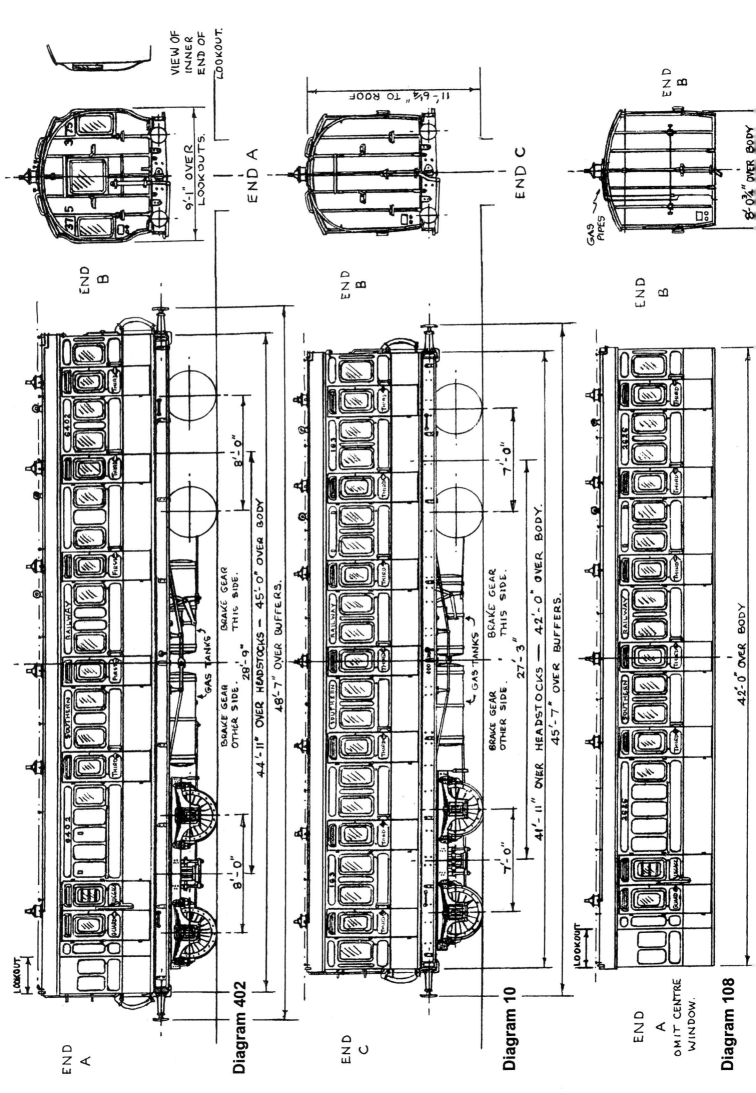

VIEW OF INNER END OF LOOKOUT.

9'-1" OVER LOOKOUTS.

END A

END B

375

375

6402

RAILWAY

SOUTHERN

THIRD

FIRST

THIRD

GUARD

6402

LOOKOUT

BRAKE GEAR OTHER SIDE.

BRAKE GEAR THIS SIDE.

GAS TANKS

28'-9"

44'-11" OVER HEADSTOCKS — 45'-0" OVER BODY

48'-7" OVER BUFFERS.

8'-0"

8'-0"

END A

Diagram 402

11'-6¾" TO ROOF

END C

END B

163

RAILWAY

SOUTHERN

THIRD

THIRD

163

BRAKE GEAR OTHER SIDE.

BRAKE GEAR THIS SIDE.

GAS TANKS

27'-3"

41'-11" OVER HEADSTOCKS — 42'-0" OVER BODY.

45'-7" OVER BUFFERS.

7'-0"

7'-0"

END C

END B

Diagram 10

8'-0¾" OVER BODY

GAS PIPES

END A

END B

2826

RAILWAY

SOUTHERN

THIRD

THIRD

2826

LOOKOUT

GUARD

42'-0" OVER BODY

END A

OMIT CENTRE WINDOW.

Diagram 108

The set chosen for pull-push conversion was one of the arc-roofed type with end lookouts and it was a fairly simple matter to fit three-wire apparatus, driving controls and a centrally placed window in the leading end of the brake composite coach. The Stokes Bay service ran only until 1915, but that between Gosport and Fareham continued well into Southern Railway days. Apart from being noted at Eastleigh Carriage Works in 1927, the set has not been recorded at any other location. No LSWR set number was allocated, at least not in the P-suffixed series, while after the Grouping it became SR set number 375. With seating for only 12 first and 80 third class passengers the accommodation was not generous and at some time before 1923 a similar, 42ft seven-compartment third class coach was equipped with three-wire gear to run either within or coupled to the set. The set was recorded by the November 1928 list (see Appendix 1) as a three-coach formation, but it was not detailed for conversion to air-control, and in fact, it appears that it was last used in pull-push mode during 1927. Almost certainly, if still at Gosport at that date, then its place was taken by one of the 1926 bogie 'block' conversions. By the September 1931 carriage working notice the set is listed as a two-coach local set, non-auto fitted and was withdrawn from service soon after.

The only other LSWR non-corridor vehicles to carry the three-wire apparatus (such as it was for an intermediate coach — just guide eyes and wire) were four 48ft thirds to SR diagram 12 (SR Nos 188, 219, 292 and 497) and 42ft brake third No 2631 to SR diagram 109. The date of fitting is not recorded, but was probably c1919-21. All these were used as strengthening coaches, placed between the locomotive and the pull-push set, and all were stripped of the gear during 1930. As noted in Chapter 5, these ran mostly with the 'block' sets. It was not long, however, before several more diagram 12 vehicles were equipped with air-control pipework, to fulfil exactly the same function. Two more diagram 12 vehicles were converted in 1931 for inclusion in pull-push sets 649/50, coupled to ex-LBSCR arc-roofed coaches. These will be detailed further in Chapter 9.

The next all-LSWR non-corridor pull-push sets were not formed until February 1935, almost four years after the demise of set 375. SR order L802 was issued in March 1934 to cover the construction of sets 652-5 for the Allhallows branch, although they may have only worked there but briefly. In fact, the carriage working notices for January 1935, printed while the stock was being converted, show their initial allocation to be South Eastern section relief duties, only to be transferred to Allhallows at the commencement of the summer service.

For those unfamiliar with the location, Allhallows is close to the Isle of Grain and adjacent to the Thames estuary. In the late

1920s there was a proposal to develop a holiday resort in the vicinity and the Southern Railway, ever ready for development opportunities, obliged by constructing a new line from Stoke Junction on the Port Victoria branch northwards across the marshes and this opened to Allhallows in May 1932. An optimistic train service, including through trains to London, was provided at the opening but by 1935 it was already apparent that only the summer service was likely to be profitable and the line became the almost undisputed domain of pull-push stock from thence until closure at the end of 1961.

Although nominally of LSWR origin, sets 652-5 were of somewhat mixed parentage. The four driving brake composites (SR Nos 6428-31) started life as 'emigrant' thirds in 1905. At that time there was a considerable traffic in refugees from Eastern Europe towards America and many of these landed at east coast ports, making their way by train to Southampton, Plymouth, Bristol or Liverpool for onward transit. To cater for the traffic, the LSWR built a number of coaches to a composite loading gauge so that they could run almost anywhere in the country. Their dimensions were 46ft 6in long, 8ft 3¾in wide and 11ft 8½in high — all dimensions somewhat less than the LSWR standard. The 1905 coaches also had one other unusual feature — corridors within the carriages, but no gangways at the ends. The later 1907/08 vehicles did have gangways and enter the pull-push story as true corridor vehicles, to be described in the next chapter.

The 1905 train became SR stock as set 337, but by 1926 the emigrant traffic had waned and the two brake thirds (SR Nos 3079/80) were modified in March 1927 for Hurstbourne-Fullerton Junction services (a line seemingly never to see pull-push operations). The other coaches continued to run in excursion and other seasonal traffic until 1934, when it was decided to reframe the similar corridor coaches and take four of the surviving non-gangwayed thirds for conversion to driving brake composites (SR Nos 6428-31). These were also reframed using new underframes supplied by the Birmingham Railway Carriage & Wagon Company and extensively modified for their new use. The accompanying full thirds (SR Nos 1-4) were provided by taking four LSWR 50ft composites and mounting these on standard SR 58ft underframes, splicing in an additional compartment (plus a 1ft void) into the bargain. The result was something of a hybrid, as can be seen from the photographs — the different lengths, widths and height of the two vehicles being most obvious. Despite the apparent discord, all four sets remained mostly on South Eastern or Central section workings until withdrawn in 1959-62, although sets 652/4 each underwent a change in formation during 1958. Those lines which saw these

Plate 63 Several 48ft eight-compartment thirds to diagram 12 were equipped for pull-push operation, both during the three-wire and air-control eras. No good photographs have come to light but this is an identical unfitted example, SR No 540, at Guildford *circa* 1933. This is a gas-lit vehicle, but some of the pull-push vehicles had electric lighting. For a drawing of these vehicles, refer to Figure 36. *D. Cullum collection*

Figure 11 The solitary arc-roofed LSWR pull-push set, later SR set 375.

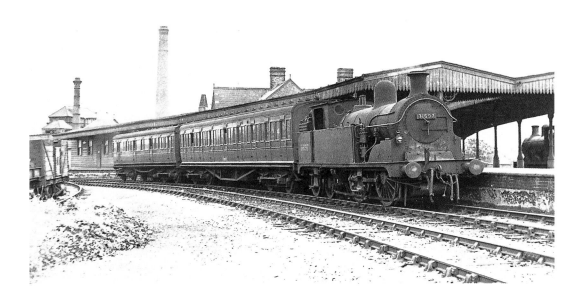

Plate 64 'Allhallows' set 653 and 'R1' class 0-4-4T No 31697 at Gravesend West Street on 24 June 1950. The set is in BR lined crimson lake livery. *R. Cogger*

Plate 65 The 'corridor' side of coach No 6429, in lined crimson lake, at Eardley Sidings on 27 April 1952. One third class compartment and a lavatory previously occupied the guard's/driver's accommodation at the left-hand end. *D. Cullum*

Plate 66 Set 653 again, showing the compartment side of the driving brake, in BR green livery at Horsham, circa 1958. Note the different proportions of the two vehicles. *Author's collection*

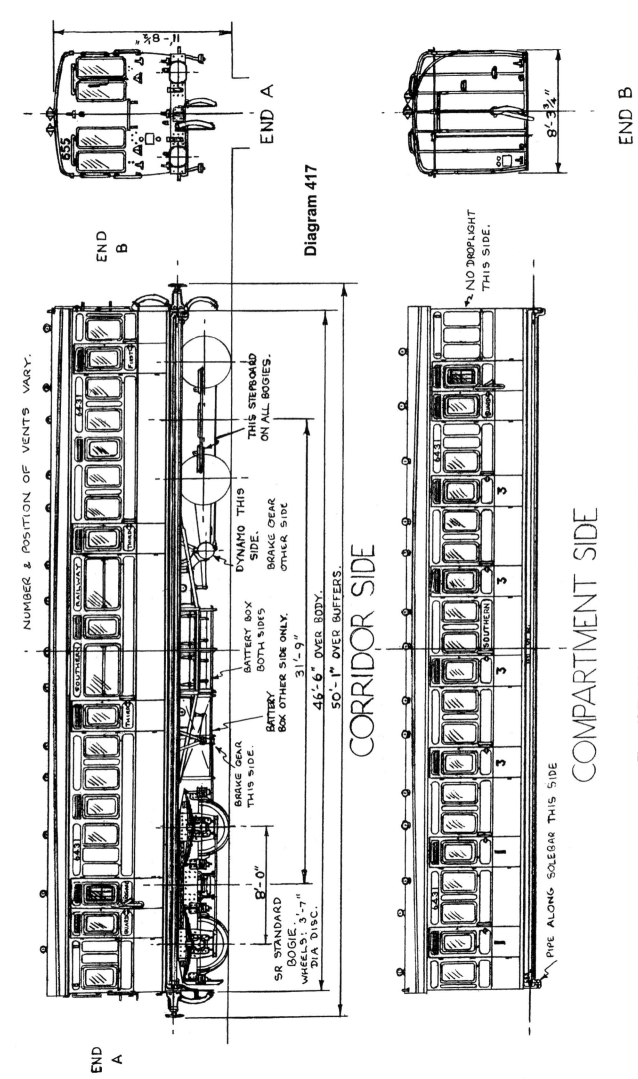

Figure 12 The driving brake composite for sets 652-5, on BRCW underframes; SR diagram 417.

NUMBER & POSITION OF VENTS VARY.

END B

Diagram 417

END A

END A

SOUTHERN RAILWAY

THIRD

FIRST

THIRD

GUARD

THIS STEPBOARD ON ALL BOGIES.

DYNAMO THIS SIDE.

BRAKE GEAR OTHER SIDE

BATTERY BOX BOTH SIDES

BRAKE GEAR THIS SIDE.

BATTERY BOX OTHER SIDE ONLY.

31'-9"

46'-6" OVER BODY.

50'-1" OVER BUFFERS.

8'-0"

SR STANDARD BOGIE. WHEELS: 3'-7" DIA DISC.

CORRIDOR SIDE

END A

11'-8¾"

655

END A

8'-3¾"

END B

NO DROPLIGHT THIS SIDE.

SOUTHERN

3

3

3

3

3

1

1

PIPE ALONG SOLEBAR THIS SIDE

COMPARTMENT SIDE

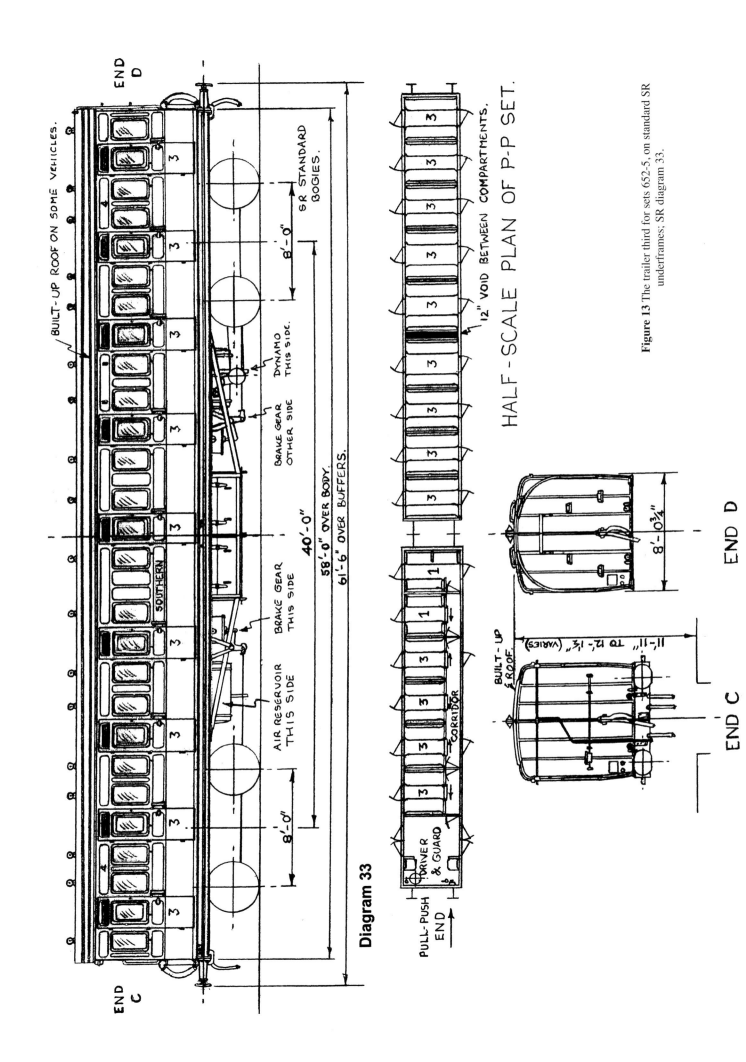

BUILT-UP ROOF ON SOME VEHICLES.

END D

END C

SR STANDARD BOGIES.

8'-0"

DYNAMO THIS SIDE.

BRAKE GEAR OTHER SIDE.

40'-0"

58'-0" OVER BODY.

61'-6" OVER BUFFERS.

SOUTHERN

3

BRAKE GEAR THIS SIDE.

AIR RESERVOIR THIS SIDE.

8'-0"

Diagram 33

3

12" VOID BETWEEN COMPARTMENTS.

HALF-SCALE PLAN OF P-P SET.

1

3

CORRIDOR

DRIVER & GUARD

PULL-PUSH END

BUILT-UP ROOF

8'-0¾"

END D

11'-11" TO 12'-1½" (VARIES)

END C

Figure 13 The trailer third for sets 652-5, on standard SR underframes; SR diagram 33.

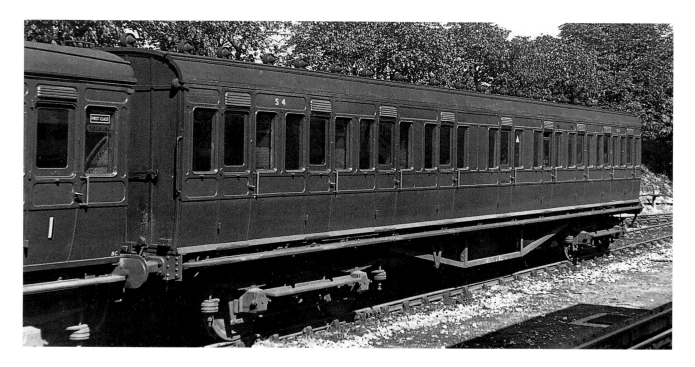

Plate 67 Diagram 33 third No 4, in malachite green livery, also at Horsham but on 3 September 1949. Note the neatly panelled-over void section between the fourth and fifth compartments. *H. C. Casserley*

sets include Hawkhurst, Maidstone West–Paddock Wood, Gravesend West Street, Eastbourne–Hailsham, Brighton–Horsham and later, Oxted–Tunbridge Wells West. However, set 652 was allocated to the Bentley–Bordon branch between 1945 and 1949 — a rare example of one of these sets running on the South Western section, while set 654 was noted on the Midhurst–Petersfield service during 1947.

The next three LSWR non-corridor conversions were again hybrids, but in a slightly different form. Order L964 was issued in April 1937 to produce sets 656-8, utilising three underframes left spare after the Micheldever train fire of August 1936. In each case the driving brake composite coach was formed using the body of an LSWR 50ft composite to diagram 272 mounted on one end of the second-hand underframe. One compartment was removed and a new guard's van grafted onto this end, being either 13ft or 14ft long, depending on the underframe chosen (either a 57ft 'Ironclad' for vehicles Nos 6406/7 or a 58ft Maunsell for coach No 6408). The accompanying trailer third in each case was an ex-SECR 60ft 1in ten-compartment vehicle — known to many staff as a 'long ten', and the first of several such conversions of these coaches. These three sets were then allocated to South Eastern or Central section workings, rarely being seen on the South Western section. No changes in formation occurred until withdrawal, although set 656 was replaced in 1956 by a 'new' set 656 formed entirely of SECR vehicles, as described in Chapter 12.

Electrification of the outer suburban lines on the South Western section reached Alton in July 1937, resulting in a changed pattern of services in this area. Pull-push operation now took over the whole of the Meon Valley line duties (previously there had been some through trains over the route) and the same process was applied over the mid-Hants line to Winchester and Eastleigh. From January 1939 the Ascot–Aldershot service was also given over to electric traction. Former LSWR pull-push services radiating northwestwards from Guildford then shrank to just a single duty — the rather isolated Bentley-Bordon working. At first bogie 'block' sets took over all the new workings, but as their withdrawal was imminent, slightly more modern LSWR sets 1-6 and 31-36 were converted as replacements, the former in 1937 and the latter in 1939, both for these and the Bournemouth/Swanage/Lymington line duties. These 12 sets remained associated with Hampshire and Dorset branch lines right up to withdrawal in 1958-62, rarely being seen elsewhere.

Sets 32 and 36 were noted at Bordon (albeit still in Hampshire) in the 1950s, while sets 1 and 35 travelled west to Seaton in 1958-61. The only real migrant was set 1 which, in its revised LSWR/SECR form, ended its days on the Oxted line in 1962.

Sets 1-6 were originally formed of a 56ft brake composite and a 48ft brake third and, along with similar sets 7-21, were reformed in 1936 with a rebuilt 58ft brake third replacing the shorter LSWR vehicle. Pull-push conversion (of sets 1-6 only) took place in 1937, with the previously unaltered brake composite becoming the driving trailer coach. These sets therefore had guard's/luggage accommodation in both vehicles, unlike many other motor sets. The brake thirds also retained lookouts, making these vehicles SR route restriction 3, which effectively confined them to the South Western section.

Numbers 31-36 followed in 1939, but in this case the 56ft brake thirds became the driving vehicles, being somewhat modified in the process, and also ending up with a large van space, but in the one vehicle only. The trailer composites were rebuilt 58ft vehicles of 1936 vintage and were of two types. Those in sets 31-33 were to SR diagram 286 (ex-diagram 285 composites with one first class compartment downgraded to third) and those in sets 34-36 were to diagram 287 (ex-full thirds upgraded to composite). Nine of the 12 coaches came from former 3-LAV sets 152-4, with the balance being former loose thirds Nos 5, 6 and 7. Rather curiously, the former thirds were afforded route restriction 0, but the composites were to restriction 1, yet both were identical in dimensions!

Set 31 acquired a replacement SECR driving brake third in 1951, but remained in the Hampshire/Dorset area and could often be found on Swanage, Bournemouth–Wimborne–Brockenhurst or Alton-Eastleigh services in this form. Other set formation changes took place from 1956 onwards — sets 1 and 6 both acquiring a South Eastern 'long ten' in place of the brake third (by now reclassified as second class), while sets 2, 35 and 36 all received at least one replacement LSWR vehicle. All these changes are recorded in Table 3. By the late 1950s several more 'long tens' were converted for use as strengthening coaches; most of the sets were by then running in BR crimson lake livery. Inclusion of an 'air-control van' — one of the SECR 'utility' vans — was a regular occurrence on the Bournemouth–Brockenhurst service. This would often be referred to by the staff as the pram van — giving an idea of its usual cargo. Details of these are included in Chapter 14.

Plate 68 Hybrid LSWR/SECR set 656 at Lewes on 21 May 1952, carrying malachite green livery. See Plate 169 for the SECR vehicle. *G. A. Hookham*

Plate 69 Diagram 420 driving brake third No 6407 of set 657 at Tonbridge in the late 1950s. The ex-LSWR 'Ironclad' underframe, with characteristic bogies, is obvious. *J. H. Aston*

Plate 70 A close-up of the driving brake end of set 657, at Ashford on 30 June 1951. Malachite green livery. *A. E. West*

Plate 71 Coach No 6408 of set 658 utilised a second-hand Maunsell underframe, so was one foot longer. Here the set is seen at Allhallows on 18 August 1947. *The Lens of Sutton Association*

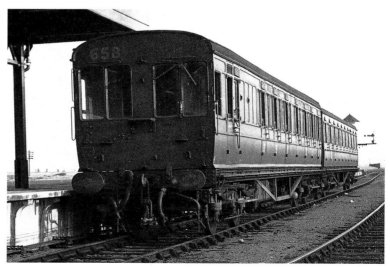

Figure 14 The driving brake composites for sets 656-8, SR diagrams 420 and 428. The accompanying diagram 52 thirds appear in Chapter 12.

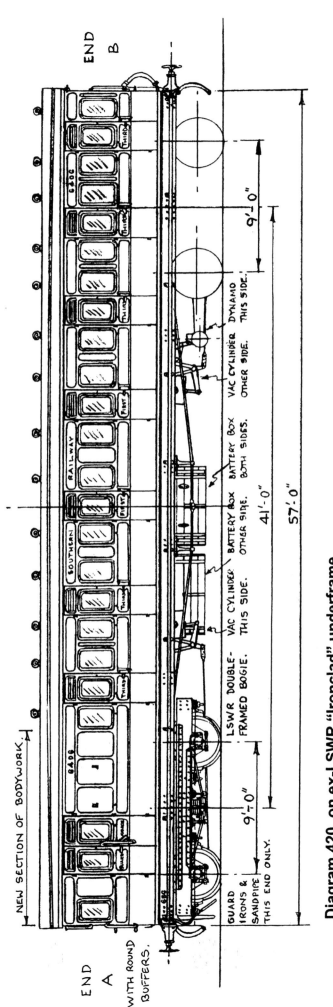

END B

NEW SECTION OF BODYWORK.

VAC CYLINDER DYNAMO OTHER SIDE. THIS SIDE.

BATTERY BOX BOTH SIDES.

VAC CYLINDER BATTERY BOX THIS SIDE. OTHER SIDE.

LSWR DOUBLE-FRAMED BOGIE.

GUARD IRONS & SANDPIPE THIS END ONLY.

9'-0"

9'-0"

41'-0"

57'-0"

END A WITH ROUND BUFFERS.

Diagram 420, on ex-LSWR "Ironclad" underframe

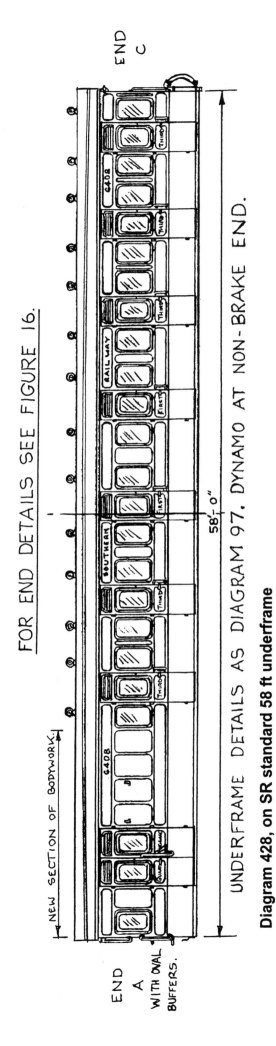

END C

NEW SECTION OF BODYWORK.

58'-0"

END A WITH OVAL BUFFERS.

FOR END DETAILS SEE FIGURE 16.

UNDERFRAME DETAILS AS DIAGRAM 97. DYNAMO AT NON-BRAKE END.

Diagram 428, on SR standard 58 ft underframe

SEE FIGURE 46 FOR THE SECR TRAILERS.

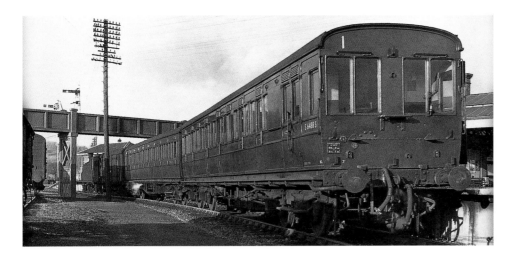

Plate 72 Set No 1 at Seaton Junction on 9 December 1961, formed of LSWR brake No 6488 and SECR third No 1066 and carrying Southern Region post-1956 green livery. The SECR air-control van, along with set 1, is well away from its usual Hampshire stamping grounds. *A. E. West*

Plate 73 Set 1 again, this time on a rail tour at Windsor & Eton Riverside on 19 March 1961, showing the opposite side of the driving brake composite. *P. H. Swift*

Plate 74 Set 2, with trailer brake third No 2604 nearest the camera, seen at Eastleigh on 29 October 1949 in SR malachite green livery, with 'S' prefix to the number. Note that the position of the pressed-steel lookout varies from one side to the other on these 58ft rebuilds. *A. E. West*

Plate 75 In 1958 set 2 received a diagram 31 replacement coach (as did 'Allhallows' set 654). Similar vehicle No 225 is seen at Eastleigh station coupled to pull-push set 36, despite the fact that this coach was not pull-push fitted. *The Lens of Sutton Association*

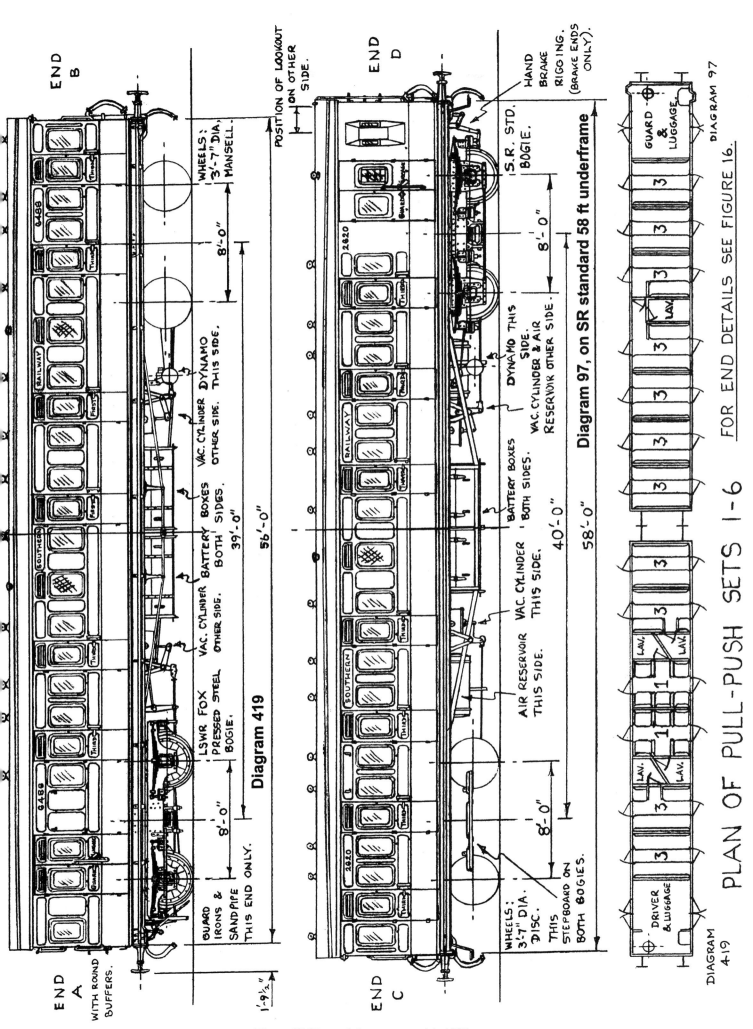

Figure 15 SR sets 1-6, as converted in 1937.

Plate 76 Set 36 at Wimborne circa 1958, formed of Nos 3070 and 4752. The triangular weatherboard moulding along the bottom edge of the body easily identifies the 58ft rebuilt vehicle. This was necessary because the SR underframe was fractionally wider than the LSWR bodywork. *The Lens of Sutton Association*

Plate 77 In December 1949, the driving brake third of set 31 was unexpectedly withdrawn from service and it was over a year before a replacement coach (of SECR origin) was provided. In the meantime the composite coach No 4744 was stored at Henfield – presumably out of the way yet reasonably convenient for Lancing Works. It is seen at this location on 22 April 1950. *D. Cullum*

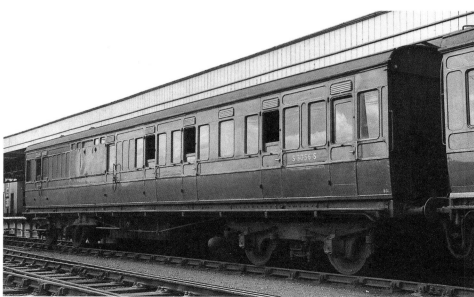

Plate 78 Diagram 235 driving brake third No 3056 of set 35 at Seaton in July 1958, carrying unlined crimson lake livery. *A. E. West*

Plate 79 Accompanying diagram 290 trailer composite No 4617 of set 35, on the same date. This coach replaced the original diagram 287 vehicle a few months earlier, but differs only in that the lavatory was sealed out of use and three first class compartments were retained. *A. E. West*

Plate 80 The 5.40pm Eastleigh–Andover Junction pull-push service leaves Eastleigh behind 'M7' No 30048 on 25 August 1959. The train is formed of set 31, the rear coach being the replacement SECR vehicle to diagram 160A. *L. Elsey*

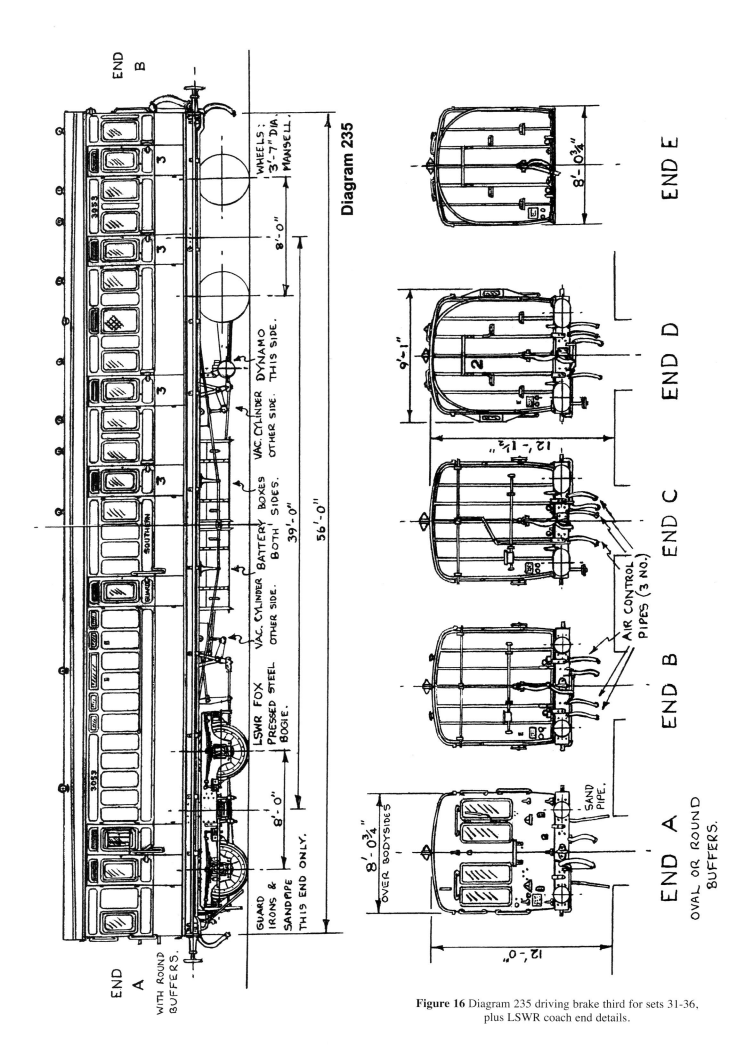

END B

3 **3** **3** **3**

3053

SOUTHERN

END A
WITH ROUND BUFFERS.

WHEELS: 3'-7" DIA. MANSELL.

Diagram 235

8'-0"

VAC. CYLINDER DYNAMO THIS SIDE. OTHER SIDE.

39'-0"

56'-0"

VAC. CYLINDER BATTERY BOXES OTHER SIDE. BOTH SIDES.

LSWR FOX PRESSED STEEL BOGIE.

8'-0"

GUARD IRONS & SANDPIPE THIS END ONLY.

8'-0¾"

END E

9'-1"

2

END D

12'-1½"

END C

AIR CONTROL PIPES (3 NO.)

END B

8'-0¾"
OVER BODYSIDES

SAND PIPE.

END A
OVAL OR ROUND BUFFERS.

12'-0"

Figure 16 Diagram 235 driving brake third for sets 31-36, plus LSWR coach end details.

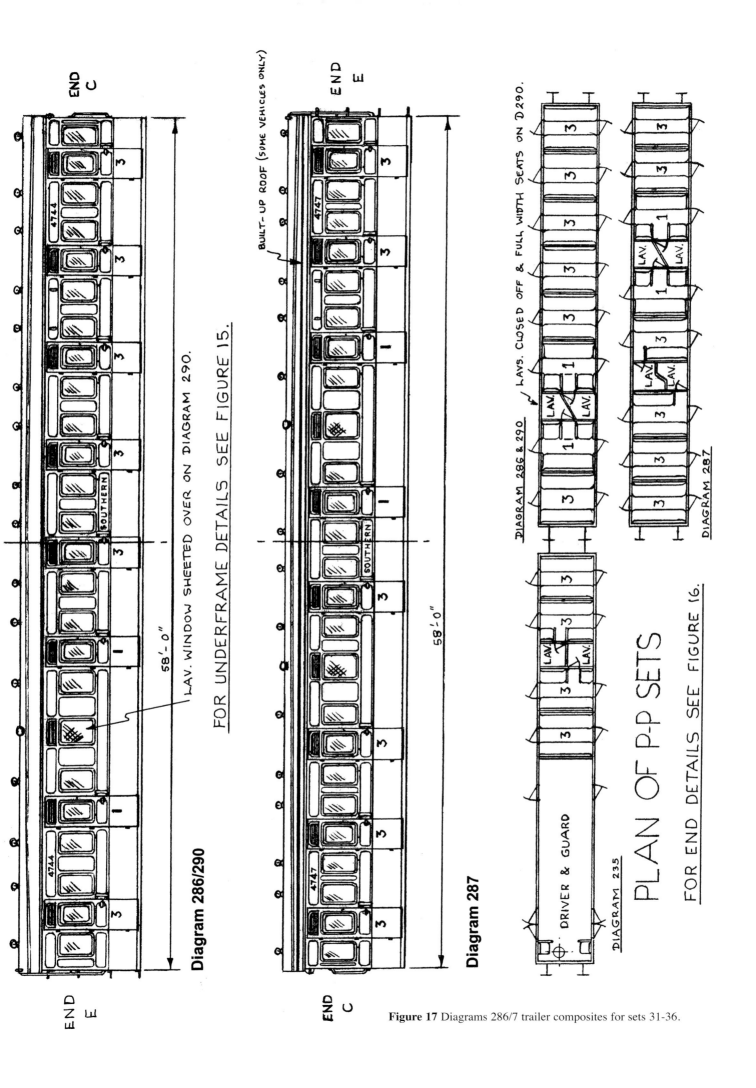

END C

Diagram 286/290

4744

3

3

SOUTHERN

3

3

1

4744

3

END E

58'-0"

LAV. WINDOW SHEETED OVER ON DIAGRAM 290.

FOR UNDERFRAME DETAILS SEE FIGURE 15.

END E

BUILT-UP ROOF (SOME VEHICLES ONLY)

4747

3

3

1

1

SOUTHERN

3

3

4747

3

END C

58'-0"

Diagram 287

PLAN OF P-P SETS

FOR END DETAILS SEE FIGURE 16.

LAVS. CLOSED OFF & FULL WIDTH SEATS ON D290.

3 | 3 | 3 | 3 | 3 | 3 | 3 | 1 | 1 | LAV. | LAV. | 1 | 3

DIAGRAM 286 & 290

3 | 3 | 3 | 3 | LAV. | LAV. | 1 | 3 | LAV. | LAV. | 1 | 3 | 3 | 3

DIAGRAM 287

3 | 3 | 3 | 3 | LAV. | LAV. | 3 | DRIVER & GUARD

DIAGRAM 235

Figure 17 Diagrams 286/7 trailer composites for sets 31-36.

Table 3
Ex-LSWR Non-Corridor Stock Sets

SR Set No.	Running dates	SR coach Nos* BT	C	Usual 1950s Allocation	Remarks
1	6/37-7/58	2620	6488		
	7/58-7/62	1066	6488		Coach No 1066 is ex-SECR, diagram 52
2	4/37-8/56	2604	6487	Alton-Fareham	
	8/56-7/58	2614	6487	(one set)	Replacement coach to diagram 97
	7/58-6/60	373	6487	Alton-Eastleigh	Replacement coach to diagram 31
3	5/37-1/59	2609	6490	(four sets)	
4	6/37-11/58	2605	6491	Gosport-Fareham	
5	4/37-9/58	2621	6495	or Swanage	
6	5/37-10/57	2612	6496	(one set)	
	5/58-4/59	1103	6496		Coach 1103 is ex-SECR, diagram 52
31	6/39-12/49	3053	4744	Bournemouth West-	
	c6/51-12/57	3474	4744	Brockenhurst	Coach 3474 is ex-SECR, diagram 160A
	6/58-3/61	3474	4730	(three sets)	Replacement coach to diagram 290
32	7/39-5/59	3055	4745	Lymington	
33	6/39-2/60	3069	4746	(one set)	
34	6/39-9/58	3054	4747	Swanage	
35	7/39-11/57	3056	4748	(one set)	
	5/58-5/60	3056	4617	Alton-Fareham or Swanage	Replacement coach to diagram 290
36	6/39-11/56	3070	4749	(one set)	
	11/56-6/59	3070	4752		Replacement coach to diagram 287
375*	c1914-10/31	2626	6406 or	Gosport-Fareham &	Three-wire control only. Not pull-push after 1927
		2626 163	6406	Stokes Bay (1914)	Arc-roof stock. Ran as two- or three-coach set
652	2/35-8/57	6428	1		
	1/58-8/62	6428	1074	Set 652 at Bordon	Coach 1074 is ex-SECR, diagram 52
653	2/35-2/61	6429	2	in late 1940s,	
654	2/35-6/58	6430	3	otherwise all on	
	7/58-3/59	6430	219	SE Section	Replacement coach to diagram 31
655	2/35-11/60	6431	4		
656	11/37-10/56	6406	1057	SE Section	Coach 1057 is ex-SECR, diagram 52
657	12/37-8/60	6407	1077	SE Section	Coach 1077 is ex-SECR, diagram 52
658	12/37-7/58	6408	1088	SE Section	Coach 1088 is ex-SECR, diagram 52

* No LSWR set number allocated. LSWR coach numbers were 1935 (2626), 676 (163), 3543 (6406).

Table 3.2
Carriage Summary

SR Diagram	SR Nos	Date of Pull-Push conversion	Dimensions L x W	Seats 1	3	Remarks
10	163 (LSWR 676)	pre-1923	42ft x 8ft		70	Arc-roof. Ran with set 375. 3-wire P-P gear until c1927.
12	188, 219/92, 497 (LSWR 71,168,250,550)	c1919/20	48ft x 8ft		80	Three-wire P-P gear until c1931. Loose coaches.
12	328/83/93, 438/9/80, 500	1930-onwards	48ft x 8ft		80	Air control gear. All withdrawn by 1939. Loose coaches.
31	219, 373	7/58	58ft x 8ft		88	Replacements. On SR standard u/frames.
33	1-4	Rebuilt 2/35	58ft x 8ft		90	For sets 652-5. On SR standard u/frames.
52	1057/77/88	11-12/37	60ft 1in x 8ft		100	Ex-SECR vehicles for sets 656-8.
52	1066/74, 1103	1958	60ft 1in x 8ft		100	Replacements. Ex-SECR vehicles.
97	2604/5/9/12/20/1	4-6/37	58ft x 8ft		68	For sets 1-6. On SR standard u/frames.
97	2614	8/56	58ft x 8ft		68	Replacement.
108	2626 (LSWR 1935)	c1914	42ft x 8ft		50	Arc-roof. In set 375. 3-wire P-P gear until c1927.
109	2631 (LSWR 1649)	c1920	48ft x 8ft		50	Three-wire P-P gear until 10/30. Loose vehicle.
235	3053-6/69/70	6-7/39	56ft x 8ft		38	Ex-diagram 126.in sets 31-6.
160A	3474	6/50	60ft 1in x 8ft		80	Replacement. Ex-SECR vehicle — in set 31 from c6/51.
286	4744-6	6-7/39	58ft x 8ft	12	60	Ex-diagram 285, on SR standard u/frames. In sets 31-3.
287	4747-9	6-7/39	58ft x 8ft	12	58	Ex-diagram 32, on SR standard u/frames. In sets 34-6.
287	4752	c1956	58ft x 8ft	12	58	Replacement, ex-diagram 32. On SR standard u/frame.
290	4617, 4730	5-6/58	58ft x 8ft	18	50	Replacements, ex-diagram 285. On SR standard u/frame.
402	6406 (LSWR 3543)	c1914	45ft x 8ft	12	30	Arc-roof. In set 375. 3-wire P-P gear until c1927.
417	6428-31	Rebuilt 2/35	46ft 6in x 8ft 3in	13	32	Ex-diagram 18 'emigrant' thirds. For sets 652-5.
419	6487/8/90/1/5/6	4-6/37	56ft x 8ft	10	38	Ex-diagram 408. For sets 1-6.
420	6406/7	11-12/37	57ft x 8ft	16	50	On secondhand LSWR "Ironclad" u/frames. For sets 656/7.
428	6408	12/37	58ft x 8ft	16	50	On secondhand SR standard u/frame. For set 658.

Vehicles with lookouts (SR diagrams 97, 108/9, 402/19) were 9ft wide overall and to SR route restriction 3, diagrams 235/86/90, 417/20/28 were to route restriction 1, the remainder were restriction 0.

Two other diagram 12 vehicles were converted for pull-push operation in 1931, for LBSCR sets 649/50 — see Chapter 9. Coach No 500 later in set 649.

Chapter 7.

LSWR Corridor Stock

The first gangwayed LSWR vehicle to receive any form of pull-push fittings, if one considers the 'gate' stock separately, was ex-'Eagle Express' saloon No 72, recorded as being equipped to run as a strengthening coach for the Seaton branch set in 1916. No other LSWR corridor vehicles appear until 1943, when all the surviving 1907/08 'emigrant' coaches were converted for pull-push operation.

As noted in the last chapter, these coaches were built to a composite loading gauge, 46ft 6in long, 8ft 3¾in wide and 11ft 8½in high to enable them to travel almost unrestricted over any line in the country. The 1907/08 coaches came to the Southern as sets 473/4 and were, by the 1930s, mostly being used for excursion and special traffic duties. In 1934 all were reframed on new underframes supplied by the Birmingham Railway Carriage & Wagon Company and for this reason alone were going to remain serviceable for some time to come, albeit not for long as true corridor vehicles.

In September 1942, order L2246 was issued to convert all 18 vehicles into nine two-coach pull-push sets, allocated set numbers 731-9. This process was to be fairly extensive, since there were, in 1942, only four brake thirds, 12 thirds and just two composites which needed to be turned into nine driving brake thirds and nine trailer composites. Several different alterations would be necessary to achieve this objective, resulting in four different types of pull-push coach, as illustrated in **Figures 18-21**. The work was carried out between January and April 1943, with five of the full thirds being rebuilt as brake thirds similar but not quite identical to the four converted from existing brake vehicles. The remaining thirds became composites, having two compartments upgraded to first class. In all coaches, the outer end gangway connections were removed and the lavatories stripped out, resulting in sets which had seating for just 12 first and 64 third class passengers — even fewer than non-corridor set 375 described in Chapter 6.

Plate 81 Former 'emigrant' set 734 at Brookwood on 19 July 1952, just before final closure of the Bisley branch. The set is in lined crimson lake, with left-hand positioned numerals. *The Lens of Sutton Association*

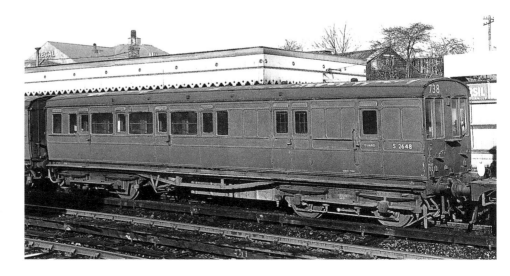

Plate 82 Driving brake third No 2648 of set 738 at Gravesend Central on 2 February 1952. This was rebuilt from a brake third, whereas coach No 2644 in Plate 81 started life as a corridor third. Note the different arrangement of corridor side doors. *D. Cullum*

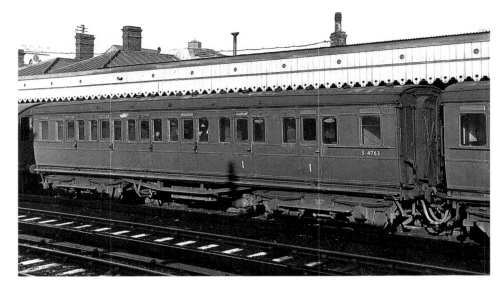

Plate 83 Trailer composite No 4763 of set 738, again at Gravesend Central on 2 February 1952. This was always a composite, confirmed by the wider spacing of the two right-hand compartments. *D. Cullum*

Plate 84 Trailer composite No 4762 of set 737, at Allhallows about 1960, in Southern Region green livery. This was formerly a corridor third; hence all compartments are of the same width. *The Lens of Sutton Association*

This ensured that the sets were used on the most rural of lines, but for modelling purposes they provide the perfect compact pull-push train, usually powered by an 'M7', 'O2', 'R', 'R-1' or 'H' class 0-4-4 tank.

The sets were by no means confined to the South Western section; indeed, most ran elsewhere on the Southern Railway/Region. Sets 731-3/7 were initially allocated to the Central section, sets 736/8/9 to the South Eastern, leaving only sets 734/5 based on the South Western section. The latter were usually kept as spare sets at Exeter Central, so could provide relief cover at such places as Turnchapel, Callington (not working pull-push), Yeovil or Seaton (in off-peak periods). When not required for these duties they could turn up on ordinary loco-hauled services to Exmouth, Sidmouth or Honiton, along with other stock. The pair was also a popular choice for Bisley NRA special traffic between 1947 and 1952. Those on the Central section tended to favour the Eastbourne–Hailsham, Brighton–Horsham, Midhurst and Tunbridge Wells West–Oxted services, while the Eastern section sets ran mostly on the Gravesend West Street, Allhallows and Hawkhurst branches. Set 738 appeared on a rail tour from Bournemouth to several Dorset branches on 7 July 1958, still absolutely resplendent in lined BR crimson lake.

Being of fairly recent rebuild, they all lasted well and could still be seen at work until 1959-61. No changes of formation were ever recorded and almost all returned to Southern Region green livery before withdrawal.

The last LSWR sets to be converted were very different from all previous pull-push conversions. These could in fact be described as the first 'modern' stock to be utilised in this manner. 'Ironclad' two-coach corridor sets 381-5 were originally completed in 1925, each formed of a six compartment brake third and a similar brake composite, for through services between Waterloo, Lymington Pier, Swanage and the West of England. The arrival of new Bulleid stock in 1946-48 and, in particular, two-coach sets 63-75, rendered the 'Ironclads' surplus to this requirement and they were 'cascaded' off front-line duties. Set 385 found alternative employment for a while on a Bournemouth–Chester through train, but for the remainder order L3434 was issued for their conversion into pull-push sets, retaining the same carriage and set numbers. This work took place between October 1948 and September 1949, as the vehicles became due for their next works visit. This is apparent in the paint finish applied, as the early conversions retained malachite green, while the later ones had BR crimson lake applied, either with or without lining.

The work involved the removal of all gangway connections and the conversion of both former lavatories into third class coupés (half-compartments), while a standard SR pull-push driving end was inserted into the guard's van end of the brake third. The luggage van of this vehicle was also reduced in size by converting part of it into an additional third class compartment. Sets 381-4 were initially allocated to Seaton, Gosport, Yeovil and the Bordon branch respectively, while set 385 eventually

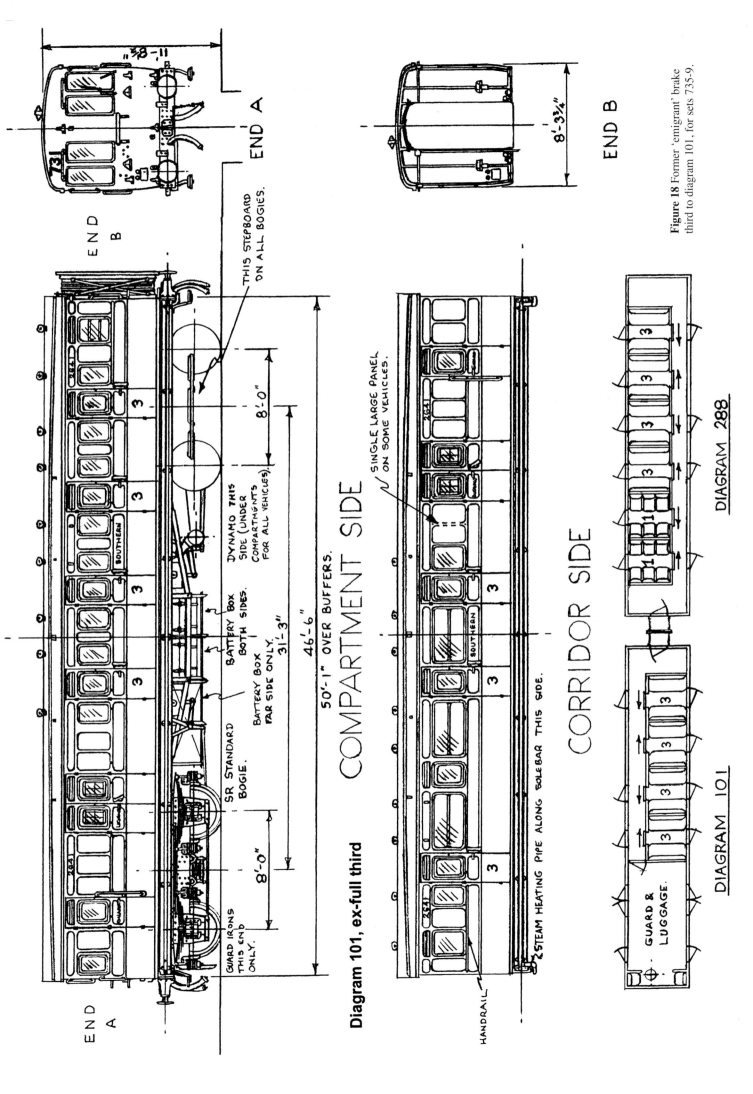

END B

731

END A

Diagram 101, ex-full third

COMPARTMENT SIDE

GUARD IRONS THIS END ONLY.

SR STANDARD BOGIE.

BATTERY BOX FAR SIDE ONLY.

BATTERY BOX BOTH SIDES.

THIS STEPBOARD ON ALL BOGIES.

DYNAMO THIS SIDE (UNDER COMPARTMENTS FOR ALL VEHICLES).

SOUTHERN

8'-0"

8'-0"

31'-3"

46'-6"

50'-1" OVER BUFFERS.

3

ENDA

CORRIDOR SIDE

SINGLE LARGE PANEL ON SOME VEHICLES.

SOUTHERN

STEAM HEATING PIPE ALONG SOLEBAR THIS SIDE.

HANDRAIL.

END B

8'-3¾"

8'-11"

DIAGRAM 288

3 3 3 3 3 3

1 1 3

3 3 3 3 3

GUARD & LUGGAGE.

DIAGRAM 101

Figure 18 Former 'emigrant' brake third to diagram 101, for sets 735-9.

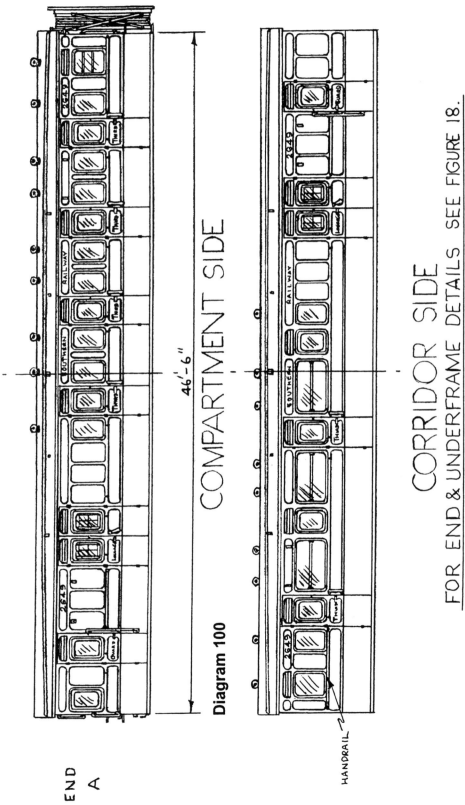

Figure 19 Former 'emigrant' brake third to diagram 100, for sets 731-4.

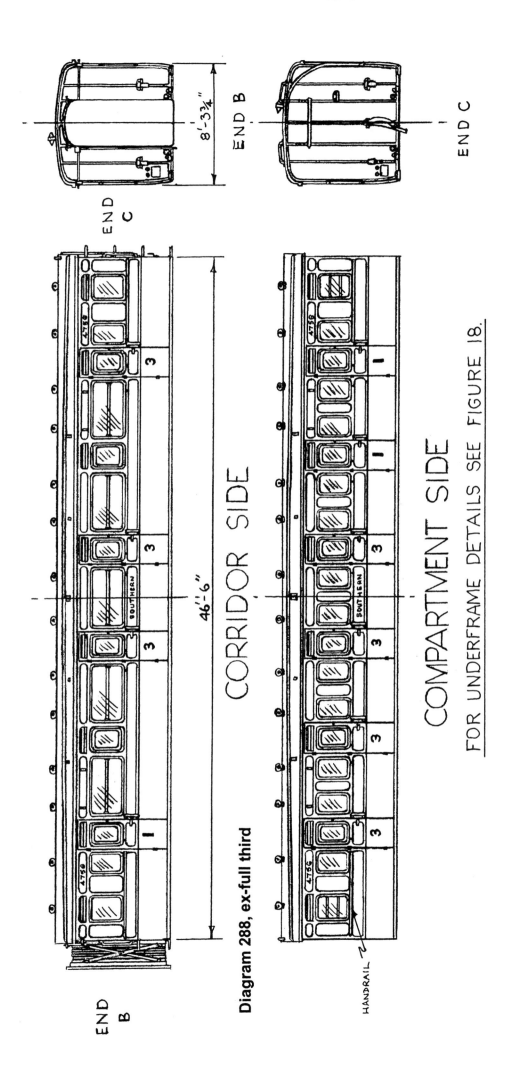

END C

END B

END C

8'-3¾"

CORRIDOR SIDE

46'-6"

SOUTHERN

3

3

3

1

4756

4756

Diagram 288, ex-full third

END B

COMPARTMENT SIDE

FOR UNDERFRAME DETAILS SEE FIGURE 18.

SOUTHERN

1

1

3

3

3

3

4756

4756

HANDRAIL

Figure 20 Former 'emigrant' composite to diagram 288, for sets 731-7.

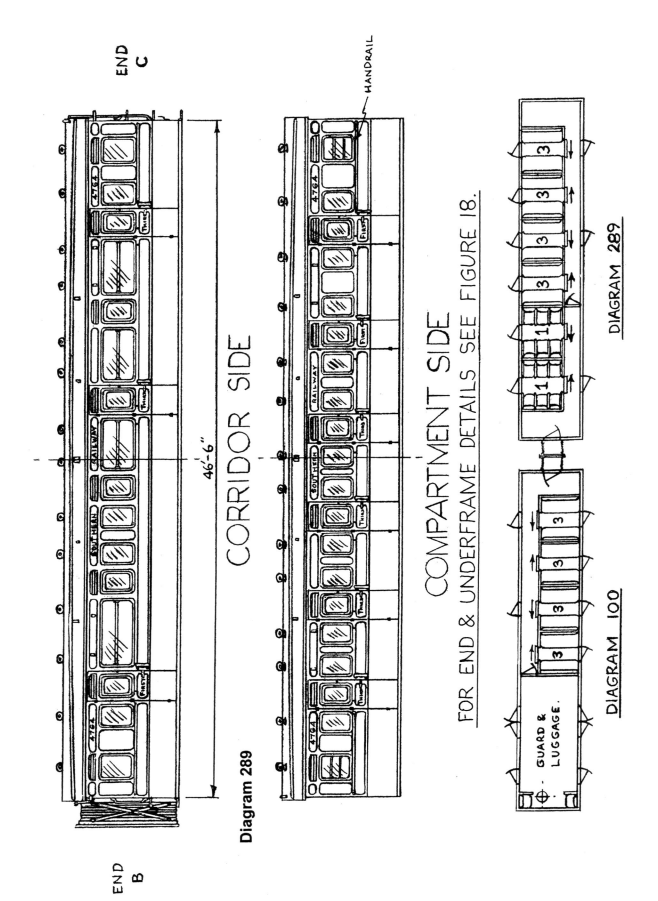

END
C

HANDRAIL

CORRIDOR SIDE

46'-6"

Diagram 289

END
B

COMPARTMENT SIDE

FOR END & UNDERFRAME DETAILS SEE FIGURE 18.

DIAGRAM 289

DIAGRAM 100

GUARD &
LUGGAGE.

Figure 21 Former 'emigrant' composite to diagram 289, for sets 738-9.

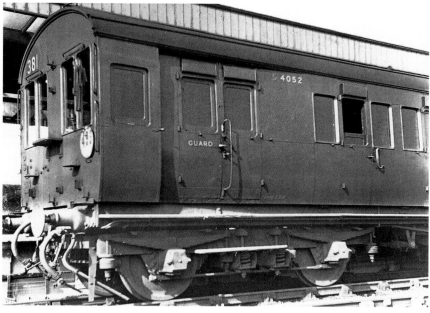

Plates 85 & 86 Close-up views of the driving end of 'Ironclad' brake third No 4052 of set 381, at Seaton on 12 March 1952. This was the second conversion and carried malachite green livery, as did set 383. *Both A. E. West*

caught up with the rest in March 1952, under order L3735, then being allocated to Bournemouth West for either the Swanage branch or general relief work. The latter usually meant the Bournemouth West–Brockenhurst via Wimborne service. After Gosport closed in 1953, set 382 moved to Lymington Pier, while set 384 migrated to Bournemouth-Brockenhurst after closure at Bordon in 1957 and so could be swapped easily with 382. Set 383 was also noted at Swanage from time to time, but none of the sets seem to have been recorded at other locations and never off the South Western section, apart from overhaul visits to Lancing.

Set 382 suffered fire damage at Bournemouth West in August 1959 and was the first to be withdrawn, but the others outlived almost all other Southern pull-push sets barring the Maunsell 1959/60 conversions, being withdrawn in late 1962. All four had by then returned to green livery. It is perhaps of interest to note that those sets serving Lymington Pier, Swanage and Seaton were probably unique in being used both for the through service to Waterloo early in their career and for the local service at the end. No set number or changes of formation occurred throughout. Table 4 gives full details of both the 'Ironclads' and the former 'emigrant' sets.

Plate 87 Set 382 appeared in July 1949, in lined crimson lake livery with left-handed numerals. Soon after entering traffic, the set leaves Fareham with an Alton to Gosport through service – not a line normally associated with the 'Ironclads'.
T. A. Barry collection

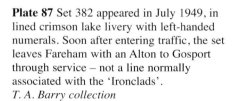

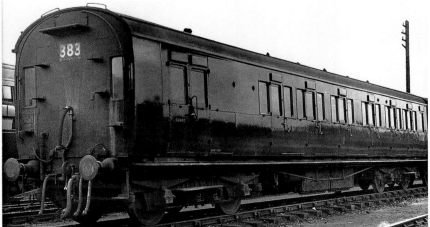

Plate 88 The 'locomotive' end of set 383/coach No 6562 at Eastleigh on 1 June 1962, not long before withdrawal. Southern Region green livery, with the set number painted at both ends. This was a characteristic of the 'Ironclad' sets, probably because both vehicles were brake coaches. *A. E. West*

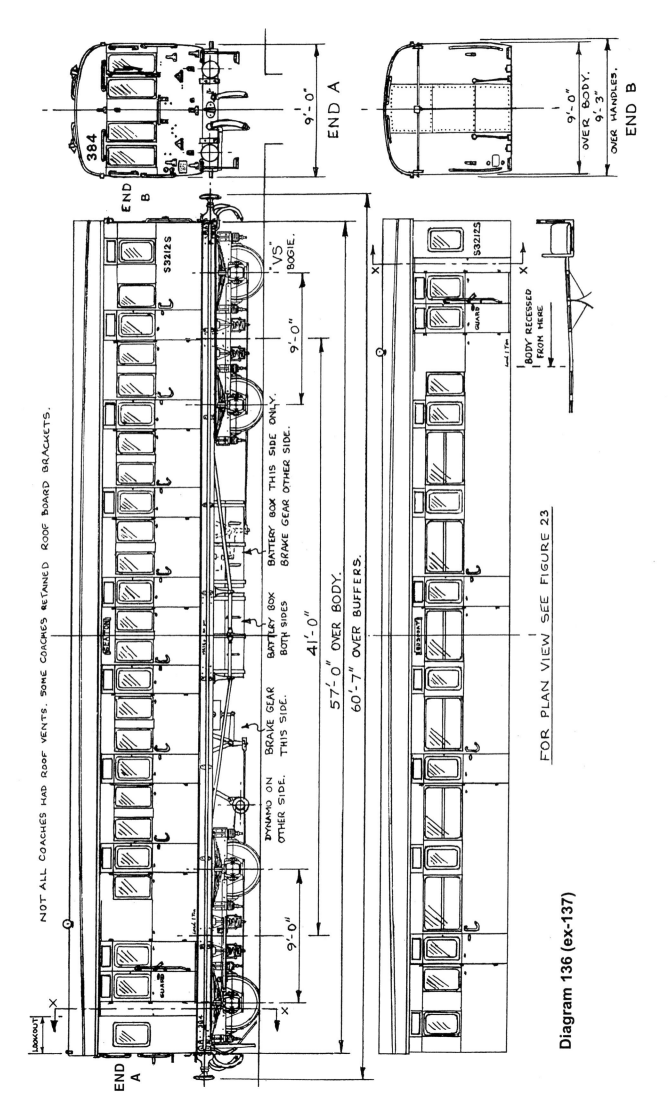

Figure 22 The 'Ironclad' driving brake third; SR diagram 136.

NOT ALL COACHES HAD ROOF VENTS. SOME COACHES RETAINED ROOF BOARD BRACKETS.

END A

384

END B

S3212S

"VS" BOGIE.

9'-0"

BATTERY BOX THIS SIDE ONLY.
BRAKE GEAR OTHER SIDE.

BATTERY BOX
BOTH SIDES

BRAKE GEAR
THIS SIDE.

DYNAMO ON
OTHER SIDE.

41'-0"

57'-0" OVER BODY.

60'-7" OVER BUFFERS.

9'-0"

GUARD

LOOKOUT

END A

9'-0" OVER BODY.

9'-3" OVER HANDLES.

END A

END B

S3212S

GUARD

BODY RECESSED FROM HERE

X

X

FOR PLAN VIEW SEE FIGURE 23

Diagram 136 (ex-137)

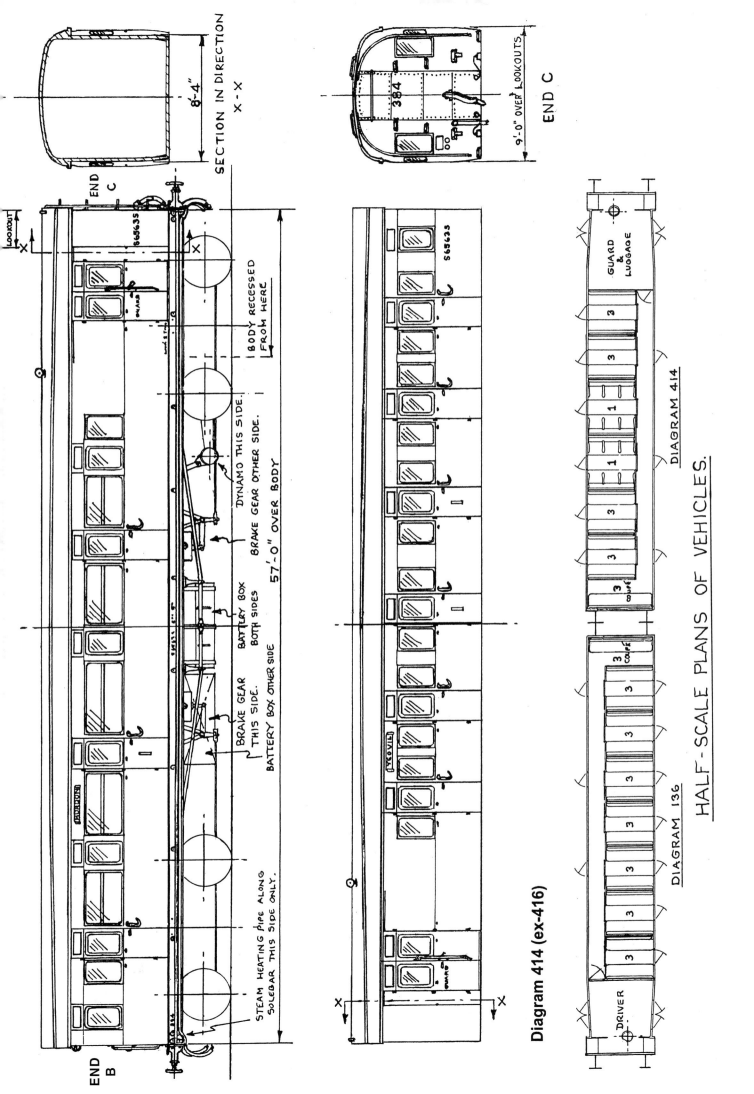

SECTION IN DIRECTION X - X

8'-4"

END C

9'-0" OVER LOOKOUTS

END C

LOOKOUT

END C

S65635

BODY RECESSED FROM HERE

DYNAMO THIS SIDE.

BRAKE GEAR OTHER SIDE.

57'-0" OVER BODY

BRAKE GEAR THIS SIDE.

BATTERY BOX BOTH SIDES

BATTERY BOX OTHER SIDE

STEAM HEATING PIPE ALONG SOLEBAR THIS SIDE ONLY.

END B

S65635

YEOVIL

GUARD

Diagram 414 (ex-416)

S65635

GUARD & LUGGAGE

3 3 1 1 3 3 3 3 COUPÉ

DIAGRAM 414

3 COUPÉ 3 3 3 3 3 3 3 3

DRIVER

DIAGRAM 136

HALF-SCALE PLANS OF VEHICLES.

Plate 89 Bordon station on 9 May 1956, with set 384 ready to leave on the 11.9am service to Bentley. Apart from the two enthusiasts, there was not a passenger in sight. *J. H. Aston*

Table 4
LSWR Corridor Stock

SR Set No	Running dates	SR coach Nos BT	C	Original allocation	Remarks
731	1/43-5/59	2641	4756	Pulborough-Midhurst	Noted later at Gravesend West Street and Horsham
732	1/43-12/60	2642	4757	Eastbourne-Hailsham	Noted later at Horsham & Tunbridge Wells West
733	2/43-10/60	2643	4758	Eastbourne-Hailsham	
734	4/43-7/59	2644	4759	SW section-Exeter relief	
735	4/43-2/61	2645	4760	SW section-Exeter relief	
736	4/43-10/59	2646	4761	Hawkhurst Branch	
737	2/43-5/60	2647	4762	Pulborough-Midhurst	Noted later at Allhallows, Brighton and Tonbridge
738	2/43-6/60	2648	4763	Gravesend West Street	Noted later at Tunbridge Wells West
739	3/43-1/60	2649	4764	Hawkhurst Branch	
		BT	BC		
381	12/48-12/62	4052	6560	Seaton Branch	
382	7/49-10/59	4053	6561	Gosport Branch	Later on Lymington Branch
383	10/48-12/62	3211	6562	Yeovil Town	Later on Swanage Branch
384	6/49-12/62	3212	6563	Bordon Branch	Later Bournemouth West–Brockenhurst or Lymington
385	3/52-8/62	3213	6564	Bournemouth West-relief	Often on Swanage branch, later at Yeovil

No changes of formation recorded

Table 4.2
Carriage Summary

SR Diagram	SR Nos	Date of P-P conversion	Dimensions L x W	Seats 1	3	Remarks
100	2646-9	2-3/43	46ft 6in x 8ft 3in		32	Former 'emigrant' diagram 128 brake thirds
101	2641-5	1-3/43	46ft 6in x 8ft 3in		32	Former 'emigrant' diagram 20 thirds
136*	3211-3, 4052-3	10/48-3/52	57ft x 9ft		62	Ironclad stock, ex diagram 137
288	4756-62	1-4/43	46ft 6in x 8ft 3in	12	32	Former 'emigrant' diagram 20 thirds
289	4763-4	2-3/43	46ft 6in x 8ft 3in	12	32	Former 'emigrant' diagram 276 composites
414*	6560-4	10/48-3/52	57ft x 9ft	12	38	Ironclad stock, ex-diagram 416

* Second allocation of this diagram number to pull-push vehicles.
Ironclad vehicles were to SR route restriction 4, the former emigrant coaches were to restriction 1.

Chapter 8.

LBSCR 'Balloon' Stock

We must now return to the dawn of pull-push operation in Southern England — to 1905 in fact. The evaluation trials of September–December 1905 between steam railmotors, petrol railcars and pull-push trains (as described in Chapters 1 and 3) convinced Douglas Earle Marsh and others on the LBSCR where the future lay. The 'Terrier + Balloon' combination tested between Brighton and Worthing was clearly the way forward and within three years another 15 auto-fitted 'Balloon' trailers and 20 locomotives were at work on the line.

During 1906, six slightly different trailers were completed, seating 60 third class passengers (the 1905 prototypes seating only 52 passengers), while in 1907, a further nine coaches were completed, to yet another slightly different design, but again having seats for 60 passengers. Initially, these ran between Chichester and Portsmouth, Brighton and Seaford, Brighton and East Grinstead, the Epsom Downs branch, plus local duties around both Horsham and Tunbridge Wells, along with the 1905 prototypes, which covered the Brighton–Worthing service as well as trips to Kemp Town and The Dyke.

Whatever their differences, all were to the same overall dimensions of 54ft long, 8ft 10in wide and 12ft 11in to roof — making full use of the generous LBSCR loading gauge and, incidentally, ensuring they did not travel far off the Brighton system after 1923. These dimensions were exceeded by very few other Brighton coaches, while their size was undoubtedly accentuated by the diminutive 'A1' class locomotives converted to work with them. Provided the coaches ran singly then these locomotives were adequate, but once two or four-coach trains were envisaged then the 'D1' class 0-4-2 tanks were substituted with complete success.

The new services were to some extent 'marketed', not only by the opening of small unstaffed halts on the routes served (listed in Appendix 2) but also by the issue of specially printed and coloured tickets which drew attention to the frequent services and discounted fares available. To be fair, this same process was adopted by other companies and also by the LBSCR for the railmotor and railcar services as well, but without the same levels of reliability these soon lost their initial popularity.

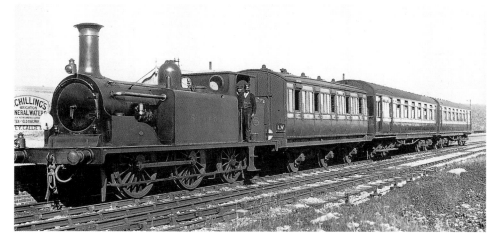

Plate 90 Both original 1905 'Balloon' trailers together at The Dyke, but not operating in pull-push mode, as 'D1' tank No 228 *Seaford* was not auto fitted until 1923. Neither was 6-wheeled second No 182 at the front of the train. Note the 'LV' (last vehicle) board on the carriage end. The date is *circa* 1906-10 and is probably a Saturday afternoon or Sunday, when patronage of the branch was most popular.
W. J. Reynolds

Plate 91 One of the 1906 'Balloon' trailers, LBSCR No 1331/SR No 3834 (to SR diagram 191), enters Brighton from Kemp Town, hauled by 'Terrier' No 681, while running as a 2-4-0T. The date is therefore not later than 1913.
Author's collection

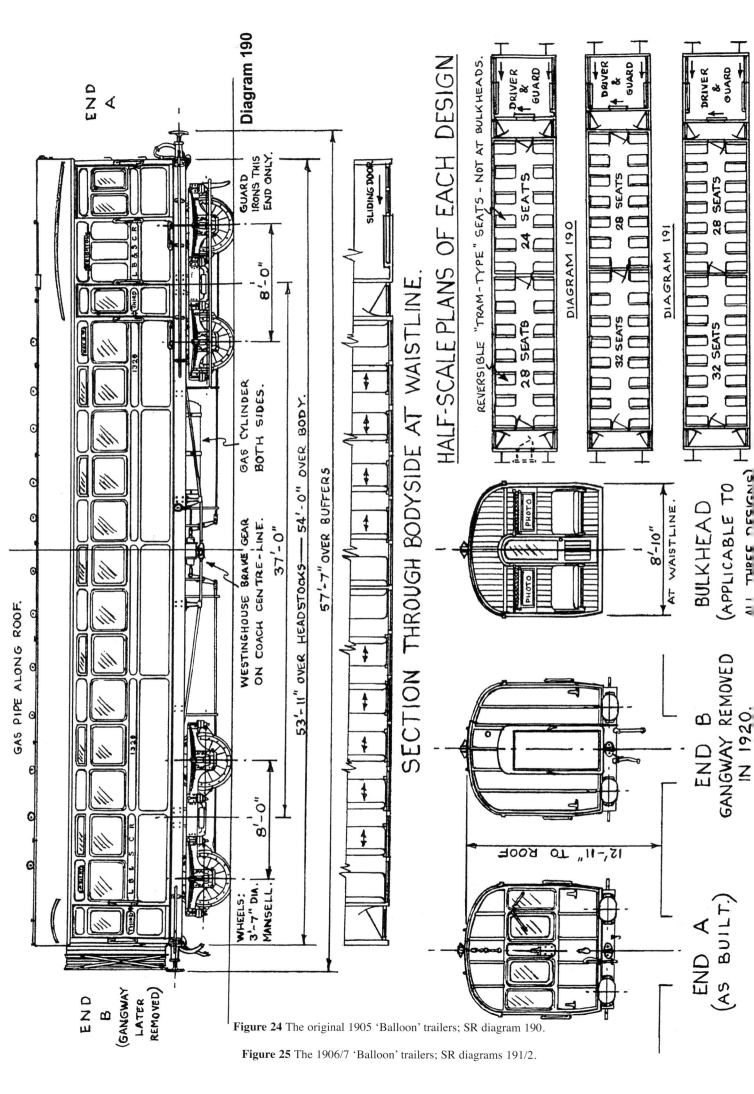

Figure 24 The original 1905 'Balloon' trailers; SR diagram 190.

Figure 25 The 1906/7 'Balloon' trailers; SR diagrams 191/2.

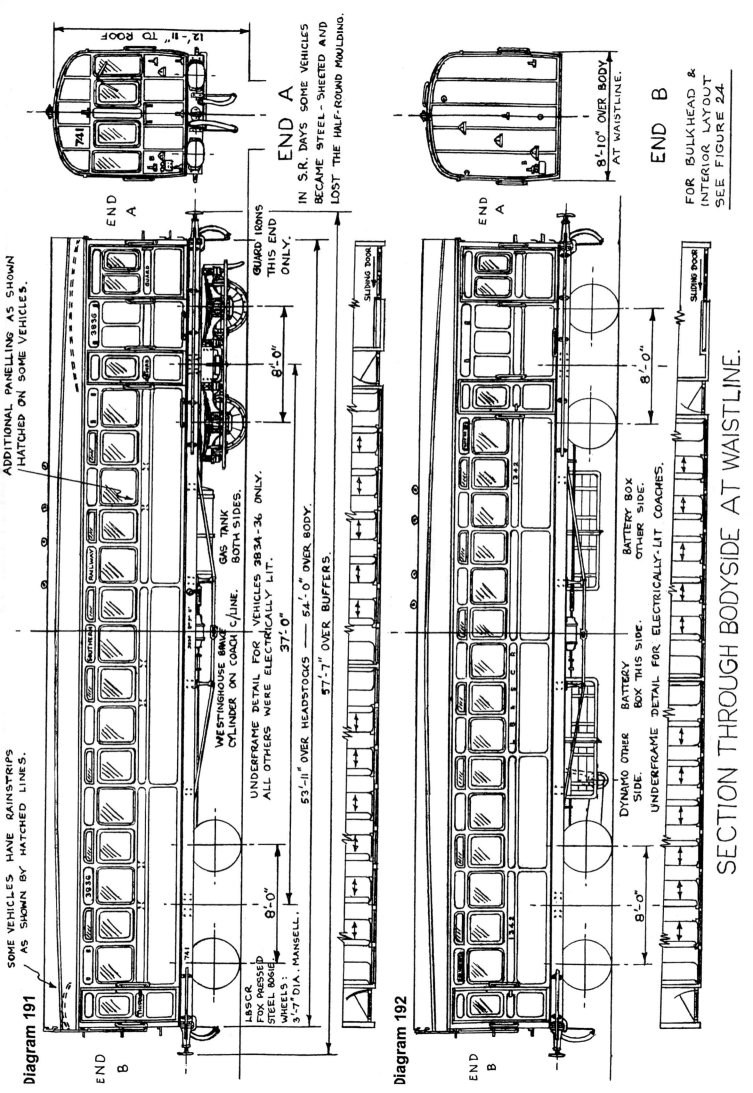

Diagram 191

SOME VEHICLES HAVE RAINSTRIPS AS SHOWN BY HATCHED LINES.

ADDITIONAL PANELLING AS SHOWN HATCHED ON SOME VEHICLES.

12'-11" TO ROOF

END A

IN S.R. DAYS SOME VEHICLES BECAME STEEL-SHEETED AND LOST THE HALF-ROUND MOULDING.

GUARD IRONS THIS END ONLY.

8'-0"

8'-0"

WESTINGHOUSE BRAKE CYLINDER ON COACH C/LINE.

GAS TANK BOTH SIDES.

UNDERFRAME DETAIL FOR VEHICLES 3834-36 ONLY. ALL OTHERS WERE ELECTRICALLY LIT.

53'-11" OVER HEADSTOCKS — 54'-0" OVER BODY.

37'-0"

57'-7" OVER BUFFERS.

LBSCR FOX PRESSED STEEL BOGIE. WHEELS: 3'-7" DIA. MANSELL.

SLIDING DOOR

END B

Diagram 192

END A

8'-10" OVER BODY AT WAISTLINE.

END B

FOR BULKHEAD & INTERIOR LAYOUT SEE FIGURE 24

8'-0"

8'-0"

BATTERY BOX OTHER SIDE.

DYNAMO OTHER SIDE.

BATTERY BOX THIS SIDE.

UNDERFRAME DETAIL FOR ELECTRICALLY-LIT COACHES.

SLIDING DOOR

END B

SECTION THROUGH BODYSIDE AT WAISTLINE.

Plate 92 Interior of a 'Balloon' trailer third, showing the rattan-covered seating with reversible backs. Note the elaborate LB&SCR monogram over the bulkhead doors and the straps for standing passengers.
As the vehicle is gas-lit, it is probably one of the 1905 vehicles. *LBSCR*

In order to emphasise the competition with other forms of transport, the seating was arranged in open saloons and on rattan-covered seats, with reversible tram-type seat backs on all except those against fixed bulkheads, as seen in **Plate 92**. The three carriage variations are drawn in **Figures 24** and **25**.

The two original vehicles were equipped with gangways at the 'locomotive' end. However, no matching trailer cars were ever built to work with them and the gangways were removed from both cars in August 1920, possibly without ever being used. All 'Balloon' pull-push services were originally third class only and it was not until 1916 that any other coaches were adapted to run with them. In that year one arc-roofed third (LBSCR No 1734) and two similar composites (LBSCR Nos 538/40) were through piped to provide additional accommodation. However the composites were primarily intended to run with other arc-roofed stock rather than the 'Balloons', as some of these pull-push vehicles did include first class accommodation. For this reason no LBSCR set numbers were allocated, while the cars were regularly moved around the Brighton system from one duty to another. Off-peak workings into London termini were not unknown by 1910-12, even if this might have occurred only once per day. **Plate 93** illustrates such a working and also the fact that a few six-wheeled trailer coaches could be pressed into service as strengthening vehicles. At this date and away from the London area, with the possible exception of Midhurst, most lines would see a motor train at some time during the day. The only restriction applied to the coaches at this time was that they could not run through Bopeep Tunnel into Hastings. That said,

however, the author has seen correspondence between the LBSCR and the SECR, indicating that infringements did occur and that the South Eastern's management let their displeasure be known on several occasions!

Mechanical control linkage was used initially, but once the 1909 arc-roofed coaches and 'D1' class locomotives were introduced, air-control gradually took over, although there were two versions of this and what eventually became the SR standard did not fully evolve until 1914, as described in Chapter 2.

The October 1912 locomotive workings list some 23 motor train duties, but being primarily concerned with motive power matters, do not necessarily detail the rolling stock involved. By this time there were 17 'Balloon' trailers at work, as well as 22 other arc-roofed vehicles fitted with pull-push gear — the latter capable of working a minimum of 11 other duties (if all were working in pairs). These are summarised as follows:

Base	Duties
Brighton	Six (at least two with arc-roofed 1911 stock)
Eastbourne	One (with arc-roofed 1912 stock)
St Leonards	One (with arc-roofed 1912 stock)
Tunbridge Wells	Two
Horsham	Two
Bognor	One
Fratton	Two
New Cross Gate	One (possibly with 1909 arc-roofed stock)
Coulsdon	One (with 1909 arc-roofed stock)
West Croydon	Six (at least two with 1909 arc-roofed stock)

Plate 93 Diagram 192 trailer LBSCR No 1341/SR No 3844 passes Balham Intermediate signalbox, *circa* 1910-12, with what may be the 3pm Victoria–Banstead service, part of West Croydon motor duty No 3 (weekdays) which gave the London terminus the sight of a pull-push train. A three-compartment six-wheeled brake third trails the locomotive, possibly one of those originally fitted to run with the steam railmotors between Eastbourne and St Leonards. *F. Moore*

From photographic evidence, it would seem that a combination of a 'Balloon' driving brake third and a 1909 arc-roofed brake composite coach was occasional, and mostly confined to the London area. The Dyke service was, at this time, not detailed for pull-push working, but from photographic evidence was often provided with the 1905 cars, but hauled in the conventional manner by a non-fitted locomotive. Many of the above duties were straightforward, such as those at Fratton, which simply ran to and from Chichester all day, but those at Brighton in particular might encompass locations as diverse at Seaford, Lewes, Haywards Heath and Uckfied in a single day. In contrast, one coach ran no further than Kemp Town, albeit many times in the course of the day.

By October 1916 and February 1921, the picture is much clearer and the relevant carriage workings give the following allocations for 'Balloon' trailers:

In 1923, the newly formed Southern Railway decided to form permanent two-coach sets and equipped arc-roofed composites Nos 6033-45/55/7, plus thirds Nos 2063, 2166 and 2271 for the purpose. **Figure 26** details these additional vehicles. Three of these coaches (Nos 2166 and 6038/40) were already through piped for strengthening duties, so not all vehicles needed any additional work in order to form SR sets 736-50 and 979/80. The last two sets were third class only, hence the different number sequence, and these were primarily reserved for services between Brighton and The Dyke or Kemp Town, where the short duration of the journey did not warrant the provision of first class seating.

The July 1924 carriage working notices list the sets so formed, but with the carriage numbers in a mixture of LBSCR and SR identities. Set 736 alone was already in SR livery, while set 737 had just the 'Balloon' driving brake third with its SR number, the

Vehicle Nos	October 1916 duty	February 1921 duty
1326/7	Brighton and The Dyke	Spare cars
1328	Brighton and Haywards Heath	Brighton and Seaford
1329	Horsham and Guildford	Brighton and Seaford
1330	Spare car (London district)	Brighton and East Grinstead
1331	Brighton and Kemp Town	Brighton and The Dyke
1332	Spare car	Spare car
1333	Brighton and Uckfield	Spare car
1334	Spare car	Tunbridge Wells and Crowborough
1335	Tunbridge Wells and Oxted	Portsmouth and Emsworth
1336	Brighton and Seaford	Tunbridge Wells and Oxted
1337	Coulsdon and Crystal Palace	Coulsdon and Crystal Palace
1338	Tunbridge Wells and Crowborough	Brighton and The Dyke
1339	West Croydon and Banstead*	Brighton and Kemp Town
1340	Horsham and Three Bridges	Horsham and Three Bridges
1341	Streatham and East/West Croydon	Spare car
1342	Bognor Branch	West Croydon and Sutton/Crystal Palace

*Certain trips with arc-roofed bogie third No 1734 attached.

Undoubtedly, these allocations could change as necessary, for example due to works visits etc. while at a location such as Brighton with six or more workings, it would not be at all difficult to swap duties. The locomotive and coach at Bognor would travel between there and Barnham Junction, Ford, Littlehampton and Arundel during the day, picking up through coaches from London on various trips as required, the through coaches trailing the locomotive or coach depending on the direction of travel.

arc-roofed trailer still being in LBSCR livery. Set 979 was exactly the reverse, with just trailer third No 2166 renumbered. All the other sets were identified by their LBSCR numbers, but all had SR set numbers painted on. Set 980 is shown formed with a 54ft nine-compartment third (LBSCR No 1381/SR No 2271, to SR diagram 71) as trailer. However, soon after this it was decided to utilise these 90-seat thirds for electric trailer sets (making better use of their slightly greater seating capacity) and eight-compartment third SR No 2063 was substituted early in 1925.

Plate 94 A Haywards Heath–Brighton working, seen just south of Hassocks, formed of diagram 192 'Balloon' brake No 1342/3845 and an unidentified composite, propelled by 'D1' class locomotive No 214, circa 1923. Both coaches are in the lined umber livery, adopted after 1911.
H. Gordon Tidey/The Lens of Sutton Association

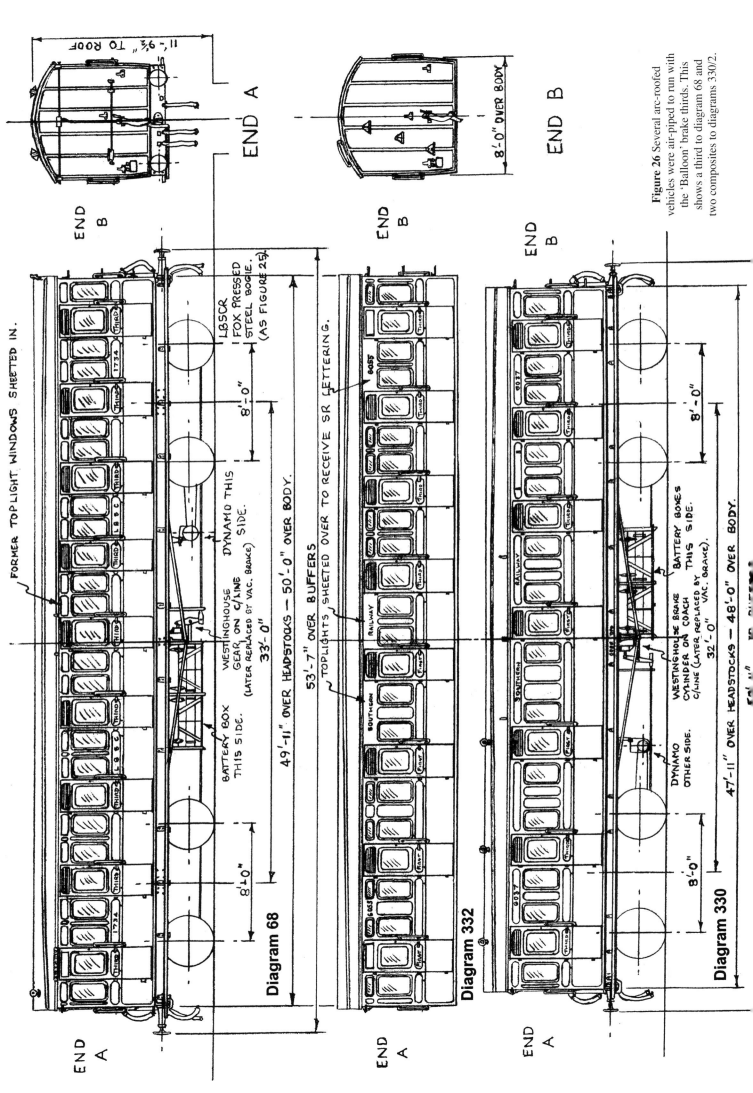

11'-3¾" TO ROOF

END A

END B

END B

END A

END B

FORMER TOPLIGHT WINDOWS SHEETED IN.

LBSCR FOX PRESSED STEEL BOGIE. (AS FIGURE 25).

8'-0"

WESTINGHOUSE DYNAMO THIS GEAR ON C/LINE SIDE. (LATER REPLACED BY VAC. BRAKE)

33'-0"

BATTERY BOX THIS SIDE.

49'-11" OVER HEADSTOCKS — 50'-0" OVER BODY.

8'-0"

Diagram 68

53'-7" OVER BUFFERS

TOPLIGHTS SHEETED OVER TO RECEIVE SR LETTERING.

Diagram 332

END B

END A

8'-0"

BATTERY BOXES THIS SIDE.

WESTINGHOUSE BRAKE CYLINDER ON COACH C/LINE (LATER REPLACED BY VAC. BRAKE).

32'-0"

DYNAMO OTHER SIDE.

47'-11" OVER HEADSTOCKS — 48'-0" OVER BODY.

8'-0"

Diagram 330

8'-0" OVER BODY

END B

Figure 26 Several arc-roofed vehicles were air-piped to run with the 'Balloon' brake thirds. This shows a third to diagram 68 and two composites to diagrams 330/2.

These 'Balloon'/arc-roofed pairings hardly matched each other in terms of appearance but were to remain so formed for almost ten years. By 1931, the shorter Brighton bogie coaches were being withdrawn from service (quite a few were gas-lit) and the opportunity was taken to replace them with some 'Balloon' compartment coaches then being made redundant by the introduction of Maunsell corridor stock and the forthcoming electrification of the Brighton main line. Although these were only 8ft 6in wide (instead of 8ft 10in for the 'Balloon' auto-trailers) at least they would match them in appearance. Set 980 had been disbanded in 1928, coach No 3830 being retained as a single vehicle for the Kemp Town branch, in 1928, making no fewer than 30 round trips in a day! Trailer No 2063 was at first retained as a strengthening vehicle at Brighton, but by 1931 had been sent to Chertsey for augmenting the Weybridge–Virginia

Water shuttle — quite a contrast to the LSWR 'bogie' block sets otherwise used on that service. By this time most LBSCR stock had received vacuum brakes, so transfer between sections no longer constituted a problem. At about the same date the five gas-lit 'Balloon' brake thirds (SR Nos 3829/30/4-6) had this replaced by electricity. Quite why this distinction had been made in 1905/06 is not clear, especially as three of the 1906 cars had electric lighting from new. Loose coach No 3830 later moved to Arundel for the Littlehampton shuttle service and it was at the latter station where it suffered collision damage in February 1936, being withdrawn soon after.

SR order L670 was issued in July 1931 for the conversion of 28 additional vehicles to pull-push working and this included the 16 'Balloon' compartment coaches for sets 736-50 and 979, together with replacements for the 48ft arc-roofed thirds in sets

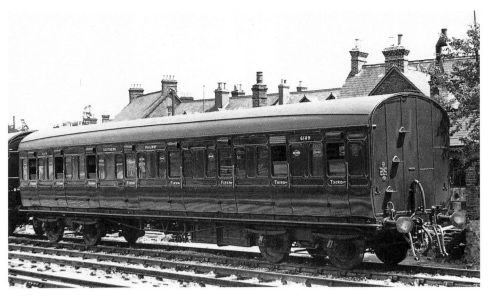

Plate 98 The other half of set 750, diagram 366 composite No 6189 in similar condition, at Horsham on 16 July 1938. *H. C. Casserley*

Plate 99 Also at Horsham, but prior to the rebuilding for the mid-Sussex electrification in 1938, 'D1' class No 2254 waits to leave with a Dorking North service. The composite is to diagram 355A/B, so the set is either of Nos 743, 744 or 745. *The Lens of Sutton Association*

Plate 100 A close-up of the end of diagram 70 third No 2180 at Bognor in August 1937. The three air-control connections and their cast-iron descriptive labels are visible on the headstock. *E. R. Lacey*

751-9 (described in the next chapter) as well as 'new' sets 649-51, also described in Chapter 9. Two vehicles were full thirds (for sets 738 and 979), while the other 14 composites were to seven different diagrams, although basically only of four types, but by the time that various downgradings of first class compartments and the fact that some had either 8ft or 10ft wheelbase bogies had been taken into account, the number of diagrams allocated reached this figure. Alongside the fitting of air-control pipes, all vehicles had their lavatories blanked off and the frosted windows replaced by steel sheeting. This work was completed by May/June 1932. Set 979 was renumbered 733 during 1937, as part of a move to clear the upper range of the steam stock set list for additional electric stock trailer units, numbered downwards from 1000.

Two additional 'Balloon' pull-push sets were formed in 1934, Nos 734/5, utilising some more compartment vehicles now made redundant by the Brighton electrification. The order number used for these is not clear, but it may have been an extension of order L670. In each case the driving trailer was formed using a six-compartment third brake, coupled with a suitably matched composite. All four vehicles were slightly different, although in traffic this was perhaps academic, but it did add three more diagrams to the total of 'Balloon' pull-push stock. One of the composites was a former third, resulting in somewhat cramped conditions for the unfortunate first class passenger when presented with set 735, yet in most other sets the eagle-eyed third class traveller could enjoy compartments of first class dimensions at no extra cost, if he were careful! These two compartment 'Balloon' sets were based originally at Bognor, later at Horsham.

Plate 101 Diagram 357A composite No 6286 at Eastbourne in August 1938, formed as part of set 736. *E. R. Lacey*

Plate 102 A Ford-bound motor service leaves Barnham propelled by 'D1' class No 2289 on 16 April 1938. The pull-push set is one of Nos 736/7/9, formed of a diagram 357A composite and a diagram 191 driving brake third. *K. O'B. Nicholls*

Sets based at Horsham, prior to electrification, could travel in all four directions: northwards to Dorking, eastwards to Three Bridges, southwards to Brighton and Pulborough, and westwards to Guildford. This last destination gave one of few occasions when the sets would be seen off the Central section (just!), and apart from this, the ex-LSWR Midhurst–Petersfield branch was about the only other location where a 'Balloon' pull-push set might work away from former LBSCR lines.

Electrification of the mid-Sussex line in 1938 resulted in a surplus of these sets and withdrawal commenced soon after, being completed in January 1943, with set 750, in a revised form, being the last to go. This was the only later change of formation recorded, in contrast to the many previous alterations. After withdrawal a number of carriage bodies were grounded at various locations around the Southern, while coach No 3841 from set 750 remained on its bogies as a 'mobile store' within Lancing Works. In reality, it was not at all mobile, certainly not by 1963 when the Bluebell Railway C&W staff inspected it with a view to possible preservation. Regrettably, it was considered beyond saving at that time. Considering what has now been achieved at Horsted Keynes and elsewhere, one wonders if the same decision would be reached had the carriage still existed today? In those early days of preservation, the economics were rather different.

Carriage and set formation details follow in Table 5, together with allocations for 1931, 1935 and 1939, while that for November 1928 appears in Appendix 1.

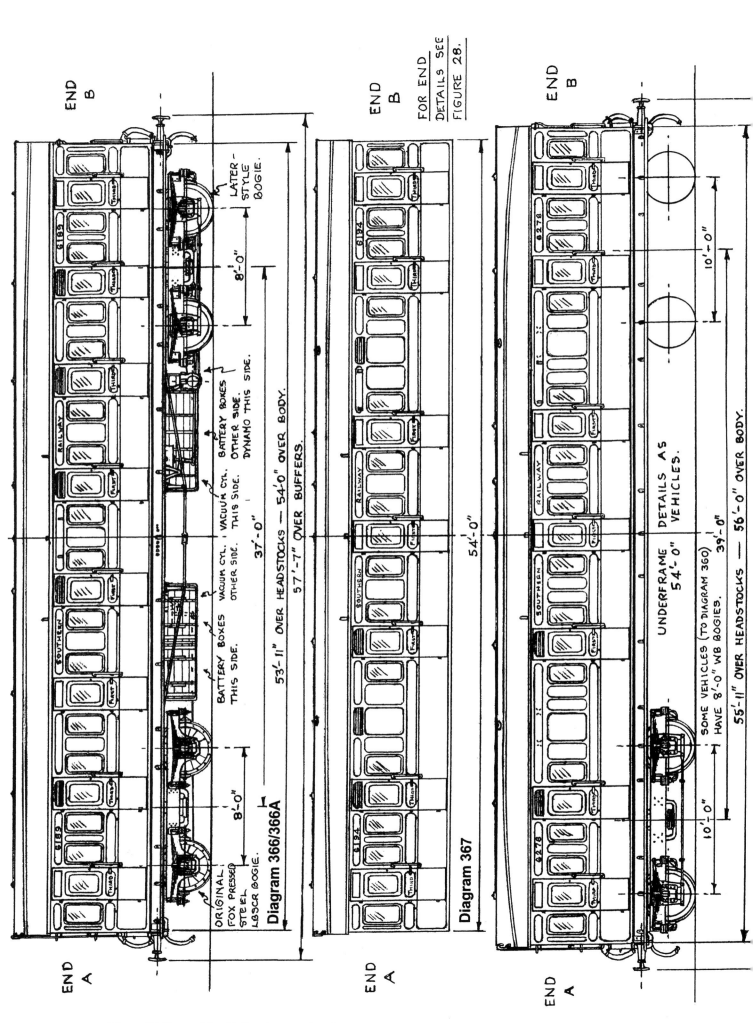

Figure 27 Three of the 'Balloon' composites formed into pull-push sets from 1931, covering diagrams 355/60/6/7.

Plate 103 Compartment 'Balloon' brake third No 3819 at Horsham on 19 June 1938, to diagram 229. Coach No 3816 to diagram 228 was almost identical externally. *E. R. Lacey*

Plate 104 Diagram 360A composite No 6271, at Lancing Works in 1951, after relegation to departmental stock as No 1635S. It formerly ran in set 734 until 1941. *J. H. Aston*

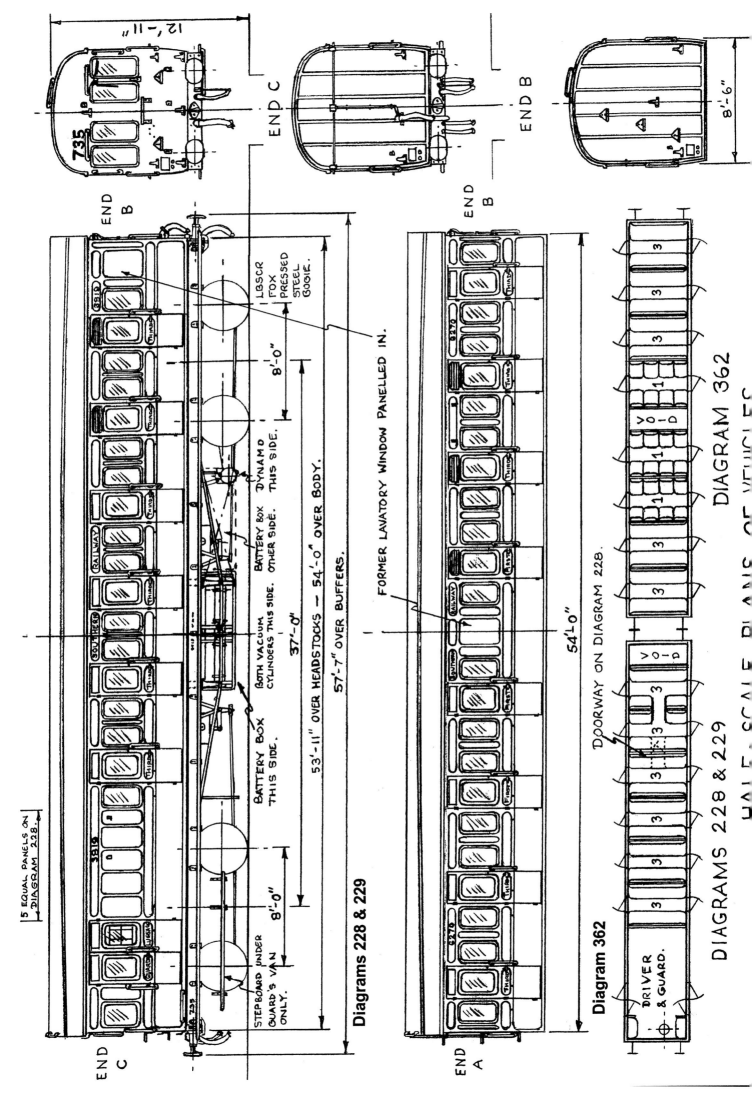

12'-11"

END B

735

END C

END B

8'-6"

5 EQUAL PANELS ON DIAGRAM 228.

END B

3819

THIRD

THIRD

THIRD

RAILWAY

THIRD

SOUTHERN

THIRD

3819

GUARD

L.B.S.C.R FOX PRESSED STEEL BOGIE.

8'-0"

DYNAMO THIS SIDE.
BATTERY BOX OTHER SIDE.

BATTERY BOX THIS SIDE.

BOTH VACUUM CYLINDERS THIS SIDE.

37'-0"

53'-11" OVER HEADSTOCKS — 54'-0" OVER BODY.

57'-7" OVER BUFFERS.

8'-0"

STEPBOARD UNDER GUARD'S VAN ONLY.

END C

Diagrams 228 & 229

END B

8270

THIRD

THIRD

THIRD

RAILWAY

FIRST

FIRST

THIRD

THIRD

8270

FORMER LAVATORY WINDOW PANELLED IN.

54'-0"

Diagram 362

END A

3   3   3

3

3

V O I D

1   1

3   3

3   3

V O I D

3

3

DOORWAY ON DIAGRAM 228.

3   3   3   3   3   3

DRIVER & GUARD.

DIAGRAM 362

DIAGRAMS 228 & 229

HALF SCALE PLANS OF VEHICLES

Table 5
LBSCR 'Balloon' Stock Sets

SR Set No	Running Dates	SR BT	Coach Nos C or T	Allocation 1931	Allocation 1935	Allocation 1939	Remarks
733	1937-7/42	3829	2179			Midhurst	Ex-set 979 in 1937. Third class only.
734	2/34-5/41	3816	6271		Bognor	Horsham	Compartment stock
735	4/34-10/41	3819	6270		Bognor	Horsham	Compartment stock
736	1923-12/31	3831	6033	Bognor			Composite is arc-roofed
	1/32-8/40	3831	6286		Bognor	Pulborough	
737	1923-2/32	3832	6034	Littlehampton			Composite is arc-roofed
	2/32-12/42	3832	6283		Littlehampton	Horsham	
738	1923-3/31	3833	6035	Relief set			Composite is arc-roofed
	1/32-6/41	3833	2180		The Dyke	Petersfield	Third class only from 1/32
739	1923-10/31	3834	6036	Horsham			Composite is arc-roofed
	10/31-10/42	3834	6282		Horsham	Steyning	
740	1923-2/32	3835	6037	Horsham			Composite is arc-roofed
	2/32-12/40	3835	6190		Horsham	Horsham	
741	1923-4/32	3836	6038	Littlehampton			Composite is arc-roofed
	4/32-10/41	3836	6284		Bognor	Hailsham	
742	1923-8/31	3837	6039	Brighton			Composite is arc-roofed
	8/31-6/40	3837	6285		Littlehampton	Bognor	
743	1923-12/31	3838	6040	Brighton			Composite is arc-roofed
	12/31-10/38	3838	6278		Brighton		
744	1923-12/31	3839	6041	Relief set			Composite is arc-roofed
	12/31-8/38	3839	6279		Bognor		
745	1923-12/31	3840	6042	Relief set			Composite is arc-roofed
	12/31-8/38	3840	6280		Bognor		
746	1923-6/32	3841	6043	Relief set			Composite is arc-roofed
	6/32-7/41	3841	6194		Eastbourne	?	Coach No 3841 later to set 750
747	1923-12/31	3842	6044	Horsham			Composite is arc-roofed
	12/31-11/42	3842	6191		Relief set	?	
748	1923-12/31	3843	6045	Relief set			Composite is arc-roofed
	3/32-2/39	3843	6273		Horsham		
749	1923-3/32	3844	6056	Horsham			Composite is arc-roofed
	3/32-1/42	3844	6275		Horsham	Horsham	
750	1923-4/32	3845	6057	Horsham			Composite is arc-roofed
	4/32-7/41	3845	6189		Horsham	Horsham	
	7/41-1/43	3841	6189				Coach No 3841 ex-set 746
979	1923-11/31	3829	2166	The Dyke			Third is arc-roofed
	2/32-1937	3829	2179		Relief set		Set renumbered as 733 in 1937
980	c5/24-11/25	3830	2271	Kemp Town	Arundel		Third is arc-roofed
	11/25-1928	3830	2063	(3830 only)	(3830 only)		Third is arc-roofed, later to loose stock

Note: No LBSCR set numbers or permanent set formations allocated before 1923.
Additional loose arc-roofed coaches 2157/9/68 and 6055 ran with the 'Balloon' vehicles at various times.
All 'Balloon' coaches were to SR route restriction 5, all arc-roofed coaches to restriction 0.

Table 5.2
Carriage Summary

SR Diagram	SR Nos	Relevant LBSCR Nos	Date of P-P conversion	Dimensions L x W	Seats 1	Seats 3	Remarks
64	2063		11/25	48ft x 8ft		80	Arc-roof. For set 980, later loose coach until 4/32.
68	2157/9/66/8	1734 only	c1916 & 1930	50ft x 8ft		90	Arc-roof. Only LBSCR No 1734 P-P fitted c1916, rest 1930/1.
70	2179/80		1-2/32	54ft x 8ft 6in		90	For sets 979 and 738.
71	2271	1381*	c5/24	54ft x 8ft		90	Arc-roof. P-P fitted for set 980 until 11/25 only.
190	3829-30	1326-7	9/05	54ft x 8ft 10in		52	Prototype 'Balloon' auto trailer cars, with gangway.
191	3831-6	1328-33	6/06	54ft x 8ft 10in		60	Later 'Balloon' auto trailer cars.
192	3837-45	1334-42	6-12/07	54ft x 8ft 10in		60	Final 'Balloon' auto trailer cars.
228	3816		12/33	54ft x 8ft 6in		56	Compartment stock. Ex-diagram 186 for set 734.
229	3819		12/33	54ft x 8ft 6in		58	Compartment stock. Ex-diagram 187 for set 735.
330	6033-45	533-45*	c1916 & 1923	48ft x 8ft	12	50	Arc-roof. Only LBSCR Nos 538/40 P-P fitted c1916, rest 1923.
332	6055-7	548/9*	1923 & 1930	50ft x 8ft	32	40	Arc-roof. Coach No 6055 P-P fitted in 1930-34 only.
355A/B	6278-80		10-11/31	56ft x 8ft 6in	18/20	40	Coach No 6279 only to diagram 355B—20 first class seats. As diagram 360A but on 10ft wheelbase bogies.
357A	6282/3/6		10/31-1/32	56ft x 8ft 6in	18	50	8ft wheelbase bogies.
358A	6284/5		8/31-4/32	56ft x 8ft 6in	18	50	As diagram 357A but on 10ft wheelbase bogies.
360/A	6271/3/5		3/32-2/34	56ft x 8ft 6in	18/24	40	Diagram 360A with 24 first class seats. 8ft wheelbase bogies.
362	6270		4/34	54ft x 8ft 6in	24	50	Ex-diagram 77 third class.
366/A	6189-92		12/31-6/32	54ft x 8ft 6in	18/24	50	Diagram 366A with 24 first class seats.
367	6194		10/32	54ft x 8ft 6in	18/24	40	First class seating later 24.

* Most of these vehicles converted during 1923/4 retained LBSCR livery and numbers until first SR repaint.
Diagram 355B had just one first class compartment altered to seat 8 instead of 6 passengers.
Diagrams 360A, 366A & 367 later altered so that all first class compartments seated eight instead of six passengers.
All 'Balloon' vehicles were to SR route restriction 5 (to be confined to LBSCR lines only), arc-roofed vehicles to restriction 0.
Other examples of diagrams 64 and 71 were pull-push fitted — see Chapter 9.

Figure 28 Compartment 'Balloon' sets 734/5; SR diagrams 228/9 and 362. For the diagram 360 composite in set 734 see Figure 27

Chapter 9.

LBSCR Arc-roofed Stock

We now come to the largest single group of vehicles utilised for pull-push working — and also the ones with the longest running period, extending from 1909 until 1961 (just!). In total, there were 32 sets of LBSCR arc-roofed stock, although the final three were actually formed by the Southern Railway in 1931. Nineteen sets and ten individual coaches pre-date the Grouping and most of these were purpose-built for motor train working, in marked contrast to the pull-push stock from the other SR constituent companies. None was allocated set numbers in LBSCR days, yet it appears that the majority were permanently formed as two-coach sets and did not alter in their formations before 1923.

They may be considered in three distinct groups: those individual coaches built in 1909/11 without corridors (later incorporated into SR sets 751-60), those pairs built between 1911 and 1922 with corridors (later SR sets 981-99) and the final three 1931 conversions from former ac electric stock and other vehicles, again without corridors (SR sets 649-51). The 1909/11 vehicles were built to run singly and did not have any accompanying trailer coaches until 1924 onwards. However, no fewer than three generations of trailer were converted to run with them between then and 1932. Just to add complication, the sets numbered in the 9XX series were renumbered 714-31 and 504 in 1937, to clear this number series for additional electric trailer units, themselves numbered downwards from 1000.

1909/11 stock (SR sets 751-60)

By 1909 the 'Balloon' and 'A1' class locomotives had become well established on LBSCR pull-push services, but by then the production of these imposing-looking coaches had ceased and the company had returned to its rather outdated arc-roofed profile. When the next pull-push stock was needed, this was provided economically by mounting the bodies of some five-compartment six-wheeled thirds on new 54ft underframes and building on two additional compartments, plus a guard's/driving compartment at one end. This process was much favoured by the Brighton during the 1908-11 period to 'modernise' its carriage stock fleet. Ten driving brake composites, of two types, were produced in this manner in 1909 and 1911, one type having three first and four third class compartments, the other having two firsts and five thirds. In this way, mixing and matching could provide variable amounts of first class accommodation to suit the requirements of the particular route. This was the first time that the LBSCR had provided accommodation for both classes in a pull-push train.

The coaches were equipped with the initial form of air-control from the start and usually ran as a two-coach formation with a 'D1' class locomotive in the centre. The driver thus travelled in the leading end of one coach regardless of the direction of travel, with the fireman remaining alone on the engine. **Plate 19** illustrates one of the first pairings together with the short-lived L&B lettering style applied to the first four 1909 'D1' conversions. The guard's/driver's compartment was accessed via large sliding doors on each side and the usual four end windows were provided — a feature later adopted as standard on almost all SR pull-push sets. The first combination entered service in October 1909 between Epsom Downs and Sutton and there seems to have been a deliberate policy of keeping these vehicles to the suburban areas rather than out in the countryside. Allocations in 1916 were as follows:

Nos 630/3	Wimbledon and Streatham
Nos 631/2	Wimbledon and West Croydon
Nos 634/5	Epsom Downs and Sutton
Nos 636-9	West Croydon, Crystal Palace and Coulsdon

Plate 105 A Sutton–Wimbledon motor train leaving Mitcham, formed of two trailer brake composites to SR diagram 434 or 435, either side of a 'D1' class tank, circa 1910. *The Lens of Sutton Association*

The first two pairs had three first class compartments in each coach, the rest had just two.

Some alterations to duties must have occurred from time to time, as the Wimbledon–Streatham service was suspended for a period during World War 1 and the Wimbledon–West Croydon route reverted to normal locomotive haulage in 1917/18. A few loose thirds and composites were through piped around 1916 for strengthening purposes and these are detailed in Table 5 at the end of Chapter 8 as they could also run with the 'Balloon' stock.

In 1924, the Southern Railway decided to form the ten vehicles into permanent sets 751-60 and proposed to equip ten 54ft nine-compartment thirds (LBSCR Nos 1382-91/SR Nos 2272-81) to run with them, both groups of vehicles being formed in numerical order. This work commenced in May 1924 and the new SR set formations are listed in the July 1924 working notices, with all sets save 757 still shown with their LBSCR carriage numbers. Allocation details were given as:

Set Nos	Allocation	Workings
751	Eastbourne	Hailsham, Haywards Heath, Horsted Keynes, Seaford, Uckfield
752-4	Brighton	Relief set
755	West Croydon	Relief sets
756	Horsham	Brighton, Guildford, Three Bridges, Midhurst (+ 6w van)
757	Horsham	Relief set
758	Eastbourne	Relief set
759-60	Three Bridges	Relief sets

As only two sets were shown with regular workings, it is probable that few were expected to be available for traffic at that date. Just how many were actually formed as such, or indeed how long the formations were maintained is debatable, as very soon afterwards the decision was taken to use all the nine-compartment 54ft thirds as electric stock trailers. Their greater seating capacity could be put to better use in this way, so between November 1925 and January 1926, sets 751-60 were reformed using eight-compartment vehicles to diagram 64 instead. These coaches were selected at random, probably as they were outshopped at Lancing Works after overhaul. In each instance the 48ft third was freshly repainted in SR green livery, but at least two of the 54ft driving brake composites retained LBSCR umber for another couple of years.

It was in this form that set 754 (coaches Nos 6930 and 2038) was selected for air-control trials in August 1928, being equipped with vacuum braking and coupled to 'D1' class 0-4-2T No 234 for the purpose. Between November 1928 and February 1929 the combination toured a number of South Eastern and South Western routes, before official sanction of the overall adoption of LBSCR air control was given in March 1929. The other nine sets were similarly equipped between December 1929 and March 1930 and from this point onwards could be used anywhere on the system where pull-push operation was envisaged. Most sets found their way onto the Eastern section after 1935, but apart from running into Guildford from Horsham, were a rare sight on South Western lines.

Plate 106 It is perhaps not surprising that none of the 54ft nine-compartment thirds were photographed in pull-push form, as they only ran thus for about 18 months. However, the replacement 48ft vehicles are equally elusive. Non-motor fitted diagram 64 third No 2057 illustrates the type, at Brighton, *circa* 1930. *P. Coutanche*

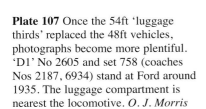

Plate 107 Once the 54ft 'luggage thirds' replaced the 48ft vehicles, photographs become more plentiful. 'D1' No 2605 and set 758 (coaches Nos 2187, 6934) stand at Ford around 1935. The luggage compartment is nearest the locomotive. *O. J. Morris*

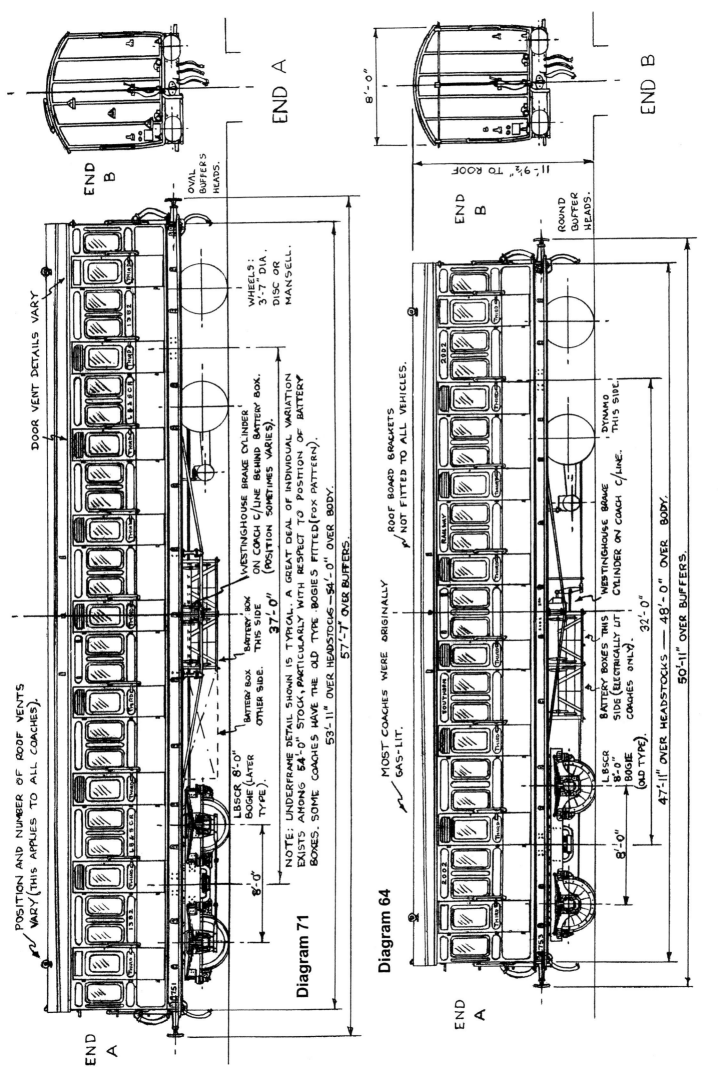

Figure 29 The 54ft nine-compartment third and 48ft eight-compartment third, to SR diagrams 71 and 64 respectively, used to make up sets 751-60 between 1924 and 1932.

Diagram 71

POSITION AND NUMBER OF ROOF VENTS VARY (THIS APPLIES TO ALL COACHES).

DOOR VENT DETAILS VARY

END B

END A

OVAL BUFFERS HEADS.

WHEELS: 3'-7" DIA. DISC OR MANSELL.

WESTINGHOUSE BRAKE CYLINDER ON COACH C/LINE BEHIND BATTERY BOX. (POSITION SOMETIMES VARIES).

BATTERY BOX THIS SIDE

BATTERY BOX OTHER SIDE.

LBSCR 8'-0" BOGIE (LATER TYPE).

8'-0"

37'-0"

NOTE: UNDERFRAME DETAIL SHOWN IS TYPICAL. A GREAT DEAL OF INDIVIDUAL VARIATION EXISTS AMONG 54'-0" STOCK, PARTICULARLY WITH RESPECT TO POSITION OF BATTERY BOXES. SOME COACHES HAVE THE OLD TYPE. BOGIES (FOX PATTERN).

53'-11" OVER HEADSTOCKS — 54'-0" OVER BODY.

57'-7" OVER BUFFERS.

END A

Diagram 64

ROOF BOARD BRACKETS NOT FITTED TO ALL VEHICLES.

MOST COACHES WERE ORIGINALLY GAS-LIT.

END B

8'-0"

11'-9½" TO ROOF

ROUND BUFFER HEADS.

DYNAMO THIS SIDE.

WESTINGHOUSE BRAKE CYLINDER ON COACH C/LINE.

BATTERY BOXES THIS SIDE (ELECTRICALLY LIT COACHES ONLY).

LBSCR 8'-0" BOGIE (OLD TYPE).

8'-0"

32'-0"

47'-11" OVER HEADSTOCKS — 48'-0" OVER BODY.

50'-11" OVER BUFFERS.

END A

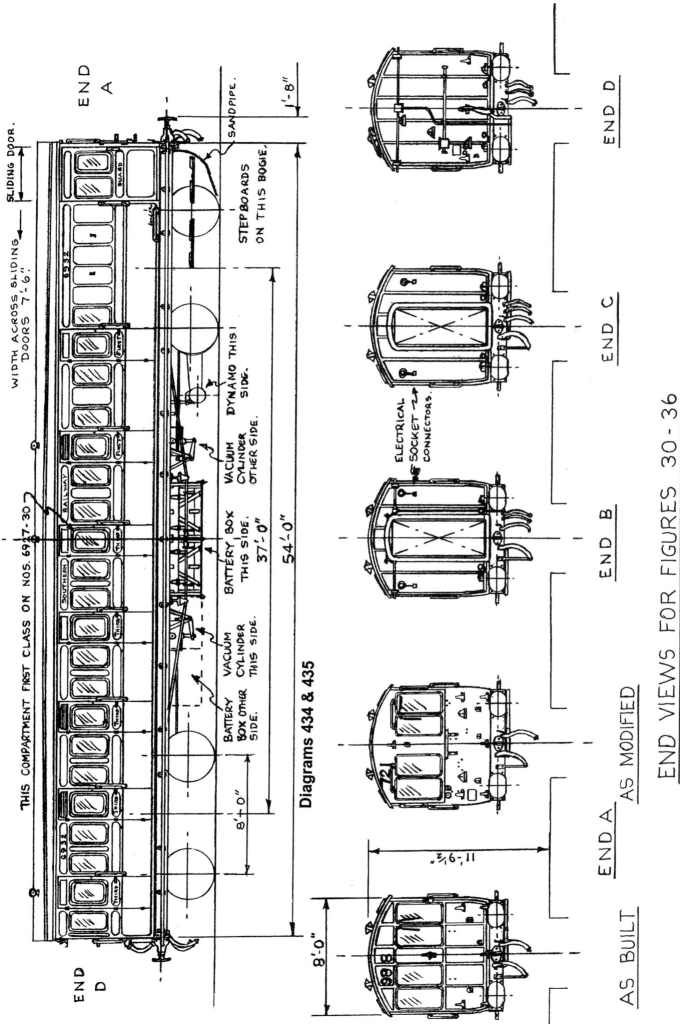

END A

SLIDING DOOR.

WIDTH ACROSS SLIDING DOORS 7'-6"

END D

SANDPIPE.

STEPBOARDS ON THIS BOGIE.

1'-8"

DYNAMO THIS SIDE.

VACUUM CYLINDER OTHER SIDE.

BATTERY BOX THIS SIDE.

54'-0"

37'-0"

8'-0"

VACUUM CYLINDER THIS SIDE.

BATTERY BOX OTHER SIDE.

THIS COMPARTMENT FIRST CLASS ON NOS. 6927-30.

Diagrams 434 & 435

ELECTRICAL SOCKET CONNECTORS.

END D

END C

END B

END A

AS MODIFIED

END VIEWS FOR FIGURES 30-36

11'-9½"

8'-0"

AS BUILT

Figure 30 The 1909/11 driving brake composites; SR diagrams 434/5, plus ends for LBSCR arc-roofed vehicles.

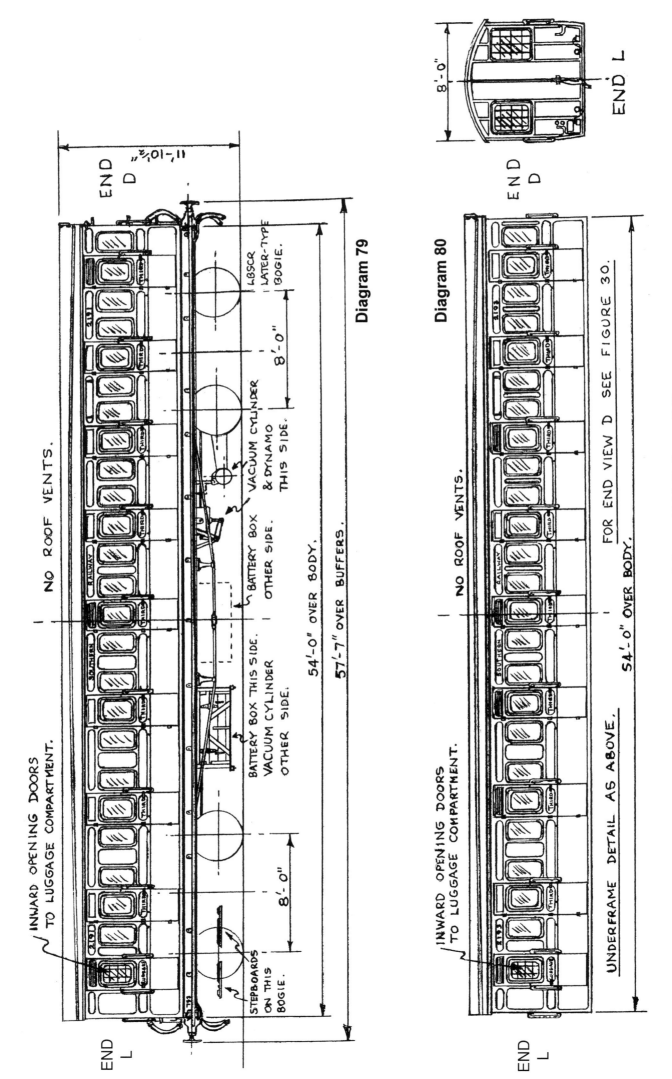

Figure 31 The 54ft 'luggage thirds'; SR diagrams 79/80.

The policy decision to withdraw all the shorter LBSCR carriages caught up with these sets in 1931/32, requiring the replacement of the 48ft thirds by other 54ft stock. SR order L670, issued in July 1931, called for 28 vehicles 'to be made suitable for pull-push working', but gave no individual details. Sixteen may be accounted for by the replacement 'Balloon' coaches described in the previous chapter, while three former ac electric stock vehicles became composite brakes for sets 649-51, to be described later. This left a further nine other conversions of former ac driving trailer composites, which, although intended for ac electric service, had never been used as such and had been in steam stock use since construction in 1915-21. These were converted into replacement vehicles for sets 751-9, leaving 1911 brake composite No 6936 (ex-set 760) to run as a loose/spare coach following the withdrawal of its companion 48ft third in April 1931. This coach remained in stock until withdrawn in March 1936. However, no allocated duty has been found for the vehicle during this period. Almost certainly, it was kept as a spare at or around Brighton and was the first withdrawal of these pull-push driving trailers.

The nine conversions, unlike those for sets 649-51, were trimmed as all-thirds, but retained the former driving compartment at one end for luggage — the former driving end windows being retained with the addition of protective grilles over the inside. In fact two types of coach were involved, with slightly different compartment dimensions depending on their origins, but for all practical purposes this was immaterial since both types seated 80 third class passengers — the same as the 48ft vehicles they had replaced. Just how much use was made of the luggage compartment is not known. However, photographs of the coaches in BR days show the luggage doors to be unlabelled and quite possibly locked out of use. Other photographs of this period show some sets running with the luggage compartment inboard, ie facing the driving trailer, instead of at the 'locomotive' end of the set, or with the end windows either painted out or sheeted over.

Withdrawal was a rather protracted process, as sets 751/2/4/6 went between 1938 and 1944, leaving the other five to run well into the 1950s, with the last not being taken out of service until 1959. Latterly, only set 755 remained on the South Eastern section, based at Ashford for New Romney and Hastings services; the rest returned to their native Central section and worked mostly from Horsham on services to Brighton or Guildford. Although set 759 was withdrawn in 1954, its trailer third saw further use in set 37, coupled to an ex-SECR driving trailer, described in Chapter 12. Table 6 at the end of this chapter summarises the many set formation changes and carriage details.

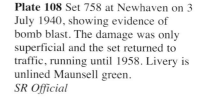

Plate 108 Set 758 at Newhaven on 3 July 1940, showing evidence of bomb blast. The damage was only superficial and the set returned to traffic, running until 1958. Livery is unlined Maunsell green. *SR Official*

Plate 109 A close-up of the luggage compartment of diagram 79 third No 2187 at Tunbridge Wells West on 11 September 1948. *D. Cullum*

Plate 110 The driving end of coach No 6929 of set 753 at Horsham on 6 May 1950, in SR malachite green livery. *K. G. Carr*

Plate 111 Diagram 80 'luggage third' No 2193 of set 759 at Horsham on 27 May 1950, one of the vehicles with only three compartments of first class dimensions. This was an early BR repaint in malachite green that omitted the third class door designations and 'Southern' title, but with the 'S' prefix to the number. *K. G. Carr*

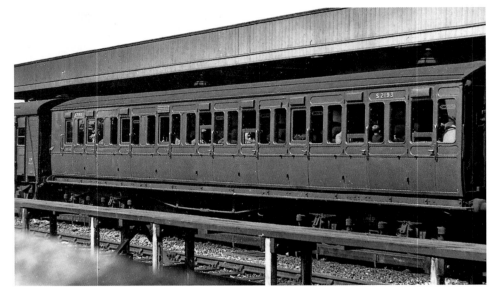

1911 Brighton–Worthing two-coach sets (SR sets 995-8)

We now return to 1911, when traffic levels between Brighton and West Worthing had increased beyond that capable of being dealt with by the single 'Balloon' trailers. In that year four two-coach sets were completed for these services. They were the first of what eventually totalled 19 sets of various types and all were equipped with gangway connections between the coaches, together with side corridors giving access to all compartments, facilitating ticket issue by the guard en route.

Like the 1909 brake composites, the driving brake thirds had seven passenger compartments and large sliding doors for access to the driver's/guard's compartment — which incidentally in later years would give rise to complaints from the crews about draughts! The accompanying trailer composites had six thirds with three first class compartments at the 'locomotive' end, one of which was segregated for non-smokers by an extra sliding door across the corridor. Another sliding door separated the first and third class compartments. The brake thirds also had a sliding door across the corridor to segregate smokers from the two end compartments reserved for non-smokers. Modellers should perhaps note that the third class compartment adjacent to the gangway connection in each coach was slightly larger than the rest. The others, at 5ft 5in across partitions, could hardly be described as generous. No end armrests or partition were provided where the corridor passed through the compartments, so a passenger forced to sit on the end seat when the train was crowded could be guaranteed an uncomfortable journey!

The four pairs were never allocated set numbers in pre-Grouping days, but were unlikely to run in any other combination by virtue of the electrical arrangements, with the dynamo and battery boxes on the brake thirds only and plug-in connectors on the end of the composites. Underframe details generally were not consistent on these, or indeed on any LBSCR carriage, and numerous minor variations have been recorded.

After 1918 two of the pairs were transferred to West Croydon for Wimbledon–Streatham and Sutton–Epsom Downs services, while by 1924, when SR set numbers 995-8 had been applied, the allocations were:

| Sets 995/7 | Brighton–West Worthing (both sets ran together either side of the engine) |
| Sets 996/8 | West Croydon for (respectively) Epsom Downs and Wimbledon services |

From this point onwards the four sets 'did the rounds' of Central section motor services, while in February/March 1930 all sets had their Westinghouse brake replaced by vacuum. In 1937 they were renumbered as 728-31 and very soon after set 731 was modified, renumbered as set 503 and transferred to the Isle of Wight, arriving there in May 1938 as a replacement for the somewhat antiquated LCDR sets 483/4 on the Merstone–Ventnor West service. For this duty, conventional pairs of hinged doors replaced the sliding doors to the luggage van and Westinghouse braking was reinstated. One further single brake composite coach (SR No 6987) was transferred at the same time and will be described shortly.

Plate 112 Diagram 346 composite No 6203 at Tonbridge on a Maidstone West train on 17 September 1949. Malachite green livery with the word 'Southern' in early Bulleid style. An ex-SECR air-control van (No 2002) is just visible to the left, and appears in Plate 176. *K. G. Carr*

Plate 113 Diagram 189 driving brake third No 3827 of set 730 at Eridge in the early 1950s, carrying BR lined crimson lake livery and left-hand numerals. Note that the driving end still retains some timber mouldings. A further example of these sets appears in Plate 4. *The Lens of Sutton Association*

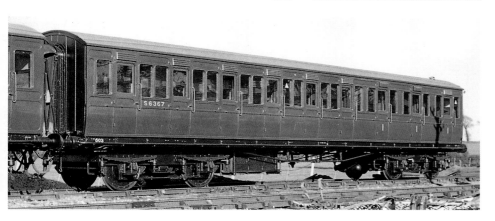

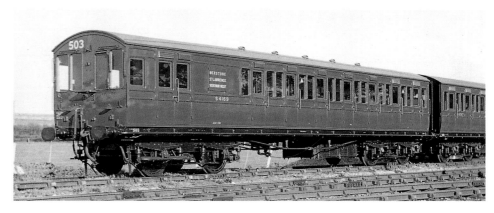

Plates 114 and 115 Isle of Wight transfer set 503 (Nos 4169 and 6367) at Merstone in April 1949, boarded for the Ventnor West branch. The set is clearly ex-works in malachite green, but with hand-painted numerals. The rebuilt luggage van side is obvious. *Both J. H. Aston*

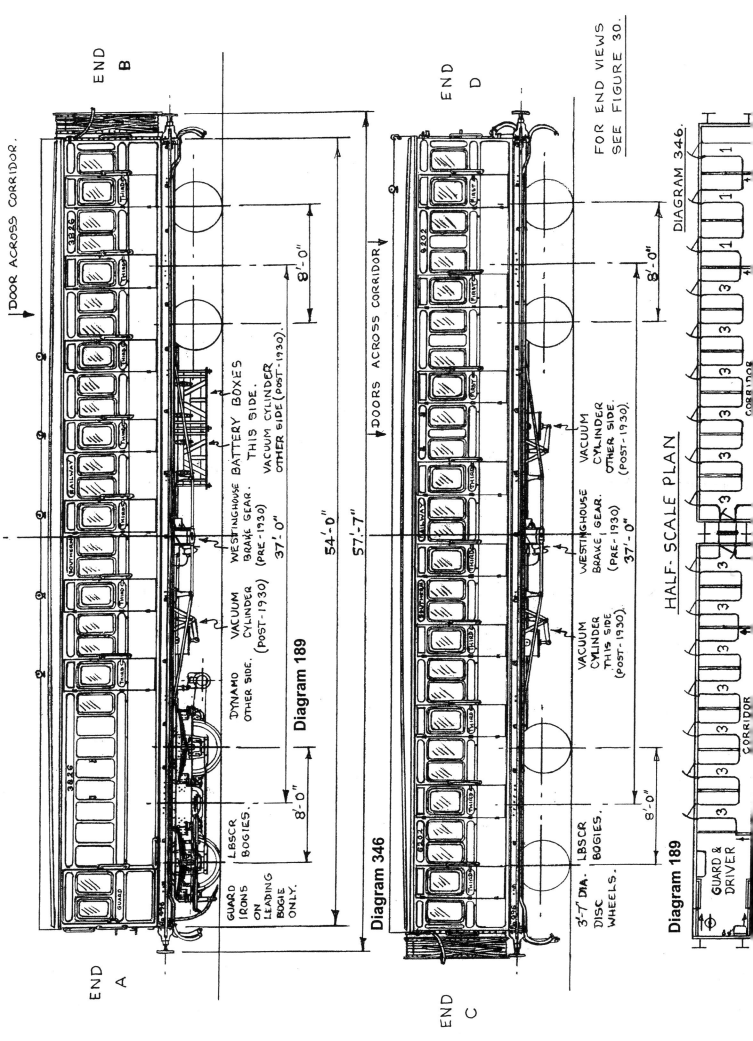

Figure 32 The 1911 Brighton–Worthing sets; SR diagrams 189 & 346.

Plate 116 A close-up of the gangway connection of set 503, photographed about 1953, possibly while it was stored pending withdrawal. Note that at least one panel has already been covered with steel sheeting. *A. Blackburn*

Plate 117 Despite the poor quality, this is the only known photograph of the driving end of a 1912 Eastbourne brake third in original condition with only two small end windows. Set 992 or 993 crosses Run Common, near Cranleigh, with a Guildford–Horsham train prior to 1930. *E. Jackson*

Set 728 was similarly modified and transferred to the Island in May 1947 as set 505, being used at either Ventnor West or on the Bembridge branch (the latter seldom in pull-push mode). At this time there were thoughts of running the Ryde–Ventnor service with six-coach pull-push trains but this came to nothing. Both sets and the loose coach were redundant after closure of their respective branch lines in 1952/53 and after a period of storage were finally withdrawn in May 1954 and sold to a scrap merchant in December 1955. Breaking up was somewhat protracted and took place at St Helens Quay during 1956, although none of the coaches had seen service since at least 1953.

The two sets remaining on the mainland fared somewhat better, which was unusual as most Island transfers outlived their mainland counterparts by many years, and lasted until 1959/60 on various Central section services. Set 730 at least ran in British Railways lined crimson lake between 1949 and 1956, as did at least one of the Island transfers in its latter years.

1912 Eastbourne–St Leonards stock and 1914 Portsmouth–Chichester set (SR sets 991-4/9)
The continuing problems with the steam railmotors operating between Eastbourne and St Leonards, plus their inability to cope with peak period loadings, resulted in the construction of four more corridor driving brake thirds during 1912. These could run

Plate 118 Guard's van and droplight detail of diagram 188 brake third No 3821 of set 726, in crimson lake livery, at Eastleigh on 2 September 1959. Withdrawal came just four weeks later. *A. E. West*

103

Plate 119 Set 727 on a rail tour at Kemp Town on 5 October 1952, resplendent in lined crimson lake livery. *D. Cullum*

Plate 120 This is 1914 Portsmouth set 504 (999/980) in its last days at Lewes, on 13 April 1958. The unique diagram 349 composite is farthest from the camera. *N. L. Browne*

singly or either side of a locomotive as necessary and featured eight third class compartments and a rather smaller guard's/driving compartment, all connected by a side corridor. The unpopular sliding doors to the latter gave way to pairs of hinged doors and, despite not being built to run as coupled pairs, an end gangway was provided which proved fortunate when some trailer composites were built in 1922 to run permanently with them.

However, for some reason the usual four windows were not fitted at the driving end. Instead there were two small windows in the same manner as many other non-motor fitted LBSCR brake coaches. At some time after 1923 (possibly when vacuum braking was provided in 1929/30) the Southern Railway rebuilt the ends to conform to the usual standard. Good photographs showing the original arrangement are conspicuous by their absence and only the SR diagrams show this detail with certainty. These four vehicles remained on the St Leonards motor service until at least 1922.

In 1914, an additional set was required for the Portsmouth–Chichester duty. The brake third (LBSCR No 1325/SR No 3820) was identical to the 1912 vehicles but a unique trailer composite (LBSCR No 644/SR No 6236) was completed to run with it. In this instance all six third class compartments were to the ungenerous 5ft 5in dimension, allowing the three firsts an extra 1½in each — not that the passengers would have noticed! Otherwise the seating and layout was the same as the 1911 composites. This set was to remain on its designated Portsmouth–Chichester working until well into the

Grouping period, being allocated SR set number 999 and receiving SR livery in December 1924. Indeed, the set was still working from Portsmouth in 1935, at that time with an LSWR diagram 12 vehicle (SR No 328) as the regular strengthening coach. Vacuum braking had been provided in February 1930.

In late 1936 or early 1937, the set was renumbered as 980, to clear the original set number for new electric stock trailer sets. Even this number was subsequently deemed needed for more electric stock, as later in 1937 the set was further renumbered as 504, within the block reserved for Isle of Wight transfers. Just whether this was the intention is not certain, but perhaps the fact that the luggage van was smaller than that in set 503 (which was sent over) might have been the deciding factor, and the set was instead diverted to the Eastern section, where it remained until returning to the Central in 1956. It ended its days based at Lewes in 1958, often on the reinstated Bluebell line service to East Grinstead. Brake third No 3820 received a further lease of life in 1959, being used for driver training purposes for the forthcoming Kent Coast electrification, along with brake composite No 6941 from set 651 (described later).

Returning now to the 1912 St Leonards stock, these were made into permanent two-coach sets in 1922 by the construction of ten new trailer composites for these, as well as for six new sets yet to be detailed. These trailer composites differed from all previous construction in having only two first class compartments, together with seven thirds. In 1923 the sets were allocated SR set numbers 991-4 and all found themselves

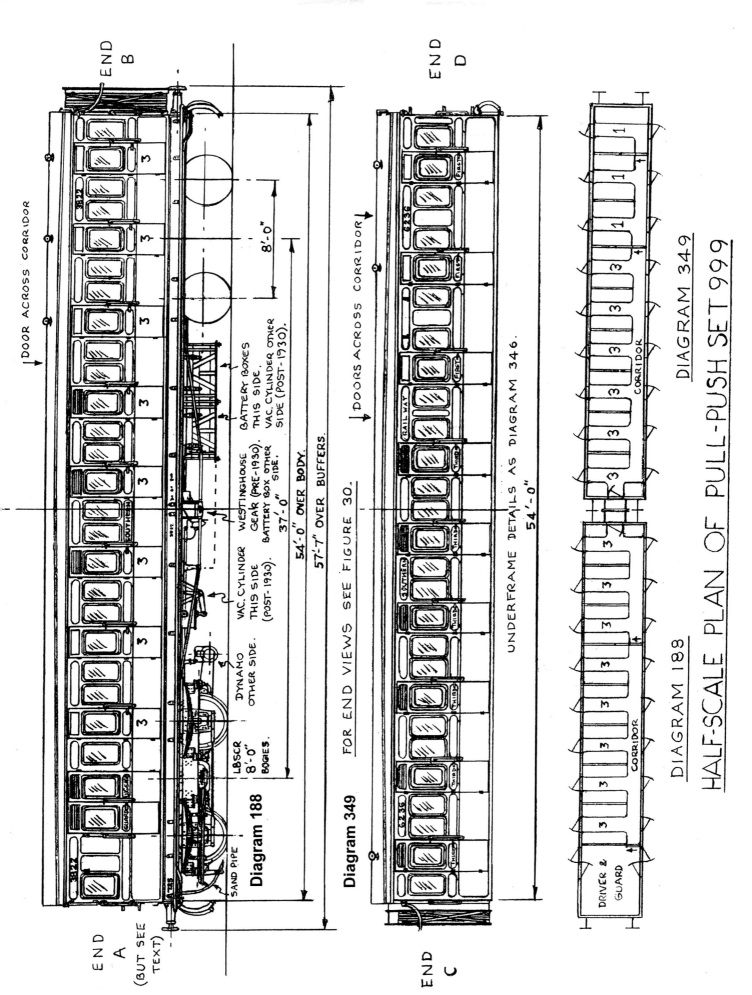

Figure 33 The 1912/14 Eastbourne and Portsmouth vehicles, to SR diagrams 188 and 349. For the 1922 trailers see Figure 35.

circulating throughout most of the Central section motor train workings over the next few years.

The July 1924 allocations were as follows:

Set No	Allocation	Workings
991	Tunbridge Wells West	Oxted and East Grinstead
992	Hastings	Eastbourne and Rye
993	Horsham	Redhill, Three Bridges, Guildford and Brighton
994	Seaford	Brighton, Haywards Heath and Horsted Keynes

Sets 993/4 both ran with a six-wheeled air-control van coupled between the set and the locomotive. These are dealt with in Chapter 14.

Vacuum braking was provided in 1929/30 and from then onwards some sets could appear on South Eastern workings, in addition to that between Hastings and Rye detailed above. Renumbering as sets 724-7 took place in 1937 and in 1939 set 727 was allocated to the Hayling Island branch (as was set 728 a little earlier). However, just whether either set ran in pull-push mode is extremely doubtful, as the only locomotives permitted over Langston Bridge were Class A1X and only those remaining on the Isle of Wight were still auto fitted at this time. In 1945, sets 724-6 were all on the South Eastern section with just 727 remaining on the Central and these allocations did not change before withdrawal between 1953 and 1959.

However, although set 724 was disbanded as early as April 1953, only the composite trailer was withdrawn, leaving just the brake third (No 3823) to be allocated to Midhurst for services between Petersfield and Pulborough. The gangway connection therefore served no useful purpose and was removed, resulting in a change of SR diagram from 188 to 188A. Just whether this alteration needed to be documented could be argued, but was typical of the meticulous record-keeping of the era. After withdrawal of passenger services to Midhurst in February 1955 the coach was variously allocated to the Eastern and later Central sections until condemned in 1960.

The brake third from set 726 (coach No 3821) also outlived its composite as a loose coach, first on the South Eastern and finally on the South Western section between 1957 and 1959. While on the South Western it wandered far and wide, being recorded at Portsmouth, Eastleigh, Salisbury and Exeter in company with reframed LSWR 58ft third No 253, nominally still described as set 726, but not capable of running as a pull-push set (see **Frontispiece**).

1921 two-coach sets for motor services (SR sets 981-4)

The restrictions of World War One resulted in no further pull-push construction until 1921, when four more two-coach sets were authorised, but with no specific allocation being mentioned. The eight-compartment driving brake thirds were very similar to the 1912/14 vehicles, but omitted the dividing door in the corridor to segregate smokers from non-smokers. This small change would ensure that different LBSCR and SR diagrams were allocated, as these partitions had to be thicker than the others in order to accommodate the sliding door.

The accompanying composites were rather different — having four first and only five third class compartments and therefore the proportion of first class accommodation in these sets was

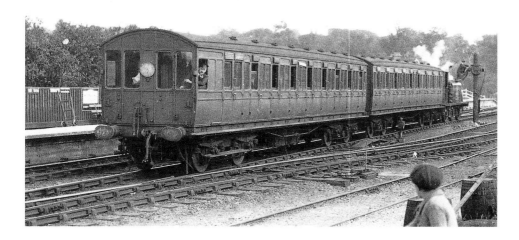

Plate 121 'D1' tank No 224 takes water at Rye before returning to Hastings or Eastbourne with 1921 pull-push set 983. The driving end retains full timber panelling and the set number is just visible above the headcode disc. *The Lens of Sutton Association*

Plate 122 Set 982 at Mitcham Junction in the final days of steam between Wimbledon and West Croydon, July 1930. This set now has steel sheeting over the driving end. *The Lens of Sutton Association*

greater than in any other LBSCR pull-push set. They were allocated SR set numbers 981-4 after the Grouping and are listed in the July 1924 working notices as being for the following services:

Set No	Allocation	Workings
981	Horsham	Guildford, Three Bridges and Midhurst (+ 6w van)
982	West Croydon	Wimbledon, Epsom Downs and Crystal Palace
983	Eastbourne	Hastings and Rye
984	Sutton	Epsom Downs and West Croydon

Vacuum braking was provided between January and May 1930, set 981 being recorded on trial with an 'M7' on the Bishops Waltham branch on 26 June of that year and various other changes of allocation occurred before the sets were renumbered as 714-7 in 1937. Until then, only set 981 had deserted the Central section for the South Eastern, being listed as a relief set with no allocated working in January 1935. Set 715 yielded its LBSCR composite for conversion to Isle of Wight driving brake composite No 6987 in 1938. Its replacement was ex-SECR 50ft composite No 5298, giving this set a hybrid appearance with one arc-roofed and one semi-elliptical roofed vehicle. As this coach was a non-corridor vehicle, the gangway at the end of the LBSCR driving brake was no longer needed and it was removed during 1939.

The LBSCR composite was required to provide a single pull-push coach for Isle of Wight services between Merstone and Ventnor West and was rebuilt with guard's/driver's accommodation in place of two first class compartments. The usual four end windows were fitted at the driving end and the coach was shipped to the Island in May 1938, together with set 503. Confusingly, coach No 6987 was also allocated the set number 503, despite being capable of operating as a single vehicle. Island records refer to the coach as part of this set, but whether it actually ran coupled to the other two coaches, or as a 2 + 1 formation either side of the locomotive, is unclear. Later, the set number was painted out and the coach did run as a single vehicle, especially in off-peak periods, on either the Ventnor West or Bembridge branch services. In 1949 the remaining three Island 'Terriers' were returned to the mainland in exchange for two pull-push fitted 'O2s' and it was then found necessary to remove the gangway connection at the 'locomotive' end of the coach, as this fouled the extended bunkers of the LSWR tanks; this modification dating from April 1949. In this form the coach outlived both the Ventnor West and Bembridge branches and, after a period in store, was withdrawn in May 1954 and scrapped along with the other Island pull-push sets at St Helens during 1956.

Returning to the mainland, set 715, in its hybrid form, was initially allocated to Horsham for services to Dorking North until electrification of the mid-Sussex line later in 1938, after which it migrated to the Hawkhurst branch. Sets 714/6 also ran at this time on the South Eastern section, being noted at New Romney and Hythe respectively. Set 717 alone remained on Central section workings, based at Tunbridge Wells West. Later it moved to the Bexhill West branch, being joined by set 716. After World War 2, all four sets were working on South Eastern lines with sets 714/5 operating Ashford–Hastings and St Leonards–Rye services.

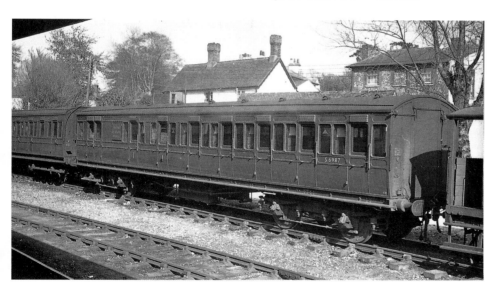

Plate 123 The solitary Isle of Wight driving brake composite conversion: coach No 6987 to diagram 439 at Bembridge in 1952. Rebuilt from composite No 6238 in April 1938, two first class compartments at the far end were turned into the guard's/driver's accommodation. The corridor is on the far side of the coach. The former position of the gangway connection is visible. *A. E. West*

Plate 124 Set 717 at Westerham in August 1947, in malachite green livery. Motive power is provided by 'R' class 0-4-4T No 1671. *HMRS collection*

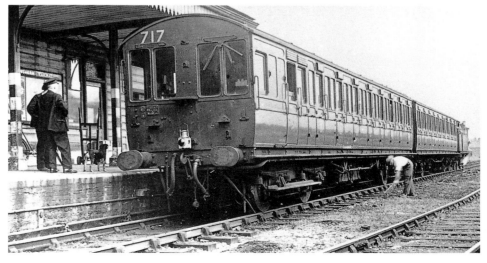

Plate 125 Diagram 350 composite No 6237 of set 714 at Horsham in June 1960. Now steel-panelled throughout and coupled to SECR driving brake third No 3467, this was the last LBSCR passenger coach to remain in mainland service. *D. Cullum*

By this time set 714 had been reformed with ex-SECR 60ft driving brake third no 3467 replacing the original LBSCR vehicle, giving this set a hybrid appearance similar to 715 from 1944 onwards, and any subsequent history is dealt with in Chapter 12. The ousted brake third (No 3846) went to the Midhurst branch as a single unit until withdrawn in May 1948. Set 715 saw one further change of formation when its LBSCR brake third (No 3847) was also appropriated for the Midhurst services in 1952. The replacement was another ex-SECR coach in the shape of 60ft brake third No 3475, now making this set completely of South Eastern origin and its subsequent history is also recorded in Chapter 12.

The loose LBSCR brake thirds continued to serve at Midhurst until closure in February 1955, when they were redeployed at various locations on the Eastern and Central sections until withdrawn in 1960. However, apart from finding employment on the reinstated Lewes-East Grinstead service in 1956-58, it is doubtful if any of these loose brake thirds saw much use once the Petersfield–Midhurst–Pulborough line closed.

Sets 716/7 remained in service until 1959/60, leaving just coach No 6237 in hybrid set 714 as the final example of LBSCR pull-push stock to survive into 1961. After withdrawal this coach was sent to the Ardingly branch to join another 140+ Southern Railway coaches to await the call for scrapping at Newhaven, which took place in October 1962.

1922 two-coach sets for branch line services (SR sets 985-90)
The last new LBSCR pull-push sets were authorised for construction in two batches during 1922. These comprised the balance of six of the ten composites built to strengthen the 1912 brake thirds on the Eastbourne–St Leonards service and six more new brake thirds to run with them. No specific allocation is quoted; they were described simply as being 'for branch line service'.

Plate 126 The 1922 sets had a rather larger luggage van and only six compartments in the brake third. Set 719 on the 1.35pm Brighton–Horsham is seen between Henfield and Partridge Green on 22 April 1950. Lined crimson lake livery and fully panelled brake end. Contrary to regulations, the guard has his compartment door open. *K. G. Carr*

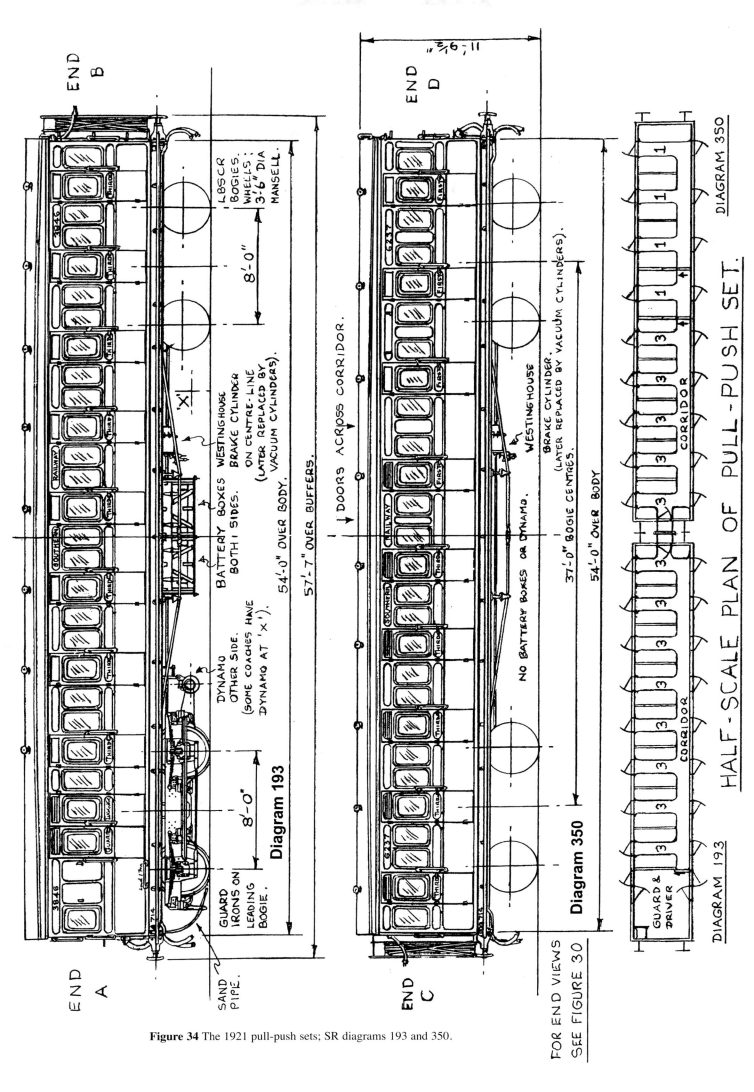

Figure 34 The 1921 pull-push sets; SR diagrams 193 and 350.

Plate 127 Set 723 was exiled to the Seaton branch from 1939 until 1949, giving the rare sight of a Brighton pull-push set in the west of England. The set is seen at Colyton with 'M7' No 49 on 28 June 1948, carrying early BR malachite green livery.
J. H. Aston

The composites have already been described, but the brake thirds had only six compartments (divided into three smoking and three non-smoking compartments). This was the first time that this particular configuration had been used in a Brighton pull-push set; consequently these had greater luggage space than all previous units. In fact they were not entirely new, as some underframes were second-hand, having been built originally for an LBSCR ambulance train several years earlier. As a result, minor detail differences, such as the type of buffer, could be identified between otherwise identical coaches. As before, the brake thirds were equipped with dynamos and battery boxes, and the composites were electrically wired only.

These sets became SR numbers 985-90 — set 985 alone receiving SR livery and carriage numbers during 1925, while the others, being fairly new, did not receive similar treatment until 1927. Vacuum braking was provided between November 1929 and June 1930. The July 1924 working notices list the allocations as follows:

Set No	Allocation	Workings
985	Portsmouth	Chichester, Pulborough and Littlehampton
986	Tunbridge Wells West	Brighton and Three Bridges
987	Horsham	Three Bridges, Chichester and Littlehampton
988	Littlehampton	Ford, Horsham and Three Bridges (+ 6w van)
989	Brighton	Worthing, Kemp Town, Seaford and Haywards Heath
990	Eastbourne	Tunbridge Wells West and St Leonards

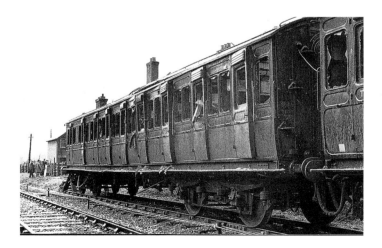

Plates 128 and 129 On 16 December 1942, set 718 was shot up by a German fighter aircraft near Bramley & Wonersh. This shows the damage inflicted, in which seven passengers died. Constructional details of the side corridor and partitions are revealed. *Both SR Official*

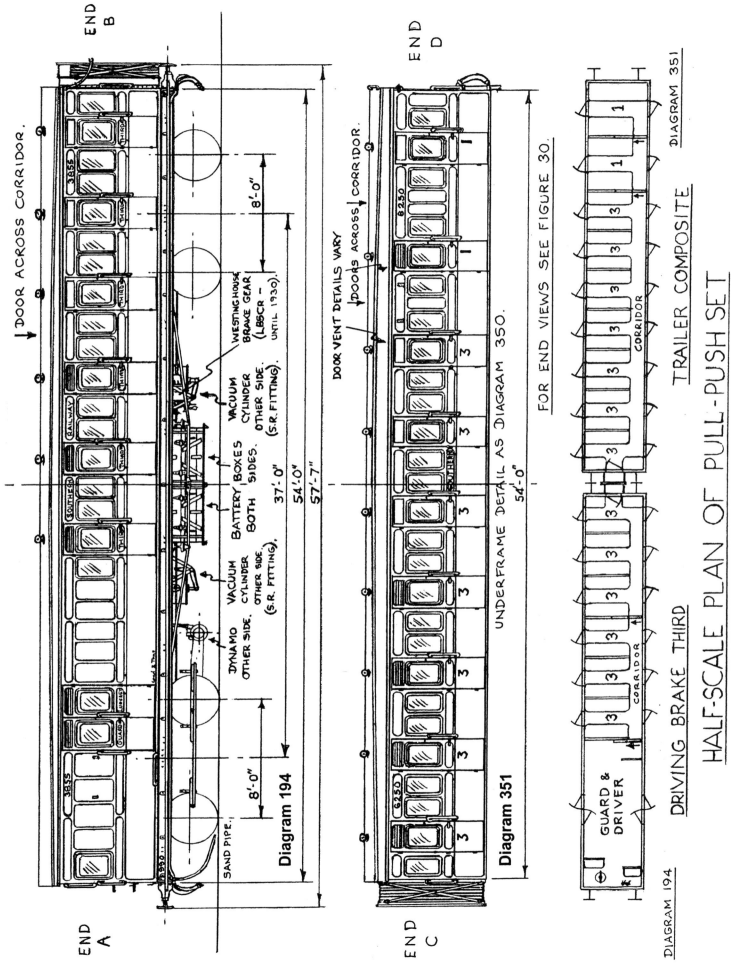

Figure 35 The 1922 pull-push sets; SR diagrams 194 and 351.

Plate 130 Diagram 351 composite No 6249 of set 722, seen at Bexhill West in July 1955. This is one of the ten trailers completed during 1922 and by the date of the photograph was steel-panelled on each side. Note the electrical connection between the two vehicles – only the brake coach carried the dynamo and battery boxes. *R. M. Casserley*

These allocations varied somewhat during the following years and at least two of the former ambulance underframes required replacement between 1931 and 1936. In both cases further second-hand underframes were substituted and this was a not uncommon situation at Lancing for former Brighton vehicles, yet was a much less common occurrence on former LSWR and SECR vehicles. In 1937, the sets were renumbered as 718-23 and soon after set 723 found itself exiled to the Seaton branch, where it remained until 1949 — almost the only example of a Brighton set travelling to the far west. The others remained evenly distributed between the Central and Eastern sections.

Set 718 was working the Horsham–Guildford service on 16 December 1942 when the train caught the attention of a German fighter aircraft near Bramley & Wonersh station. The train was badly shot up and the corridor side of the set severely damaged (see **Plates 128** and **129**). Seven passengers were killed and there might have been more fatalities had the compartment side taken the brunt of the attack. The set was not considered worthy of repair and was condemned soon after, the first complete LBSCR

arc-roofed pull-push set to be taken out of traffic. Others received war damage, but none severe enough to be withdrawn from service.

Withdrawal of the remainder commenced with set 720 in April 1948 (both coaches ran on second-hand underframes) but the other four lasted until 1957-60. Once LSWR 'Ironclad' set 381 relieved set 723 at Seaton in 1949 this returned to more familiar territory, all four sets being shared between the Central and Eastern sections. At least three (Nos 721-3) were then running with all-timber mouldings covered by steel sheeting and most sported BR crimson lake livery, either lined or unlined. Set 721 in unlined crimson provided the accommodation for a Railway Enthusiasts Club rail tour commencing and finishing at Farnborough station on 5 October 1957. Named the 'Compass Rose', this took in such unlikely locations as Tongham, Godalming Goods and Ascot, but was by no means the only occasion when a Brighton pull-push set was chosen for a rail tour. No doubt the access provided by the corridors added to the conviviality of the occasion. (See page 160.)

Plate 131 The Hythe branch train at Sandling Junction, circa 1935. 'D1' class No 2220 heads set 649, formed of LSWR third No 500 and LBSCR driving brake composite No 6939. *The Lens of Sutton Association*

1931 ac stock conversions (sets 649-51)

The final three sets to include LBSCR arc-roofed coaches were these, converted in 1931, partly under order L670. Like the nine third class trailers used in sets 751-9, three others that had never seen electrified services were converted into driving brake composites for sets 649-51 in March 1931. The space formerly taken up by the driver's position and the adjacent first class compartment was converted into an enlarged driver's/guard's compartment, leaving three firsts and all four third class compartments unaltered. Also unchanged were the two large end windows, giving these three sets a very characteristic appearance.

Sets 649/50 were each formed with an LSWR 48ft third as trailer — making these the earliest hybrid pull-push sets on the Southern — these coaches coming from the small pool of strengthening vehicles already being equipped with air-control gear. Set 651, however, did receive a 48ft LBSCR third (No 1960) as its trailer — one of eight such coaches reframed on standard Southern underframes in 1929-31. Set 649 lasted only

until August 1937, but managed to get through two different LSWR thirds in that short period, while set 650 acquired another reframed LBSCR third (No 2087) in June 1934. Having been reframed, these 48ft coaches survived the cull of shorter LBSCR stock and continued to run until the 1950s.

When first completed these sets were sent to the South Eastern section as reliefs, being used mostly on the Westerham and Allhallows branches. Set 649 was the regular Hythe set during 1934/5 but both 650/1 had moved to Bexhill West by 1939. Until about 1956 they remained on the Eastern section at locations such as Ashford for New Romney and Hastings duties, but ended their days on Central section workings in 1958/59. After withdrawal driving brake composite No 6941 was employed on driver training for the Kent Coast electrification, along with coach No 3820 from set 504. Often, these would run either side of an 'H' class tank or with the LSWR director's saloon No DS1.

Table 6 gives full details of all the many LBSCR arc-roofed coaches equipped with pull-push control gear.

Plate 132 Sets 650/1 eventually received LBSCR 48ft eight-compartment thirds as trailer vehicles, both on new SR underframes. Coach No 1960 of set 651 is seen at Lancing in 1949, wearing malachite green livery. *R. C. Riley*

Plate 133 Set 650 on a rail tour at Kemp Town on 23 June 1956, in BR unlined crimson lake livery. The distinctive, ex-ac electric stock driving end is characteristic.
R. M. Casserley

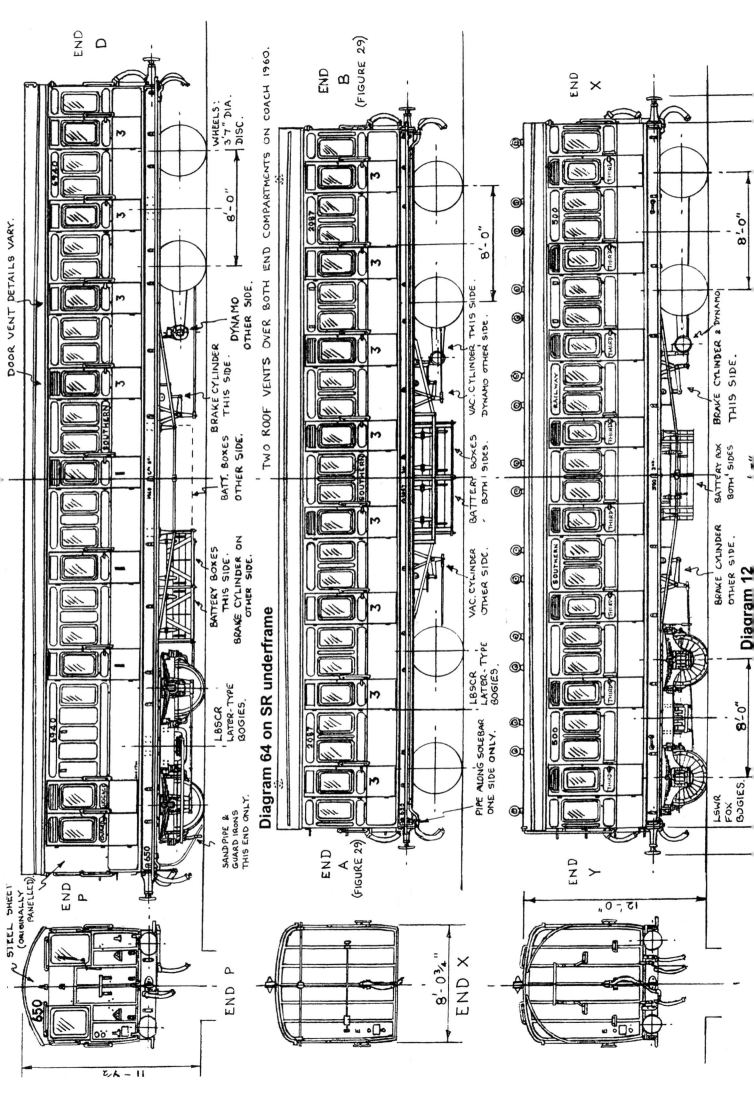

END D

DOOR VENT DETAILS VARY.

WHEELS: 3'7" DIA. DISC.

8'-0"

TWO ROOF VENTS OVER BOTH END COMPARTMENTS ON COACH 1960.

BRAKE CYLINDER THIS SIDE. DYNAMO OTHER SIDE.

BATT. BOXES OTHER SIDE.

BATTERY BOXES THIS SIDE. BRAKE CYLINDER ON OTHER SIDE.

LBSCR LATER-TYPE BOGIES.

SANDPIPE & GUARD IRONS THIS END ONLY.

STEEL SHEET (ORIGINALLY PANELLED)

END P

650

11 - 4½"

Diagram 64 on SR underframe

END B (FIGURE 29)

8'-0"

2087

END A (FIGURE 29)

VAC. CYLINDER THIS SIDE. DYNAMO OTHER SIDE.

BATTERY BOXES BOTH SIDES.

VAC. CYLINDER OTHER SIDE.

LBSCR LATER-TYPE BOGIES.

PIPE ALONG SOLEBAR ONE SIDE ONLY.

END X

8'-0¾"

END X

END X

8'-0"

500

RAILWAY

THIRD

SOUTHERN

THIRD

500

THIRD

BRAKE CYLINDER & DYNAMO THIS SIDE.

BATTERY BOX BOTH SIDES.

BRAKE CYLINDER OTHER SIDE.

LSWR FOX BOGIES.

8'-0"

END Y

12'-0"

Diagram 12

Table 6
Ex-LBSCR Arc-Roofed Sets

SR Set No.	Running Dates	SR Coach Numbers BT or BC	C or T	Allocation 1931	1935	1945	Remarks
649	3/31-9/32	6939	498	SE Relief			Third is LSWR, to diagram 12
	9/32-8/37	6939	500		Hythe		Third is LSWR, to diagram 12, ex-loose stock
650	3/31-10/34	6940	499	SE Relief			Third is LSWR, to diagram 12
	10/34-9/59	6940	2087		Westerham	SE Section	Third is reframed LBSCR 48ft vehicle
651	3/31-10/58	6941	1960	SE Relief	SE Relief	SE Section	Third is reframed LBSCR 48ft vehicle
751	5/24-10/25	6927	2272				54ft trailer third, to electric stock, 1925
	10/25-10/31	6927	2061	Eastbourne			48ft trailer third
	12/31-12/39	6927	2194		Gillingham		Ex-AC trailer third, with luggage compartment
752	5/24-10/25	6928	2273				54ft trailer third, to electric stock, 1925
	10/25-10/31	6928	2039	Horsham			48ft trailer third
	1/32-12/39	6928	2192		Horsham		Ex-AC trailer third, with luggage compartment
753	5/24-9/25	6929	2274				54ft trailer third, to electric stock, 1925
	9/25-6/32	6929	2002	Cranleigh			48ft trailer third
	4/32-3/59	6929	2191		Cranleigh	C Section	Ex-AC trailer third, with luggage compartment
754	5/24-10/25	6930	2275				54ft trailer third, to electric stock, 1925
	10/25-12/31	6930	2038	Tunbridge Wells W			48ft trailer third
	12/31-1/38	6930	2189		Ashford		Ex-AC trailer third, with luggage compartment
755	5/24-10/25	6931	2276				54ft trailer third, to electric stock, 1925
	10/25-3/32	6931	2007	Tunbridge Wells W			48ft trailer third
	4/32-11/58	6931	2188		SE Relief	Ashford	Ex-AC trailer third, with luggage compartment
756	5/24-11/25	6932	2277				54ft trailer third, to electric stock, 1925
	11/25-4/32	6932	1995	C Relief			48ft trailer third
	4/32-7/44	6932	2186		Paddock Wood		Ex-AC trailer third, with luggage compartment
757	5/24-11/25	6933	2278				54ft trailer third, to electric stock, 1925
	12/25-5/32	6933	1967	C Relief			48ft trailer third
	5/32-7/59	6933	2190		Gillingham	C Section	Ex-AC trailer third, with luggage compartment
758	5/24-12/25	6934	2279				54ft trailer third, to electric stock, 1926
	1/26-2/32	6934	1963	Westerham			48ft trailer third
	5/32-8/58	6934	2187		Gillingham	C Section	Ex-AC trailer third, with luggage compartment
759	5/24-11/25	6935	2280				54ft trailer third, to electric stock, 1926
	12/25-11/31	6935	2110	Littlehampton			48ft trailer third
	11/31-7/54	6935	2193		Gillingham	C Section	Ex-AC trailer third. Coach 2193 later to set 37
760	6/24-12/25	6936	2281				54ft trailer third, to electric stock, 1926
	12/25-4/31	6936	2048				48ft trailer third. Coach 6936 then to loose stock until withdrawn in 3/36
981/714	12/21-12/44	3846	6237	Brighton	SE Relief		Set renumbered in 1937. Coach 3846 to loose stock, based at Midhurst 1/45-5/48.
714	1/45-7/61	3467	6237			SE Section	Replacement brake third is ex-SECR
982/715	12/21-2/38	3847	6238	Seaford	Eastbourne		Set renumbered in 1937. Coach 3847 to loose stock at Midhurst 3/52-1955, then unallocated.
715	2/38-2/52	3847	5298			SE Section	Replacement composite is ex-SECR. Complete set formed of SECR stock after 2/52.
983/716	12/21-9/60	3848	6239	Seaford	Eastbourne	SE Section	Set renumbered in 1937
984/717	12/21-7/59	3849	6240	Tun Wells W	Tun Wells W	SE Section	Set renumbered in 1937
985/718	6/22-12/42	3850	6241	Bognor	Horsham		Set renumbered in 1937
986/719	6/22-11/57	3851	6242	Brighton	Hastings	C Section	Set renumbered in 1937
987/720	6/22-4/48	3852	6243	Horsham	Tun Wells W	C Section	Set renumbered in 1937
988/721	12/22-5/58	3853	6248	Littlehampton	Littlehampton	C Section	Set renumbered in 1937
989/722	12/22-1/59	3854	6249	Brighton	H Heath	SE Section	Set renumbered in 1937
990/723	12/22-9/60	3855	6250	Eastbourne	Hastings	Seaton	Set renumbered in 1937
991/724	12/22-4/53	3823	6247	Chichester	Chichester	SE Section	Set renumbered in 1937. Coach 3823 to loose stock at Midhurst, 6/53-1955, then unallocated.
992/725	12/22-12/56	3822	6244	Hastings	Seaford	SE Section	Set renumbered in 1937
993/726	12/22-6/57	3821	6245	Horsham	SE Relief	SE Section	Set renumbered in 1937. Coach 3821 to loose stock (unallocated) after 9/57.
994/727	12/22-1/59	3824	6246	Eastbourne	Littlehampton	C Section	Set renumbered in 1937
995/728	12/11-5/47	3825	6201	Brighton	Brighton	C Section	Set renumbered in 1937, to IOW 5/47
505	5/47-5/54	4167	6366	Isle of Wight (Newport)			Transferred to IOW in 5/47, ex-set 728.
996/729	12/11-6/60	3826	6202	Eastbourne	Brighton	C Section	Set renumbered in 1937
997/730	12/11-9/59	3827	6203	Brighton	Littlehampton	C Section	Set renumbered in 1937
998/731	12/11-4/38	3828	6204	Brighton	Brighton		Set renumbered in 1937, to IOW 5/38
503	5/38-5/54	4169	6367	Isle of Wight (Newport)			Transferred to IOW in 5/38, ex-set 731.
503	5/38-5/54	6987 only		Isle of Wight (Newport)			Coach ex-6237, to IOW in 5/38. IOW records show this coach as part of set 503.
999/980/504	12/14-9/58	3820	6236	Portsmouth	Portsmouth	SE Section	Set renumbered as 980 and then 504 in 1937

No set numbers allocated before 1923. For LBSCR coach numbers see summary on next page.
Many coaches ran in LBSCR livery and numbering until circa 1925-7, but with SR set numbering.

Figure 36 Diagram 437 is 54ft long over the body, the others 48ft.
The 1931 rebuilt ac stock sets; SR diagrams 64 and 437, plus LSWR diagram 12.

Table 6.2

Carriage Summary

SR Diagram	SR Nos	Relevant LBSCR Nos	Date of Pull-Push conversion	Dimensions L x W	Seats 1	Seats 3	Remarks
12	498-500		3-9/31	48ft x 8ft		80	Ex-LSWR vehicles, in sets 649/50. Coach 500 was a replacement
64	1963/7/95,2002/7, 2038/9/48/61,2110		9/25-1/26	48ft x 8ft		80	Replacements for 54ft trailer thirds in sets 751-60
64	1960, 2087		3/31 & 6/34	48ft x 8ft		80	On new SR underframes, for sets 650/1
71	2272-81	1382-91	5-6/24	54ft x 8ft		90	All to electric stock, 12/25-2/26
79	2186-92		10/31-5/32	54ft x 8ft		80	Ex-AC stock, with luggage compartment
80	2193-4		10-12/1931	54ft x 8ft		80	Ex-AC stock, with luggage compartment
166	3467		6/41	60ft 1in x 8ft		80	Ex-SECR, replacement for set 714. Ran as loose coach at Midhurst until 1/45
188	3820	1325	When built 12/14	54ft x 8ft		64*	To DS3820 10/58, for Kent Coast crew training
188	3821-4	1347-50	When built 12/12	54ft x 8ft		64*	Coach 3823 to diagram 188A in 1953
189	3825-8	1343-6	When built 12/11	54ft x 8ft		56*	Nos 3825/8 to diagram 231 in 5/47 & 5/38, for IoW
231	4167/9		5/38 & 5/47	54ft x 8ft		56*	For IoW, ex-diagram 189
193	3846-9	1401-4	When built 12/21	54ft x 8ft		64*	Coach 3847 later to diagram 193A
194	3850-5	1405-10	When built 6-12/22	54ft x 8ft		48*	No 3850 reframed in 12/36
301	5298		2/38	50ft 1in x 8ft	24	30	Ex-SECR, replacement for set 715
346	6201-4	640-3	When built 12/11	54ft x 8ft	19*	48*	Nos 6201/4 to 6366/7 in 5/47 & 5/38, for IoW
349	6236	644	When built 12/14	54ft x 8ft	19*	48*	
350	6237-40	645-8	When built 12/21	54ft x 8ft	25*	40*	No 6237 to diagram 350A after 1952 with 41 first seats. No 6238 rebuilt to diagram 439 in 4/38
351	6241-50	649-58	When built 6-12/22	54ft x 8ft	13*	56*	Nos 6241/3 reframed in 1936/31 respectively
434	6927-30	630-3	Rebuilt 12/09	54ft x 8ft	24	40	Compartment layout G1113333
435	6931-6	634-9	Rebuilt 12/09 & 6/11	54ft x 8ft	16	50	Compartment layout G1133333
437	6939-41		Rebuilt 3/31	54ft x 8ft	24	40	Ex-AC stock, for sets 649-51. No 6941 to DS6941, 10/58 for Kent Coast crew training
439	6987		Rebuilt 4/38	54ft x 8ft	12*	40*	Ex-diagram 350 composite 6238, for IoW. Gangway connection removed 4/49

* Corridor provided, with gangway at one end of coach. If gangway removed, diagram number received A suffix.
All coaches were to SR route restriction 0.

Plate 134 One of the SECR steam railmotors approaches Dover in September 1910, with a service from Sandgate and Sandling Junction. A five-compartment SER coach is trailing, possibly No 2240 listed in Table 7. *Author's collection*

Chapter 10.

SER and LCDR Stock

We return again to the first decade of the 20th century, to when the South Eastern & Chatham Railway began to develop both steam railmotor and pull-push operated services. The latter were always rather more limited in scope than on the other two Southern constituents, with a maximum of just ten (and perhaps only nine) identifiable pull-push sets in service prior to the Grouping. All except two were formed of six-wheeled stock and, not surprisingly, the six-wheelers were the first pull-push sets to be withdrawn by the Southern Railway, between 1925 and 1930. Consequently less has been recorded about them and there are a number of unanswered questions regarding their method of operation and the routes over which they were initially used.

The eight SECR railmotors were at first sufficiently successful in generating traffic to require the provision of some ex-SER six-wheeled trailer coaches and nine such vehicles are detailed in SECR carriage registers — the first six being specifically recorded as 'auto-fitted railmotor trailers'. Details are as follows:

often lost time by having to run round their trailer at the end of each journey, leads to conjecture about the amount of adaptation and/or control that was possible from the leading end. In later years (and certainly from 1912 onwards) vehicles equipped for pull-push operation had the entry 'through driving rod' made in the carriage registers; however, this is not shown against any of the coaches listed in Table 7, with the exception of coach No 2080. So, the true facts are not entirely clear.

That some of these vehicles did run in a form of pull-push mode is certain. The first SECR auto-fitted locomotives ('P' class tanks Nos 753 and 754) commenced work in February 1909 on Sevenoaks–Otford and Reading–Ash–Aldershot services — presumably utilising some of the vehicles listed below, while the former LBSCR 'Terrier' No 751 was similarly fitted in January 1910 and was put to work with coach 2101 between Beckenham Junction and Norwood Junction. By the end of that year six of the eight 'P' class tanks were at work on

Table 7
Ex-SER pull-push fitted vehicles

SECR No	Vehicle type	Date fitted	Remarks	SR No
783	33ft four-compartment brake composite	1907	For Lydd branch. Not P-P fitted after 1917	7764 (as brake 1st)
2041	33ft four-compartment brake 3rd	1906	Later with handbrake only, in set 275/654	1465 (as full 3rd)
2070	33ft four-compartment brake 3rd	1906	Not P-P fitted after 1917.	Wdn 7/26
2080	33ft four-compartment brake 3rd	1906	Later in P-P set 274/653	3600
2101	33ft four-compartment brake 3rd	1906	Not P-P fitted after 1917	3601
2111	33ft four-compartment brake 3rd	1906	Not P-P fitted after 1917	3602
2127	31ft four-compartment brake 3rd	1909*	Not P-P fitted after 1917	3603
2240	33ft five-compartment 2nd (altered to four-compartment brake 2nd in May 1918)	1909*	Not P-P fitted after 1917 Later in set 275/654	3627 (as brake 3rd)
2246	29ft four-compartment composite	1909*	Later in set 275/654	5774

*These three may have been converted to work with the 'P' class 0-6-0 tanks.

Coaches Nos 2041/70/80, 2101/11 were nominally the same and some are annotated in the registers as having 'a double compartment altered to luggage compartment and fitted with one or two drop seats to seat five or ten persons and fitted with a handbrake at exterior of luggage end. SECR diagram 3145 — either 45 or 50 seats. Two fixed and two sliding lights in end.' Coach No 783 was described similarly, but with only a single compartment rebuilt for driver/luggage.

Only vehicles Nos 2041/80, 2240/6 seem to have subsequently been formed into permanent pull-push sets and, of these, only coach Nos 2080/3600 remained so equipped by 1923, being the sole example of ex-SER stock in what, by that time, had become a group of sets consisting entirely of former LCDR vehicles. All the rest, although entering Southern Railway stock, had not been used in pull-push mode since at least 1917 and in several instances rather earlier than that.

Of those converted as railmotor trailers, some were at least equipped with a form of driving control, yet photographs of them being propelled by the railmotors are conspicuous by their absence. This, plus contemporary reports that the railmotors

motor-fitted services, including a second duty between Ash and Aldershot, the Sheppey Light Railway and the Chatham Central branch, although no other pull-push fitted coaches are recorded prior to 1912. From photographic evidence, it can be stated that by the time steam railmotors Nos 1, 5 and 6 were in store at Crystal Palace after 1915, at least three of the trailer cars were in store with them. Of the rest, we shall meet four of them again in SECR sets 274/5.

From 1912 onwards, records become more definite. In May of that year ex-LCDR bogie coaches were equipped with pull-push controls, end windows and 'through driving rods' beneath the carriage floors and, as two pairs, were coupled one either side of 'P' class locomotives 325 and 555 for the Nunhead–Greenwich Park service (see **Plates 135** and **136**). These were described in *The Locomotive* magazine for 15 July 1912, where it was stated that each driving compartment was fitted with a regulator, brake valve, hand brake and communication cord connection to the whistle. Each pairing consisted of a seven-compartment brake third and a six-compartment brake composite, the latter providing first and

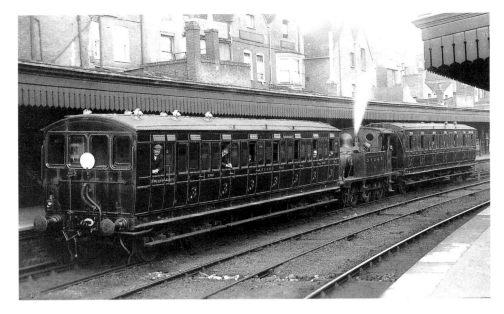

Plate 135 Greenwich Park station in June 1912, with 'P' class tank No 325 sandwiched between LCDR brake third No 3396 and brake composite No 2713, both coaches resplendent in SECR crimson lake livery. The two vehicles later became SECR set 271/SR set 732. Another view of this train appears in Plate 10. *F. Moore*

Plate 136 A further view at Greenwich Park in June 1912. Close examination shows at least two through cables – presumably the whistle cord and bell connection. Other control rodding passed beneath the carriage floors. *F. Moore*

second class accommodation. Both types had been converted from existing stock, one former passenger compartment in each coach being given over to the driver and guard's accommodation. In this respect they were unusual as, in theory at least, the locomotive could be coupled in the centre or at either end of the set and still operate in pull-push mode.

By 1915 the two pairs had become SECR sets 271/2 and remained on the Greenwich Park service, along with a few trips into Victoria until the branch closed as a wartime economy measure on 1 January 1917. They were then transferred to Ramsgate Town for the Margate Sands-Minster service until late 1919, when they migrated to the opposite end of the SECR system for the Ash–Aldershot shuttle, together with longer trips to and from Reading. Ex-LCDR 'R' or 'R1' class 0-4-4 tanks allocated to Reading shed now provided the motive power, as it had been found that the 'P' class could not cope with all four coaches if running together.

The pairs were allocated SR set numbers 732/3 after the Grouping and remained at Aldershot until withdrawn in 1936. SR air-control equipment was provided after October 1930 (possibly some of the last coaches to receive this under order L547), after which the usual motive power was outstationed from Guildford in the form of LSWR 'M7' tanks. By this time their duties would have taken them to Guildford and Farnham as well as to Reading. They were the last surviving ex-LCDR bogie coaches outside the Isle of Wight, being replaced during January/February 1936 by ex-LSWR bogie 'block' sets.

Between 1912 and 1914, seven three-coach sets of (mostly) ex-LCDR six-wheeled vehicles were formed for a variety of pull-push duties. These included Brixton–Moorgate Street, Victoria–St Paul's, Swanley Junction–Gravesend West Street, Sevenoaks–Otford, Ramsgate–Birchington and Aldershot–Ash–Reading services. They were allocated SECR set numbers 266-70/3/4 and were by no means all identical. In addition, SECR set 275 was formed in 1912 using three of the former SER vehicles listed in Table 7, for Dover Priory–Canterbury East local services. This last set was recorded as being pull-push fitted only between 1914 and 1917 and was certainly not being used as such by January 1918, as the carriage working notice of this date shows the set running in normal mode with the addition of two or three loose vehicles — a situation unchanged after 1923.

The Brixton–Moorgate Street service was provided by two sets, one either side of an 0-4-4 tank; the other duties were entrusted to the 'P' class 0-6-0 tanks. However, this service was short-lived and soon the stock and the 'R'/'R-1' tanks were running elsewhere, including between Snow Hill and Crystal Palace or Gravesend Central–Port Victoria. A set may have been trialled around this time on the Westerham and Hawkhurst branches and, briefly in late 1915/early 1916, on the Bexhill West line. Both Westerham and Hawkhurst had similarly formed sets allocated but not equipped for pull-push working. Indeed, set 279/655, the regular at Westerham was recorded as pull-push fitted in some SECR documents, but the carriage registers do not confirm this fact.

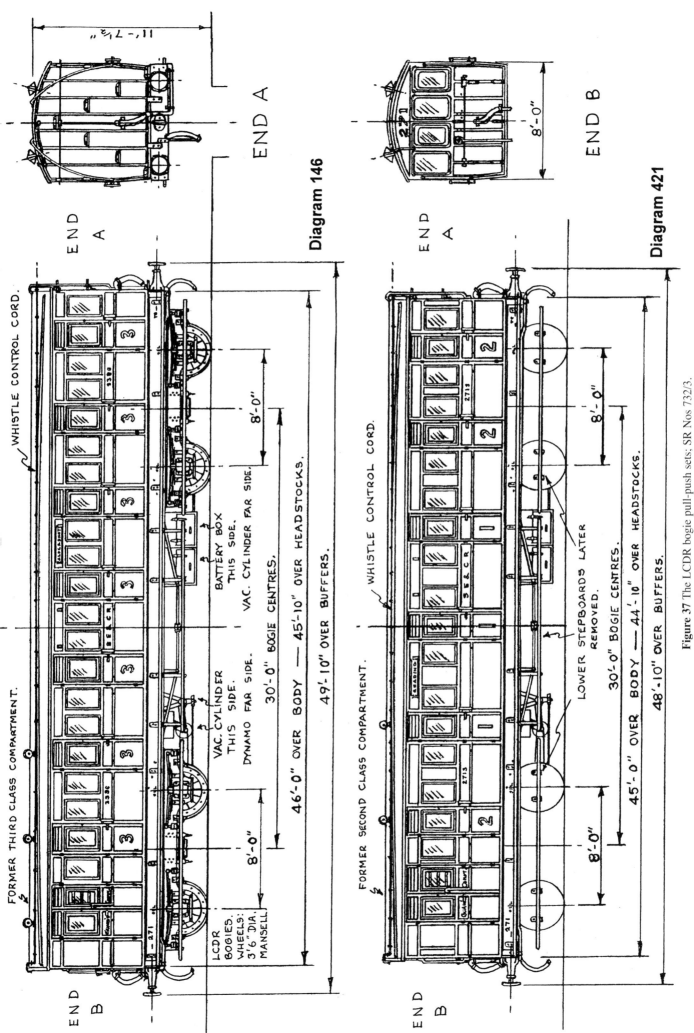

END A

Diagram 146

END B

Diagram 421

WHISTLE CONTROL CORD.

END A

FORMER THIRD CLASS COMPARTMENT.

END B

11'-7½"

8'-0"

8'-0"

8'-0"

VAC. CYLINDER THIS SIDE.
DYNAMO FAR SIDE.

BATTERY BOX THIS SIDE.
VAC. CYLINDER FAR SIDE.

30'-0" BOGIE CENTRES.

46'-0" OVER BODY — 45'-10" OVER HEADSTOCKS.

49'-10" OVER BUFFERS.

LCDR BOGIES.
WHEELS: 3'6" DIA. MANSELL.

WHISTLE CONTROL CORD.

END A

FORMER SECOND CLASS COMPARTMENT.

END B

8'-0"

8'-0"

8'-0"

LOWER STEPBOARDS LATER REMOVED.

30'-0" BOGIE CENTRES.

45'-0" OVER BODY — 44'-10" OVER HEADSTOCKS.

48'-10" OVER BUFFERS.

Figure 37 The LCDR bogie pull-push sets; SR Nos 732/3.

Plate 137 This rather interesting photograph shows LCDR set 732 being propelled by an 'M7', with four GWR coaches in tow behind, some time in the early 1930s. It is believed the location is between Guildford and Reading, but no other details of the working are known. Note that one of the driving end windows in coach No 3270 has been plated over. *HMRS collection*

Plate 138 'P' class 0-6-0T No 178 is seen at Sevenoaks Tubs Hill station, between duties on the Otford shuttle service in 1922. The stock is either SECR set 267 or 268 (SR 649 or 650), in post-war 'Wellington brown' livery. *H. P. Rutherford*

Plate 139 A similar duty on 3 April 1926; 'P' class No 323 stands in Tubs Hill station with either set 267 or 268. Both locomotive and stock remain in pre-Grouping liveries. Close examination of the carriage panelling reveals subtle differences in the mouldings. *H. C. Casserley*

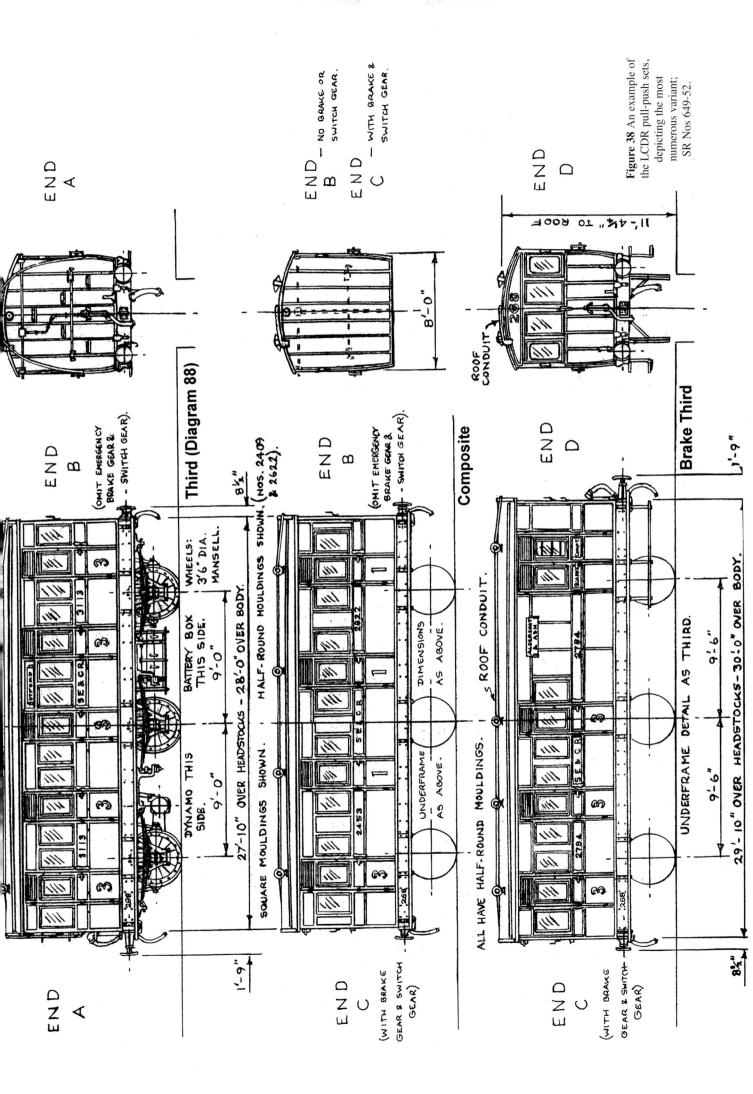

END A

END B

(OMIT EMERGENCY BRAKE GEAR & SWITCH GEAR).

Third (Diagram 88)

END B

(OMIT EMERGENCY BRAKE GEAR & SWITCH GEAR).

Composite

END D

END C

(WITH BRAKE GEAR & SWITCH GEAR)

END A

END B – NO BRAKE OR SWITCH GEAR.

END C – WITH BRAKE & SWITCH GEAR.

END D

11'-4½" TO ROOF

8'-0"

ROOF CONDUIT.

8½"

1'-9"

WHEELS: 3'6" DIA. MANSELL.

BATTERY BOX THIS SIDE.

9'-0"

DYNAMO THIS SIDE.

9'-0"

27'-10" OVER HEADSTOCKS – 28'-0" OVER BODY.

SQUARE MOULDINGS SHOWN. HALF-ROUND MOULDINGS SHOWN. (NOS. 2409 & 2622).

3 3113 S E & C R 3 3 3119 3

DIMENSIONS AS ABOVE.

UNDERFRAME AS ABOVE.

ROOF CONDUIT.

ALL HAVE HALF-ROUND MOULDINGS.

1 2622 S E C R 1 1 2453 3

END C

(WITH BRAKE GEAR & SWITCH GEAR)

Brake Third

END D

END C

(WITH BRAKE GEAR & SWITCH GEAR)

9'-6"

9'-6"

UNDERFRAME DETAIL AS THIRD.

29'-10" OVER HEADSTOCKS – 30'-0" OVER BODY.

8½"

1'-9"

S E & C R 2784 3 2784 3

Figure 38 An example of the LCDR pull-push sets, depicting the most numerous variant; SR Nos 649-52.

The most uniform of these sets were Nos 267-70, each comprising a 30ft brake second, a 28ft composite and a 28ft third — all being formed in June 1914. In 1923 the brake vehicles were reclassified as third class and all were allocated SR set numbers 649-52, although set 652 was scrapped in November 1925 without having SR carriage numbers allocated. Set 266 was similarly formed in December 1914 but had a four-compartment brake coach instead of a three-compartment vehicle as in the other sets. However, this set was stripped of pull-push gear in 1921 and was reduced to just two coaches in June 1923, as seen in **Plate 140.** It was then allocated SR set number 731, although the coaches were never actually renumbered prior to scrapping in 1926. The withdrawn vehicle developed a hot box on the journey from Swanley Junction to Ashford Works and on arrival, the axlebox and journal were so badly damaged that withdrawal was ordered. Ashford could not locate replacements quickly, so the coach (SECR No 3150) was dismantled to provide spares for other LCDR vehicles of similar vintage.

Sets 273/4 differed from the others by also having a four-compartment brake coach — that in set 274 alone being of SER origin, but this set (later SR no 653) also included a brake composite at the 'locomotive' end, making it unique on two counts. Set 273 was usually allocated to the Gravesend West Street branch and was also unique in formation, often including a fourth vehicle in the shape of an ex-LCDR saloon third, and this may explain why its allocated SR set number — 677 — was so far removed from the others. However, this coach was withdrawn at the end of 1925, so most SR set numbering lists show only three coaches in the formation.

The five remaining sets (SR Nos 649-51/3/77) were somewhat refurbished, renumbered and repainted in SR livery between December 1926 and April 1927 and were given a final lease of life on Sevenoaks-Otford, Dartford–Gillingham/Port Victoria and the Gravesend West Street branch services until late 1929, but were never included in the programme of air-control conversion, retaining their through mechanical rodding and working with 'R/R-1' class tanks to the end. By this time they were not particularly salubrious or for travel by the faint-hearted as R. W. Kidner wrote of them: 'the thirds had only half-height bulkheads; spittoons comprising hunks of cloth screwed to the floor in each corner of the compartments suggests that the stock had done a stint on the workmen's trains.' This unsavoury reminder of an earlier era must have done little to endear the sets to the general public — even in the late 1920s! No doubt all were pleased to see their passing and welcomed the LBSCR arc-roofed and LSWR bogie 'block' sets that arrived to replace them.

Perhaps remarkably, two more pull-push sets of ex-LCDR origin were formed after the Grouping and, even more remarkable, were the last to survive, in one case into modern-day preservation. Three six-wheeled saloon third class coaches and a converted saloon brake third were formed together as SECR set 40 for the Sheppey Light Railway around 1915. For the guard to issue tickets *en route*, through gangways had been provided. In April 1924 the set was taken into Ashford Works for repainting and renumbering as SR set 663 and the intention may have been for it to return to the Sheppey line, although ex-railmotor articulated sets 513/4 were then available as replacements. It may have done so briefly, but in August 1924 it was sent to Lancing for conversion to four wheels and into two two-coach pull-push sets for the Isle of Wight.

Two of the saloons became composite coaches, by having a first class compartment formed at the 'locomotive' end — the gangway connection at this end being removed in the process. The gangways between each vehicle in the set were retained to facilitate ticket issue. The other saloon was rebuilt into a saloon brake third, while the original saloon brake was rather more

Plate 141 The Otford–Sevenoaks pull-push service again, this time with 'R' class No 669 and set 649, now all in SR livery, at Sevenoaks in 1929. *P. Ransome-Wallis*

Plate 142 The LCDR four-wheeled pull-push sets on the Isle of Wight. Set 484 is seen at Ventnor West on 28 August 1936. Even the driving end has received lining out! *H. F. Wheeller*

Plate 143 Both sets sandwich 'Terrier' No 13 *Carisbrooke* at Ventnor West, on the same day. *H. F. Wheeller*

Plate 144 Interior view of coach No 4111 of set 483, on the same occasion. Although the interiors of both brake thirds were similar, the overall lengths and window layouts were different. The photographer's wife enjoys the summer sunshine. *H. F. Wheeller*

simply modified by the removal of side lookouts. Westinghouse brake gear was refitted, as this was to remain standard on the Isle of Wight. Each set seated six first and 49 third class passengers and, formed as sets 483/4, both were shipped to the Island on 31 August 1924.

At this time there were no suitably equipped locomotives to operate with them so they were used as ordinary stock, mostly on the Freshwater line until three Island 'Terriers' were fitted with the necessary pull-push equipment in February 1926. The sets then commenced work on the Ventnor West line and, despite their somewhat antiquated appearance, proved most successful and subsequently many more LCDR vehicles were transferred to the Island, although no more were equipped for pull-push working. In off-peak times one set sufficed, but in summer both were used either side of the locomotive. In 1929 the end gangways were reinstated (offset to one side to suit the seating arrangements), as there may have been a plan to run both as four-coach sets, and it may have been the intention to convert four more vehicles to run with them, but this came to nothing. In 1936 set 484 spent a few weeks on the Bembridge branch while the turntable at the terminus was rebuilt, but otherwise the sets remained on the Merstone–Ventnor West service until replaced by ex-LBSCR arc-roofed set 503, described in Chapter 9, which arrived on the Island in May 1938.

That might have been the end of the story but for the fact that all four carriage bodies were sold off and grounded at various locations on the Island. Those of set 484 survived long enough to be acquired by the Isle of Wight Steam Railway and, after much

restoration and mounting on shortened 'utility' van underframes, are now running again between Wootton and Smallbrook Junction — a unique preservation achievement. Table 8 records the various SER/LCDR pull-push sets running post-1912, including the two that were stripped of the gear prior to the Grouping.

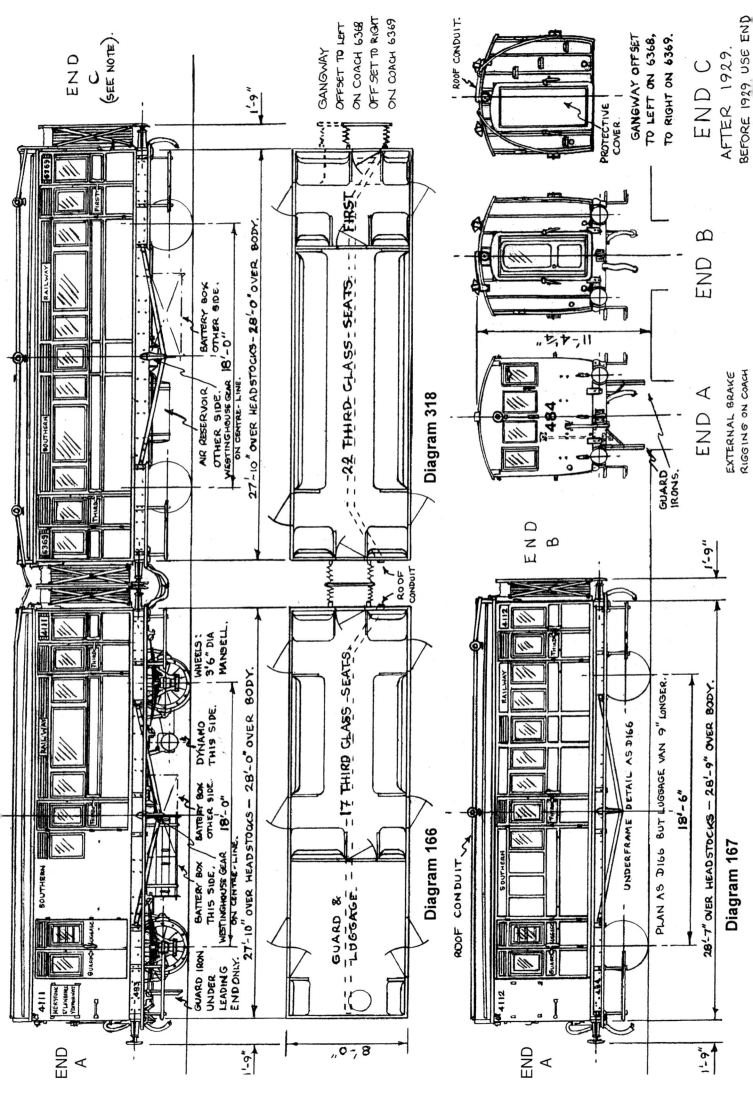

END C
(SEE NOTE).

1'-9"

GANGWAY OFFSET TO LEFT ON COACH 6368 OFFSET TO RIGHT ON COACH 6369

AIR RESERVOIR OTHER SIDE.
BATTERY BOX OTHER SIDE.
WESTINGHOUSE GEAR 18'-0" ON CENTRE-LINE.
27'-10" OVER HEADSTOCKS - 28'-0" OVER BODY.

FIRST

- 22 THIRD CLASS SEATS -

Diagram 318

ROOF CONDUIT.

PROTECTIVE COVER.

GANGWAY OFFSET TO LEFT ON 6368, TO RIGHT ON 6369.

END C
AFTER 1929.
BEFORE 1929 USE END

11'-4¼"

END B

484

END A

EXTERNAL BRAKE RIGGING ON COACH

GUARD IRONS.

END B

END A

GUARD IRON UNDER LEADING END ONLY.
BATTERY BOX, THIS SIDE,
DYNAMO THIS SIDE.
WESTINGHOUSE GEAR 18'-0" ON CENTRE-LINE.
WHEELS : 3'6" DIA MANSELL.
27'-10" OVER HEADSTOCKS - 28'-0" OVER BODY.

ROOF CONDUIT.

GUARD & LUGGAGE.

- 17 THIRD CLASS SEATS -

8'-0"

Diagram 166

ROOF CONDUIT.

1'-9"

END A

1'-9"

UNDERFRAME DETAIL AS D166
PLAN AS D166 BUT LUGGAGE VAN 9" LONGER.
18'-6"
28'-7" OVER HEADSTOCKS - 28'-9" OVER BODY.

Diagram 167

Table 8

Ex-SER/LCDR Sets

SR Set No.*	Running Dates	SR Coach Nos*	Allocation 1914	1918	1926	Remarks
483	8/24-6/38	4111, 6368	Isle of Wight	Merstone-Ventnor West		4-w saloons, ex-SECR Sheppey set 40
484	8/24-6/38	4112, 6369	Isle of Wight	Merstone-Ventnor West		4-w saloons, ex-SECR Sheppey set 40
649(267)	6/14-11/29	3605 (2749), 5769(2450), 1472(3119)	Ash	Ash	Otford	At Otford-Sevenoaks in 1929
650(268)	6/14-11/29	3606 (2784), 5770(2453), 1471(3113)	Brixton	P. Victoria	P. Victoria	At Dartford-Gillingham in 1929
651(269)	6/14-11/29	3604 (2748), 5771(2622), 1473(3178)	Brixton	Ramsgate Tn	Otford	At Otford-Sevenoaks in 1929
652(270)	6/14-11/25	(2807), (2409), (3134)	St Paul's	Ash	Dartford(1925)	SR coach numbers not allocated
653(274)	5/13-11/29	3600(2080), 1749(3343), 6922(2660)	Otford	Ramsgate Tn	P. Victoria	Coach 3600 was of SER origin
654(275)	2/12-7/30	3627 (2240), 5774(2246), 1465(2041)	Dover Priory-Canterbury East local service			SER stock. Not P-P after 1917
677(273)	4/13-1/30	3609 (3194), 1748(3342), 5741(2614)	Swanley Junction-Gravesend West Street			Saloon 7906 (2933) added as required
731(266)	12/14-8/26	(3153), (2463), (3150)	Birchington	Reading	Hayes	Not P-P after 1921. SR coach numbers not allocated. 2-coach set after 6/23.
732(271)	5/12-1/36	3270(3396), 6606(2713)	Greenwich Pk	Margate Sands	Ash	Still at Ash-Aldershot until withdrawal
733(272)	5/12-2/36	3271(3402), 6605(2711)	Greenwich Pk	Margate Sands	Ash	Still at Ash-Aldershot until withdrawal

* SECR set and coach numbers in brackets. Not all sets received SR livery or numbers.
Allocations varied considerably between 1914 and 1922, sets 266-70/4 in particular moving from one location to another frequently.

Table 8.2

Carriage Summary

SR Diagram	SR Coach Nos	SECR Coach Nos	Date of P-P fitting	Dimensions L x W	Seats# 1	3	Remarks
87	1605	2614	4/13	28ft x 8ft		40	Reclassed as composite 5741 in 1926 before renumbered
88	1471-3	3113/9/34/78	6/14	28ft x 8ft		50	Coach 3134 withdrawn 11/25 before renumbered
As 88		3150	12/14	28ft x 8ft		50	Not P-P after 1921. Withdrawn 6/23 before renumbered
88	1748/9	3342/3	4-5/13	28ft x 8ft		50	
None	1465	2041	Orig 1906	33ft x 8ft 4in		40	SER origin. With luggage compartment. Not P-P after 1917
None	3600	2080	Orig 1906	33ft x 8ft 4in		40	SER origin, in set 274/653
None	3604-6	2748/9/84, 2807	6/14	30ft x 8ft		30	Ex-brake 2nd, 6/23. Coach 2807 wdn 11/25 before renumbered
None	3609	3194	4/13	30ft x 8ft		40	Ex-brake 2nd, 6/23
None		3153	12/14	28ft x 8ft		40	Ex-brake 2nd, 6/23. Not P-P after 1921. Wdn before renumbered
None	3627	2240	Orig 1909	33ft x 8ft		40	SER origin. Ex-brake 2nd, 6/23. Not P-P after 1917
146	3270-1	3396, 3402	5/12	46ft x 8ft		70	Bogie vehicles
166	4111		8/24	28ft x 8ft		17	4w saloon, converted for IOW set 483
167	4112		8/24	28ft 9in x 8ft		17	4w saloon, converted for IOW set 484
None	5741	2614	4/13	28ft x 8ft	12	20	Allocated SR third class no. 1605 in 1923, returned to compo 1926
None	5769-71	2409/50/3, 2622	6/14	28ft x 8ft	18	10	Coach 2409 withdrawn 11/25 before renumbered
None		2463	12/14	28ft x 8ft	12	20	Not P-P after 1921. Withdrawn 8/26 before renumbered
None	5774	2246	Orig 1909	29ft x 8ft	12	20	SER origin. Not P-P after 1917
318	6368-9		8/24	28ft x 8ft	6	22	4w saloons, converted for IOW sets 483/4. From 1929 only five firsts
421	6605-6	2711/3	5/12	45ft x 8ft	18	30	Bogie vehicles. Ex-1st/2nd class in 6/23
450	6922	2660	5/13	28ft x 8ft	12	10	Lookouts removed, 1/27
610	7906	2933	4/13	28ft x 8ft		30	Saloon coach, added to set 273/677 as required. Withdrawn 12/25

Some vehicles included second class seating prior to June 1923 — the above totals show post 1923 figures only.
All coaches were to SR route restriction 0. Unless otherwise noted all were of LCDR origin.

Figure 39 The Isle of Wight LCDR sets 483/4.

Chapter 11.

SECR Railmotor Sets

The Southern Railway inherited all eight SECR steam railmotors in store with no plans for their future use. Two of them had been kept in service until February 1920, running between Hastings and Rye, but some had seen almost ten years of disuse by the Grouping. In April 1924 they were inspected and it was decided to scrap the locomotive units and convert the carriage portions into four two-coach sets — two for the Sheppey Light Railway and two for pull-push operation on the Isle of Wight.

The Sheppey Light Railway pair became SR sets 513/4 and were unique in that each set was an articulated unit, having one bogie at the centre supporting both coaches — the only vehicles of this type to run on the Southern. Despite what has been stated in several previously published accounts, they were never fitted for pull-push operation and, strictly speaking, do not form part of our story. However, brief details of the set formations, carriage numbering and workings are included, together with photographs, as they shared many details in common with the other two sets which did eventually receive pull-push equipment on their return from the Isle of Wight.

Articulated sets 513/4 remained at Sheppey until the line closed in December 1950. They were third class only, so perhaps for this reason alone were seldom, if ever, used elsewhere during the 1924-50 period, although it is unlikely that the traffic would often warrant both sets to be in service together. After this, the pair wandered around the South Western section during 1951, being noted at Portland, Hayling Island and Exmouth during this period. From 1952-6 they were allocated to the Clapham Junction–Kensington Olympia service, finally ending their days at Eastleigh for the Fawley branch between 1957 and 1959.

The other pairs were not articulated and became SR sets 481/2 in the Isle of Wight series. Presumably, it was considered that articulation might make transfer difficult and so for this reason they were treated differently from sets 513/4. There is some doubt about the intention to fit pull-push gear, but drawings exist confirming that they were to be used on the 'Yarmouth branch' — presumably the Newport–Freshwater line. This same drawing also shows the arrangements for LCDR four-wheel sets 483/4 to be used at Ventnor West. Two 'O2' class locomotives were also to be fitted with the gear to operate with them, but although some work was done at Eastleigh before they were transferred, this

Plate 145 Articulated set 514 at Leysdown on 2 June 1936 with third No 976 on the left, and brake third No 3561, right. Never pull-push fitted, these unusual coaches fit only loosely into our story. After the Sheppey Light Railway closed in December 1950, sets 513/4 travelled more widely around the Southern Region until withdrawn in 1957/59. The vacuum fitted van was provided for luggage and bicycles.
H. F. Wheeller

Plate 146 The guard issuing tickets on board articulated set 514 at Leysdown on the same day in June 1936. This shows the interior arrangements, applicable to both these and pull-push sets 481/2.
H. F. Wheeller

Plate 147 When ex-railmotor sets 481/2 were first rebuilt, they were sent to the Isle of Wight for use on the Freshwater line. However, after only a very short time they moved to the Bembridge branch, and this is one of very few photographs taken during their brief stay on the island. Seen at Brading, with IWR 2-4-0T No 14 *Shanklin*, one of these sets has a luggage van attached at the rear. Neither set was pull-push fitted until they returned to the mainland. *IWSR collection*

Plates 148 and 149 Both coaches of set 481 at Tonbridge on 29 August 1950, in SR malachite green livery. The composite coach, SR No 5580, has already been downgraded to third class, but still retains its composite series number; the other coach is No 3584. *Both D. Cullum*

work was never completed. Indeed, there is some debate about which type of control gear was to be used. Logically, the LBSCR air-control system would have been most suitable, as the decision to retain the Westinghouse brake for the Island had already been made, but Eastleigh Works would, at that time, have been more familiar with the three-wire 'over the roof' control.

The four coaches were adapted for their new role in the autumn of 1924 and, after brief trials on the Hawkhurst branch followed by a period of storage, were shipped to the Isle of Wight in April 1925. By this time there seems to have been some local publicity given to operating the Bembridge branch using pull-push trains, but whether by these sets or the LCDR four-wheelers is not entirely clear. In any event, no suitably equipped locomotives were at work on the Island until at least 1926. Sets 481/2 ran trials over both the Freshwater and Ventnor West lines. However, problems must have been encountered for the sets were soon reallocated to Ryde and were instead employed on the Bembridge branch. At this time they were only slightly longer than some recently transferred LSWR stock, but they were 6in wider — and this may have been their downfall. It

may be significant to note that when back on the mainland the coaches were afforded SR route restriction 1, whereas almost all other Island stock was route restriction 0. Whatever the problems, in May 1927 the sets were returned to the mainland and to yet another period of storage.

SR order L259 was soon issued for the fitting of vacuum brakes but for some reason this work was not undertaken immediately and it was not until September 1929 that the order was amended and reissued to include the provision of air-control pull-push gear and, presumably, a standard SR pull-push driving end. Photographs of the coaches on the Isle of Wight are rare and none show the end of the brake third vehicle clearly. The original set numbers were retained, but the coaches themselves were renumbered into the mainland series. Both were sent to the South Eastern section in April 1930, at first to the Gravesend West Street branch and Gillingham. They remained there until 1934, occasionally being noted on Swanley Junction-Sevenoaks services as well, until moving to Tonbridge for the Westerham branch, where they remained for almost the rest of their existence. Ironically, this was where at least one of the carriages

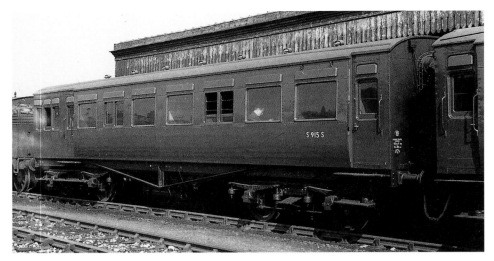

Plates 150 and 151 Both coaches of set 482 (Nos 915 and 3583) at Dunton Green on 19 April 1952, wearing BR crimson lake livery. The composite has now been renumbered into the third class sequence.
Both J. H. Aston

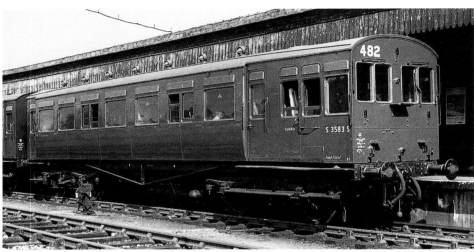

Figure 40 The ex-SECR railmotor sets 481/2.

had started life as a railmotor, some 28 years earlier. Set 481 managed to return to Gillingham just prior to withdrawal in 1959, then being seen at Allhallows and Grain (the post-1951 name for Port Victoria — now swallowed up in the oil refinery).

The only other change of note dates from 6 October 1941, when the Southern Railway decided to temporarily withdraw first class accommodation from all services that terminated within the London Passenger Transport Board area. Alone of the steam stock, this affected the Westerham branch and both trailer composite coaches were reclassified as third class. No change in numbering or seating occurred until 1952, when the change became permanent and the coaches were retrimmed and renumbered into the third class series. Table 9 gives details of the mainland set and carriage numbers.

Table 9
SECR Ex-Railmotor sets

SR Set No	SR Coach Nos BT	C or T	Running dates	Allocation 1930	1935	1957	Remarks
481	3584	5580	4/30-2/52	Gravesend W S	Westerham		Returned from Isle of Wight, 5/27
	3584	914	2/52-12/59			Westerham	Downgraded to third class, 10/41
482	3583	5581	4/30-4/52	Gillingham(relief)	Westerham		Returned from Isle of Wight, 5/27
	3583	915	4/52-3/60			Westerham	Downgraded to third class, 10/41
513	3560	975	4/24-11/57	Sheppey	Sheppey	Fawley	Articulated set, not P-P fitted
514	3561	976	4/24-10/59	Sheppey	Sheppey	Salisbury, for Idmiston	Articulated set, not P-P fitted

Isle of Wight carriage numbers for sets 481/2 were 4109/10 and 6366/7. Not pull-push fitted until 1930.

Table 9.2
Carriage Summary

SR Diagram	SR Nos	Date of Pull-Push conversion	Dimensions L x W	Seats 1	3	Remarks
214	975-6	Not fitted	48ft 4in x 8ft 6in		65	Articulated saloon third
214	3560-1	Not fitted	48ft 4in x 8ft 6in		56	Articulated saloon brake third
223	3583-4	4/30	48ft 4in x 8ft 6in		56	Driving trailer
364	5580-1	4/30	48ft 4in x 8ft 6in	15	32	Downrated to third class, 10/41, later diagram 62
62	914-5		48ft 4in x 8ft 6in		48	Ex-diagram 364, renumbered 2-4/52

Diagram 214 showed both vehicles together, described as 'twin carriages'
All vehicles were to SR route restriction 1

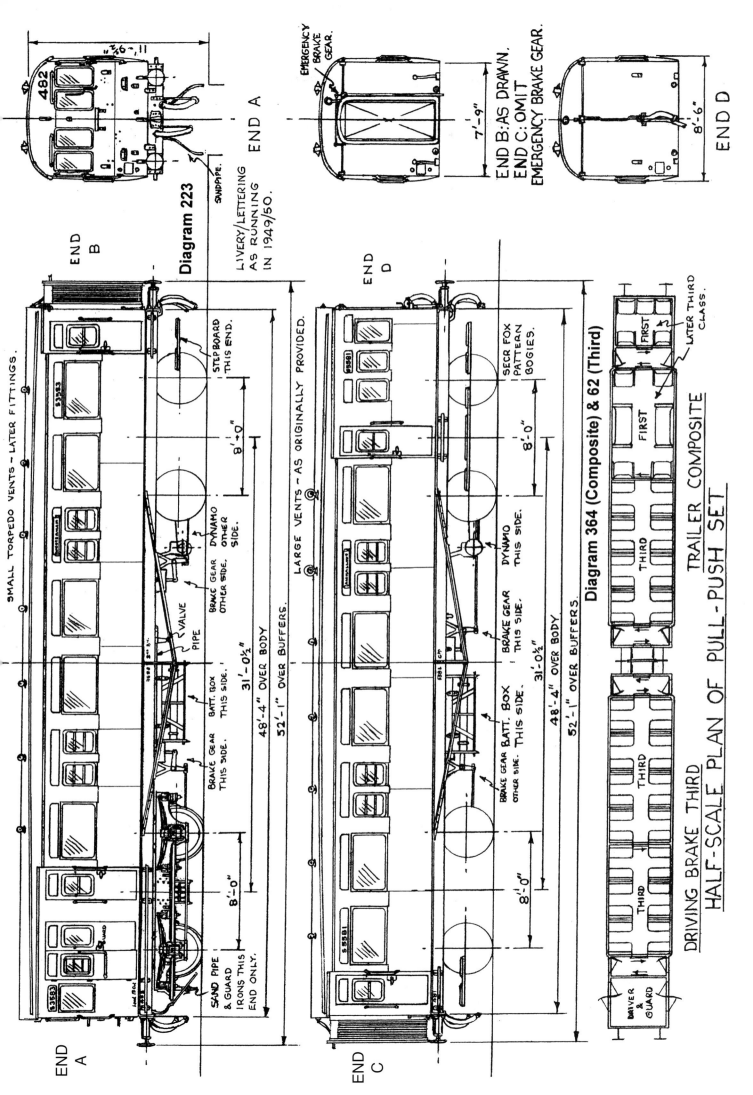

482

11'-9¾"

END A

Diagram 223

LIVERY/LETTERING AS RUNNING IN 1949/50.

END B

EMERGENCY BRAKE GEAR.

END B: AS DRAWN.
END C: OMIT
EMERGENCY BRAKE GEAR.

7'-9"

END D

8'-6"

SMALL TORPEDO VENTS ~ LATER FITTINGS.

SANDPIPE.

STEPBOARD THIS END.

8'-0"

DYNAMO OTHER SIDE.

VALVE PIPE

BRAKE GEAR OTHER SIDE.

BATT. BOX THIS SIDE.

BRAKE GEAR THIS SIDE.

31'-0½"

48'-4" OVER BODY.

52'-1" OVER BUFFERS.

8'-0"

SAND PIPE & GUARD IRONS THIS END ONLY.

S3583

END A

END B

LARGE VENTS ~ AS ORIGINALLY PROVIDED.

END D

SECR FOX PATTERN BOGIES.

8'-0"

DYNAMO THIS SIDE.

BRAKE GEAR THIS SIDE.

BRAKE GEAR OTHER SIDE.

BATT. BOX THIS SIDE.

31'-0½"

48'-4" OVER BODY.

52'-1" OVER BUFFERS.

8'-0"

S5581

Diagram 364 (Composite) & 62 (Third)

END C

FIRST

LATER THIRD CLASS.

FIRST

THIRD

THIRD

THIRD

DRIVER & GUARD

TRAILER COMPOSITE

DRIVING BRAKE THIRD

HALF-SCALE PLAN OF PULL-PUSH SET

Chapter 12.

SECR Non-corridor Stock

This stock does not enter our story until 1937, when sets 656-8 were formed using rebuilt LSWR driving brake composites and SECR ten-compartment thirds, as described in Chapter 6. However, another year was to elapse before a complete pull-push set of former SECR vehicles was formed. This was set 659, whose existence came about as a direct result of the Swanley Junction accident of 27 July 1937. This involved three-coach 'birdcage' set 535, of which one brake third was destroyed, the composite was badly damaged and the other brake third escaped practically unscathed. The latter vehicle (No 3324), together with the composite (No 5418), rebuilt as driving brake composite No 6409, were formed together as set 659 from April 1938.

This pull-push set was unique in that the brake third retained its 'birdcage' lookout — and incidentally was the last such coach running on the Southern Region when withdrawn in late 1961,

while the composite vehicle was rebuilt with a guard's/driver's compartment and standard pull-push driving end. The next two compartments also had to be rebuilt as third class, as they had been badly damaged in the accident and were previously of first class dimensions. With the exception of the driving end, all other timber bodyside mouldings were faithfully reinstated, such was the high standard of SR craftsmanship typical of the era.

The set was sent to Yeovil for the Junction–Town shuttle — the 'Yeovil bunk' as it was termed locally — where the fact that both vehicles included a guard's van proved useful for carrying the large volumes of mail and luggage regularly travelling to and from main line trains. It will be remembered from Chapter 5 that bogie 'block' set 351 had been similarly equipped with an enlarged luggage van in 1924 for exactly the same reason. Set 659 remained at Yeovil until the arrival of 'Ironclad' set 383 in October

Plate 152 The driving brake composite of set 659, No 6409, in SR malachite green, at Yeovil Junction on 8 July 1948. The Yeovil Town service had been its regular duty since conversion some ten years earlier. *J. H. Aston*

Plate 153 Companion coach No 3324 of set 659, at Tonbridge in 1959. This was the last passenger coach on the Southern Region to retain a 'birdcage' lookout. *J. H. Aston*

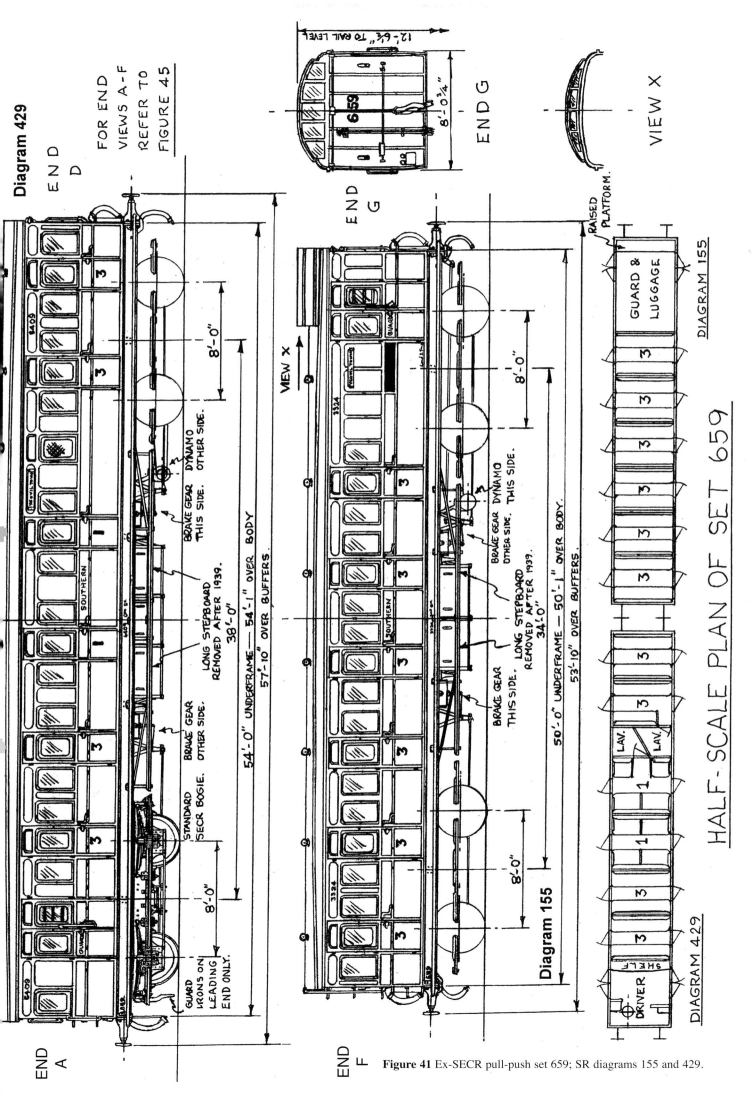

Figure 41 Ex-SECR pull-push set 659; SR diagrams 155 and 429.

Diagram 429

END D

FOR END VIEWS A–F REFER TO FIGURE 45

END G

12'-6½" TO RAIL LEVEL

659

8'-0¾"

END G

VIEW X

END A

SOUTHERN

BRAKE GEAR DYNAMO OTHER SIDE.

STANDARD SECR BOGIE.

BRAKE GEAR OTHER SIDE.

GUARD IRONS ON LEADING END ONLY.

8'-0"

8'-0"

LONG STEPBOARD REMOVED AFTER 1939.

54'-0" UNDERFRAME — 54'-1" OVER BODY

57'-10" OVER BUFFERS.

38'-0"

END F

VIEW X

SOUTHERN

3324

3324

BRAKE GEAR DYNAMO OTHER SIDE. THIS SIDE.

BRAKE GEAR THIS SIDE. LONG STEPBOARD REMOVED AFTER 1939.

34'-0"

Diagram 155

8'-0"

8'-0"

50'-0" UNDERFRAME — 50'-1" OVER BODY.

53'-10" OVER BUFFERS.

HALF-SCALE PLAN OF SET 659

RAISED PLATFORM.

3   3   3   GUARD & LUGGAGE

DIAGRAM 155

3   3   1   LAV. LAV. 1   3   3

DIAGRAM 429

3   3   1   DRIVER SHELF

DIAGRAM 429

Plate 154 Diagram 301 50ft 1in composite No 5298 from set 715, seen at Stewarts Lane in the 1950s. The livery is unlined crimson lake. Similar coach No 5301 was converted in 1942 for set 661. *The Lens of Sutton Association*

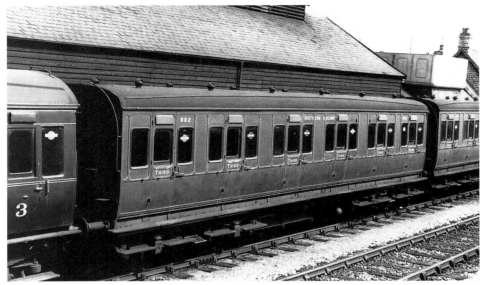

Plate 155 Around 1938/39, four 44ft SER/SECR six-compartment thirds were air piped for use as strengthening vehicles. All were ex-composites to diagram 292. No photographs are known, but this is non-fitted coach No 882 at Templecombe on 6 July 1938. All four coaches were withdrawn during 1942/43. *H. C. Casserley*

1948, when it was transferred back to home ground and could then be seen on various South Eastern section duties, being noted at Tonbridge, Westerham, Maidstone West and Hawkhurst, as well as providing some of the Kent Coast flooding emergency services during March–May 1953. A further move to Tunbridge Wells West took place in 1959 and the set ended its days as a relief on the Oxted and Three Bridges lines in November 1961. At least once during this period it was seen at Victoria, having been hastily added to the rear of a London service one busy summer Saturday.

At around the same time as set 659 was formed, similar 50ft composite No 5298 was also air piped for inclusion in LBSCR set 715, as noted in Chapter 9. A little later four 44 ft six-compartment thirds (in fact down-rated SER composites) were air piped as strengthening vehicles for, mostly, SW section duties. Coach Nos 860/3/77/83 were recorded, the latter three being noted in the 1941 carriage working notices as being allocated to the Yeovil, Swanage and Lymington branches respectively. However, all had been withdrawn in 1942/43 and their places taken by ten-compartment vehicles, of which more anon. Notably, by the late 1950s, quite a few of these 100-seaters had been air piped for use as strengtheners, and in fact, many more than were ever permanently allocated to pull-push sets.

The next three conversions took place during 1941/42, but produced three different types of set. The first was numbered as set 37 — a hybrid formed in June 1941 from an ex-SECR steel-panelled brake third converted to driving brake composite No 6410, coupled with ex-LSWR 56ft third No 608 — the only vehicle of this type to be adapted for motor train working. The set number was, in itself, unusual and rather out of sequence

for stock destined for the Central section — surely the number 660 would have been more logical? Whatever the reason, set 37 followed on from the ex-LSWR conversions of 1939 destined for Hampshire — although it is extremely doubtful if it ever saw service in that county. Based mostly at Horsham or Tunbridge Wells West, its usual duties took it to Guildford, Brighton, Tonbridge or Oxted. In 1954, the LSWR trailer coach was withdrawn and replaced by LBSCR 'luggage' third No 2193 from set 759, and described in Chapter 9, but again, making an ill-matched pair. The set continued to be based at Horsham until late 1959, when a move to Tonbridge and the Maidstone West services took it through to December 1960.

At the same time as coach No 3539 was rebuilt into No 6410 for set 37, its companion trio-C (SECR code for a three-coach set train) brake third from set 630 (coach No 3467) was also rebuilt as a loose driving brake third and allocated to Midhurst. It remained there as a single unit until December 1944, then being swapped with LBSCR brake third No 3846 in set 714 — making this set half LBSCR and half SECR in origin. No doubt the traffic volume at Midhurst was more suited to the 64-seat LBSCR vehicle than the 80-seat SECR one. Also, the Brighton coach had the added advantage of the corridor, to facilitate ticket issue by the guard. Set 714 remained a hybrid for the rest of its existence. Indeed, when withdrawn in 1961 it then included the last LBSCR coach in passenger service outside the Isle of Wight. It was seen over a variety of lines during the 1945-61 period, including Eastbourne–Hailsham, Guildford–Horsham–Brighton, Kent Coast flooding services, Tonbridge–Maidstone West and Allhallows branches.

Plate 156 Set 37 was formed in 1941 using a former SECR brake third upgraded to driving brake composite and an LSWR third. The pair are seen at an unidentified location, probably between Oxted and Tunbridge Wells West, circa 1950, in lined crimson lake, propelled by a 'D3' class 0-4-4T. *The Lens of Sutton Association*

The other two sets formed at this period came from 'birdcage' set 600 in August 1942. This had been augmented to six vehicles between 1933 and 1941, but was then disbanded and four of the coaches were used to form pull-push sets 660/1. Three of these were the original 60ft vehicles of set 600 (Nos 3433, 5473 and 3505), the fourth was 50ft composite No 5301 — this being identical to coach No 5298 converted for set 715 in 1938 and described earlier. Each set thus differed in make-up and overall length. Both brake thirds had their 'birdcage' lookouts removed and standard pull-push driving ends fitted, while the coaches in set 660 also required the removal of lavatories and these windows sheeted over. This had not been done in set 659, although the compartments had been stripped out. Several first class compartments in the composite vehicles were reclassified as third class.

Both sets were for many years allocated to the Crowhurst Junction–Bexhill West branch, where the services were timed to connect into and out of Hastings direct line trains — otherwise the patronage would hardly warrant the use of two sets. By 1942 the luxury of through trains to London from Bexhill West had almost disappeared. After dieselisation of the line in 1958, the pair moved to Tunbridge Wells West for Oxted duties, remaining there until withdrawn in 1961. By this time they contrasted unfavourably with the more modern corridor stock on London trains, but at least the first class passenger could enjoy the luxury of the saloon compartment if lucky enough to travel in set 660. Even then, there was still some character in the remaining pull-push sets!

No further conversions of SECR stock took place until after Nationalisation, when in 1950 and 1952, four coaches from steel-panelled trio-C sets 637/8 were used to form additional sets

Plate 157 The LSWR third from set 37 (No 608) was condemned in 1954 and its place was taken by diagram 80 LBSCR 'luggage third' No 2193 soon after. In its revised form the set passes the site of Teston Crossing Halt with the 3.8pm Maidstone West–Tonbridge service on 18 April 1960, propelled (chimney first) by an 'H' class tank. The conductor rails are already in place. *G. M. Kichenside*

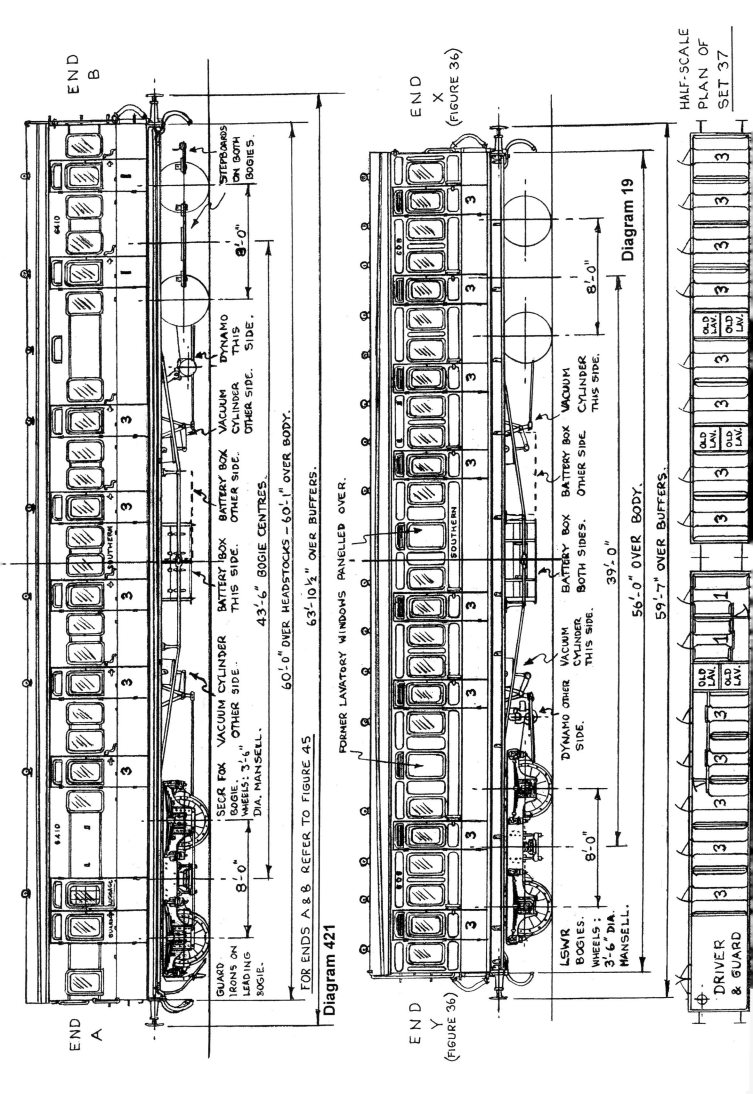

END
B

END
A

6410

3

SOUTHERN

3

3

3

3

6410

GUARD LUGGAGE

GUARD
IRONS ON
LEADING
BOGIE.

STEPBOARDS
ON BOTH
BOGIES.

8'-0"

DYNAMO
THIS SIDE.

VACUUM
CYLINDER
OTHER SIDE.

BATTERY BOX
OTHER SIDE.

'SECR FOX'
BOGIE.
WHEELS: 3'-6"
DIA. MANSELL.

BATTERY BOX
THIS SIDE.

VACUUM CYLINDER
OTHER SIDE.

8'-0"

43'-6" BOGIE CENTRES.

60'-0" OVER HEADSTOCKS - 60'-1" OVER BODY.

63'-10½" OVER BUFFERS.

FOR ENDS A & B REFER TO FIGURE 45

Diagram 421

END
X
(FIGURE 36)

3

3

3

3

609

3

3

SOUTHERN

3

3

3

3

3

END
Y
(FIGURE 36)

FORMER LAVATORY WINDOWS PANELLED OVER.

LSWR
BOGIES.
WHEELS:
3'-6" DIA.
MANSELL.

DYNAMO OTHER
SIDE.

VACUUM
CYLINDER
THIS SIDE.

BATTERY BOX
BOTH SIDES.

BATTERY BOX
OTHER SIDE.

VACUUM
CYLINDER
THIS SIDE.

8'-0"

8'-0"

39'-0"

56'-0" OVER BODY.

59'-7" OVER BUFFERS.

Diagram 19

HALF-SCALE
PLAN OF
SET 37

3   3   3   3   3   OLD
LAV.   3   OLD
LAV.   3   OLD
LAV.   3

3   3   3   3   OLD
LAV.   OLD
LAV.   3   1   1   1   OLD
LAV.   OLD
LAV.   3   3   3

DRIVER
& GUARD

Plate 158 Set 714 in hybrid form, composed of SECR driving brake third No 3467 and LBSCR composite No 6237, at Hailsham on a wet June day in 1948. Note that the set number is painted over the right-hand window instead of the more usual left-hand position. The unidentified locomotive is presumably not auto fitted, as running-round is in progress.
T. A. Barry collection

Figure 42 Set 37; SR diagrams 19 and 421. For the 'luggage third' see Figure 31.

662/3, while two single units were rebuilt from the remaining brake thirds. This work was completed under orders L3494 and L3735. Sets 662/3 were similar to set 660, but of course there were no lookouts to be removed and the bodysides were unpanelled. Set 662 was allocated to Bournemouth West and, carrying lined BR crimson lake, was usually employed on the Brockenhurst via Wimborne service. Set 663 found use at more traditional locations on the South Eastern section, ending its days on the Oxted line in 1961. Of the loose brake thirds, coach No 3474 ran alone between Petersfield and Midhurst from June 1950 until formed into LSWR set 31 about June 1951 and coach No 3475 went to ex-LBSCR set 715 in 1952, replacing the

LBSCR brake third and making this set wholly composed of SECR vehicles. In this form the set was allocated to the Central section and was used on the Stephenson Locomotive Society South London rail tour in June 1958, visiting such unlikely locations as Merton Abbey and Epsom Downs.

The last pull-push set to be formed from ex-SECR stock appeared in November 1956, this being numbered 656 — a replacement for the 1937 set that previously carried the same number. This took two coaches from steel-panelled trio-C set 633 and so was very similar to sets 662/3; however, there were detail differences between them. This set was allocated to Central and later South Eastern section duties, latterly at

Plate 159 Set 660, formed of brake third No 3505 and composite No 5473 (both ex-'birdcage' set 600) at Bexhill West in 1957, just before DEMUs took over, one of which is visible in the sidings to the right. The livery is unlined crimson lake with left-hand numerals, typical of 1949-51 repaints. *The Lens of Sutton Association*

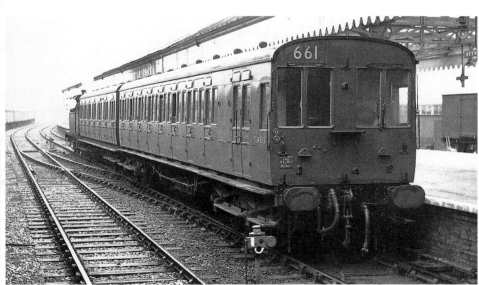

Plate 160 Companion set 661, formed of brake third No 3433 and 50ft 1in composite No 5301 (again both ex-set 600), also at Bexhill West about 1957. The livery is Southern Region post-1956 green. Sets 660/1 were regulars on the Bexhill West branch in the 1950s. *The Lens of Sutton Association*

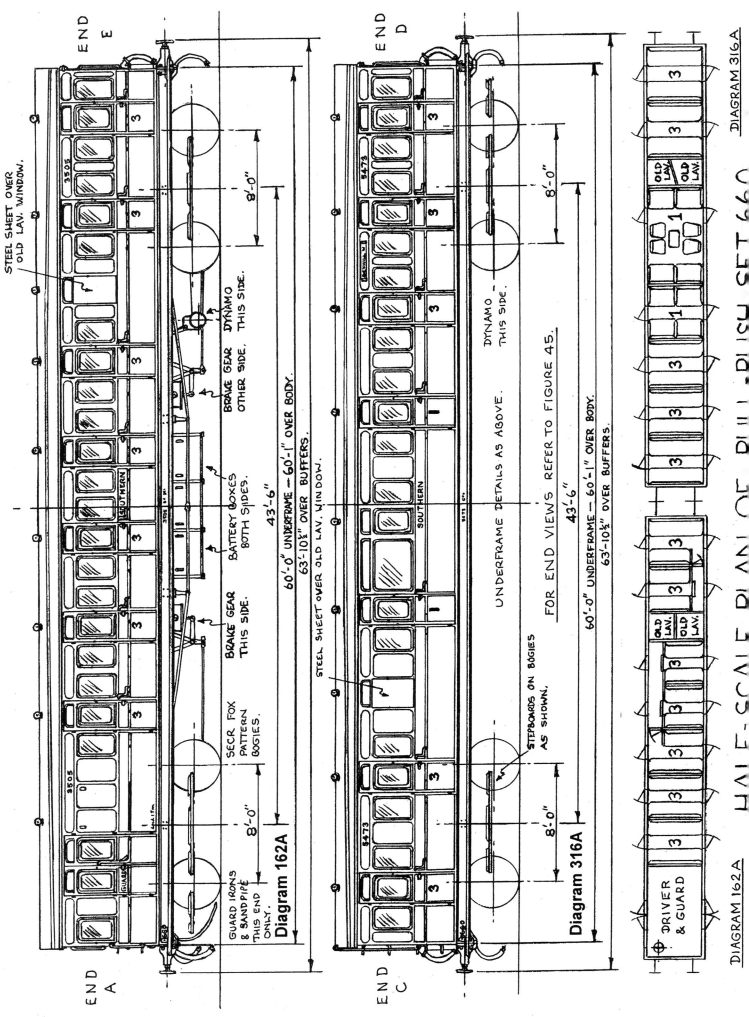

Figure 43 Set 660; SR diagrams 162A and 316A.

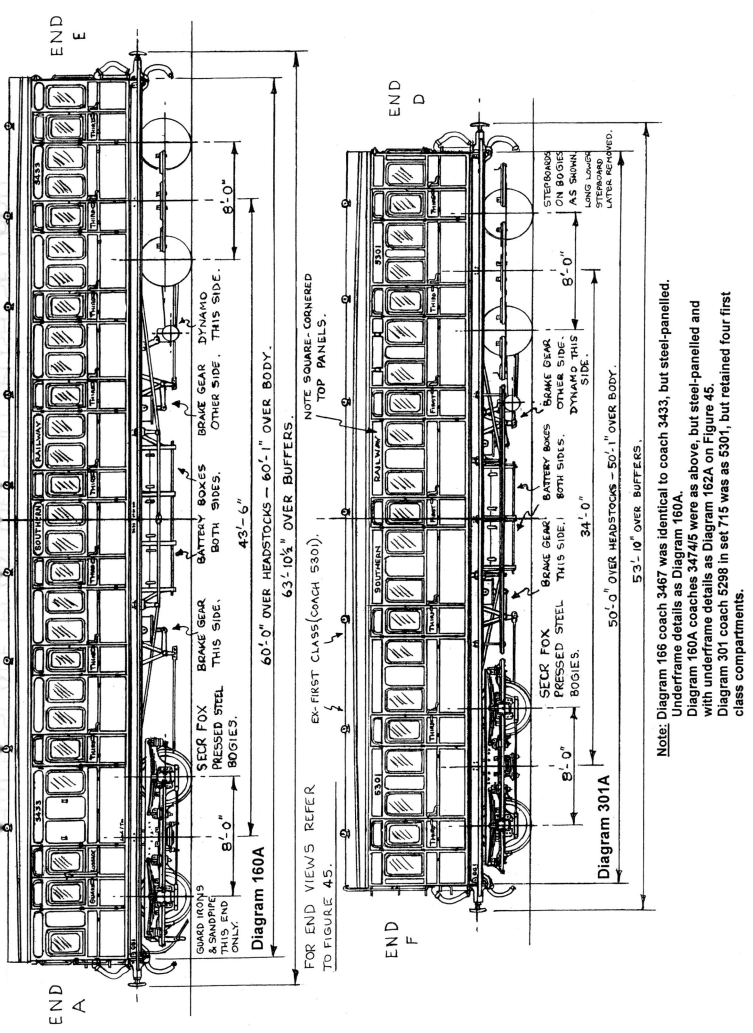

Figure 44 Set 661; SR diagrams 160A and 301A.

Plate 161 The 1950/52 conversions produced sets 662/3. Set 662 (coaches Nos 3546 and 5503) was, uncharacteristically, allocated to Bournemouth West and spent most of its working life on the Brockenhurst via Wimborne service. It is seen when new and in lined crimson lake, at Eastleigh on 29 July 1950. *A. E. West*

Plate 162 Composite coach No 5503 of set 662, now in post-1956 green livery, at Bournemouth West on 29 August 1961. This was the last ex-SECR pull-push set to remain in traffic, being withdrawn in May 1962. Just visible to the left is an ex-SECR air-control van. *A. E. West*

Plate 163 Two single units were produced using the spare brake thirds left after the completion of sets 662/3. Diagram 160A driving brake third No 3474 was allocated to Midhurst for the Petersfield service in 1950/51 and is seen at Elsted along with 'M7' No 30047. It was later incorporated into set 31. Identical coach No 3475 ran in set 715 from 1952. These two vehicles were allocated the same diagram as coach No 3433 in set 661, being steel-sheeted instead of timber-panelled. *The Lens of Sutton Association*

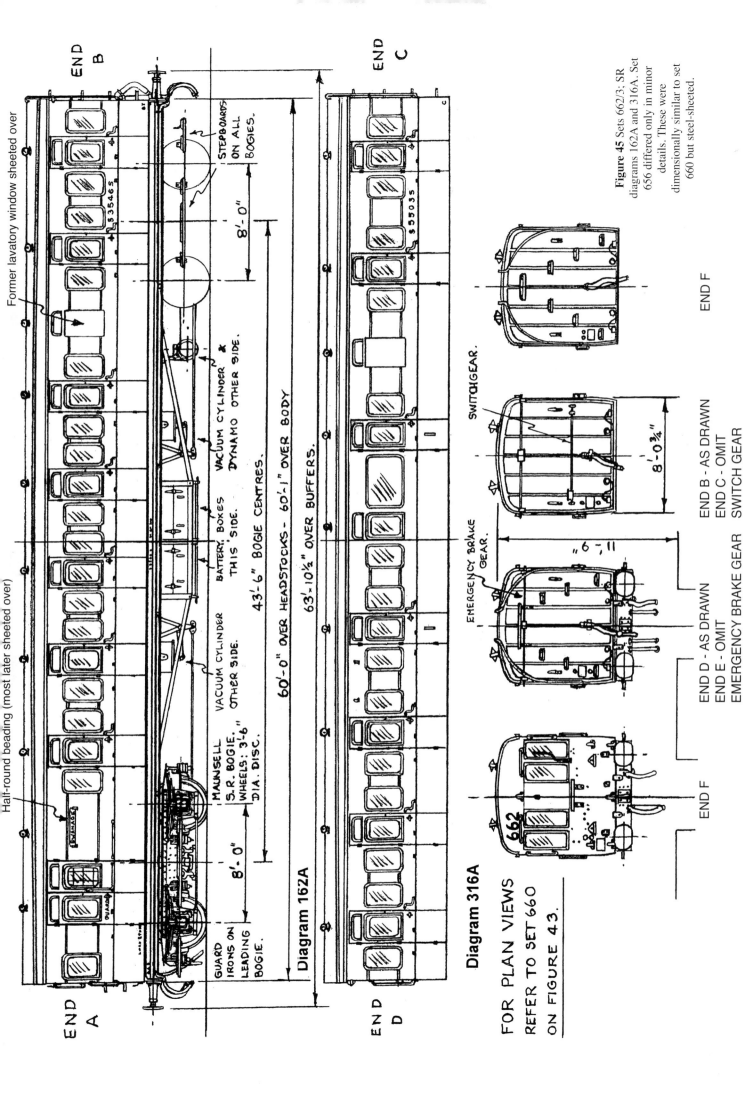

END B

END C

Former lavatory window sheeted over

STEPBOARDS ON ALL BOGIES.

8'-0"

S3546S

VACUUM CYLINDER & DYNAMO OTHER SIDE.

BATTERY BOXES THIS SIDE.

43'-6" BOGIE CENTRES.

60'-0" OVER HEADSTOCKS – 60'-1" OVER BODY

63'-10½" OVER BUFFERS.

Half-round beading (most later sheeted over)

MAUNSELL S.R. BOGIE. WHEELS: 3'-6" DIA. DISC.

VACUUM CYLINDER OTHER SIDE.

8'-0"

GUARD IRONS ON LEADING BOGIE.

END A

Diagram 162A

S5503S

END D

Diagram 316A

FOR PLAN VIEWS REFER TO SET 660 ON FIGURE 43.

SWITCHGEAR.

EMERGENCY BRAKE GEAR.

8'-0¾"

6'-11"

END F

END B – AS DRAWN
END C – OMIT SWITCH GEAR

END D – AS DRAWN
END E – OMIT EMERGENCY BRAKE GEAR

END F

662

Figure 45 Sets 662/3; SR diagrams 162A and 316A. Set 656 differed only in minor details. These were dimensionally similar to set 660 but steel-sheeted.

Plate 164 Almost at the end of South Eastern section steam working, 'H' class No 31519 sets out from Paddock Wood with the 12.30pm to Hawkhurst on 1 August 1960, hauling set 656. *G. M. Kichenside*

Plate 165 A typical scene at the buffer stops at Paddock Wood in May 1961. Set 656 awaits the next Hawkhurst departure, while replacement Maunsell set 609 stands alongside. This charming rural backwater, serving an unspoilt part of the Kentish Weald, had just one more month to live, yet on the platform one could be forgiven for thinking that it would go on for ever. This branch was the setting for the BBC TV series *The Old Pull and Push* referred to in the Introduction. *H. P. Rutherford*

Plate 166 Unique 62ft 6in composite coach No 5546 was downgraded to all-third in June 1943, then being allocated diagram 50 and running number 1050. It was then air-piped and sent to the South Western section as a pull-push strengthener. Allocated first to Yeovil, it then moved to Lymington, Seaton and Swanage until withdrawn in 1962. It took part in the 'Exeter 100' celebrations in July 1960, along with 'gate' set 373 visible behind and is seen there on 20 July in unlined crimson lake livery. *A. E. West*

Plate 167 The end view of coach No 1050, showing the three air-control pipes and the electric cable connections. *A. E. West*

Hawkhurst or Tonbridge until withdrawn in January 1962. The last former SECR pull-push set in traffic was actually 662 — withdrawn from Bournemouth in May 1962.

On page 132 it was noted that a few 44ft thirds had been air piped for strengthening duties on the South Western section and that some 100-seat vehicles had replaced them during 1942/43. One of these was the unique 'prototype splicing coach', composite No 5546 of 1924. In June 1943 this was downgraded to a full third and renumbered 1050, receiving air pipes during the conversion. It was then sent to Yeovil for augmenting the branch set (No 659), giving quite a South Eastern feel to the branch. By 1947 it had moved to Brockenhurst for either the Lymington or Bournemouth via Wimborne services, thence to Seaton in 1949, where it remained for over ten years, finally moving to Swanage until withdrawn in 1962. By then one of the last all-timber bodied coaches on the mainland, it was then dispatched to the Ardingly branch to await scrapping at Newhaven, from where the Bluebell Railway was most fortunate to purchase it in May 1963.

Also during 1943, two more 100-seat 60ft thirds (Nos 1093/8) were air piped and allocated to Swanage and Lymington respectively, remaining on these duties until the early 1960s. It was not until 1957 that any more were similarly equipped, when no fewer than 12 were done, mostly for strengthening purposes. Three went into ex-LSWR sets 1, 6 and 652 and are detailed in Chapter 6, but the rest were air piped in 1958 for South Western section branches. Most survived until 1962, latterly running with the 'Ironclad' and Maunsell conversions. Because of their steel cladding, they were more acceptable to the operating authorities, which by then were concerned about the durability of timber-bodied coaches in the event of a collision. Coaches Nos 971 and 1098 survive today on the Bluebell Railway, although devoid of pull-push fittings.

Table 10 lists the SECR vehicles equipped for pull-push operation.

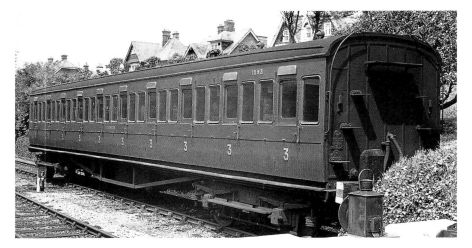

Plate 168 At Swanage is diagram 52 'long ten' – one of the matchboarded variety of SECR 100-seat thirds, on 13 June 1948. It was serving as the spare coach, hence being shunted adjacent to the buffer stops of the run-round loop – to be convenient if needed in a hurry. Malachite green livery with flat-topped '3's – some had round tops. *J. H. Aston*

Plate 169 'Long ten' No 1057 at Lewes in May 1952 – part of set 656. The accompanying LSWR driving brake composite appears in Plate 68. *G. A. Hookham*

Table 10
Ex-SECR Non-Corridor Stock Sets

SR Set No	Running dates	SR Coach Nos BT or BC	T or C	1945	Allocation 1955	1960	Remarks
37	6/41-7/54	6410	608	Horsham			Coach 608 is ex-LSWR, diagram 19
	7/54-12/60	6410	2193		Horsham	Tonbridge	Coach 2193 is ex-LBSCR, diagram 80
656	11/56-1/62	3542	5499			Tonbridge	Vehicles ex 3-set 633
659	4/38-11/61	6409	3324 (BT)	Yeovil	Tonbridge	Tun Wells W	Coach 3324 retained birdcage lookout
660	8/42-12/61	3505	5473	Bexhill W	Bexhill W	Tun Wells W	Vehicles ex 6-set 600
661	8/42-10/61	3433	5301	Bexhill W	Bexhill W	Tun Wells W	Vehicles ex 6-set 600
662	6/50-5/62	3546	5503		B'mouth W	B'mouth W	Vehicles ex 3-set 637
663	2/52-5/61	3547	5504		SE Section	C Section	Vehicles ex 3-set 638
714	1/45-8/61	3467	6237	SE Section	SE Section	C Section	Coach 6237 is ex-LBSCR, diagram 350
715	2/38-2/52	3847	5298	SE Section			Coach 3847 is ex-LBSCR, diagram 193
	2/52-3/61	3475	5298		Tonbridge	Ashford	Both vehicles now of SECR origin

Table 10.2
Carriage Summary

SR Diagram	SR Nos	Date of P-P Conversion	Dimensions L x W	Seats 1	Seats 3	Remarks
19	608	8/41	56ft x 8ft		80	Ex-LSWR vehicle for set 37
50	1050	6/43	62ft 6in x 8ft		100	Loose vehicle, ex-diagram 319 composite No 5546
52	1093/8	2-6/43	60ft 1in x 8ft		100	Loose vehicles.
52	971/3, 1056/73/81/92, 1100/4/11	3-7/58	60ft 1in x 8ft		100	Loose vehicles. Others were converted for LSWR sets 1, 6 and 652 at the same time.
57	860/3/77/83	c1938/9	44ft x 8ft		60	Ex-composites to diagram 292 in 1935-7. Wdn 1942/3
80	2193	Orig 10/31	54ft x 8ft		80	Ex-LBSCR vehicle, from set 759, for set 37
155	3324	4/38	50ft 1in x 8ft		60	For set 659 — birdcage lookout retained
160A*	3433/74/5	8/42, 6/50 & 2/52	60ft 1in x 8ft		80	Coach 3474 loose until included in set 31, c6/51
162A	3505/42/6/7	8/42, 4/57, 6/50 & 2/52	60ft 1in x 8ft		54	For sets 660/56/62/3 respectively
166*	3467	6/41	60ft 1in x 8ft		80	Loose until included in set 714, 1/45
301	5298	2/38	50ft 1in x 8ft	24	30	For set 715
301A	5301	8/42	50ft 1in x 8ft	16	50	For set 661
316A	5473/99, 5503/4	8/42, 4/57, 6/50 & 2/52	60ft 1in x 8ft	20	50	For sets 660/56/62/3 respectively
421	6410	6/41	60ft 1in x 8ft	13	40	Ex-brake third 3539, diagram 163, for set 37
429	6409	4/38	54ft 1in x 8ft	14	38	Ex-composite 5418, diagram 314, for set 659

* These two diagrams were identical.
All coaches were to SR route restriction 0 except for diagram 19, which was restriction 1.

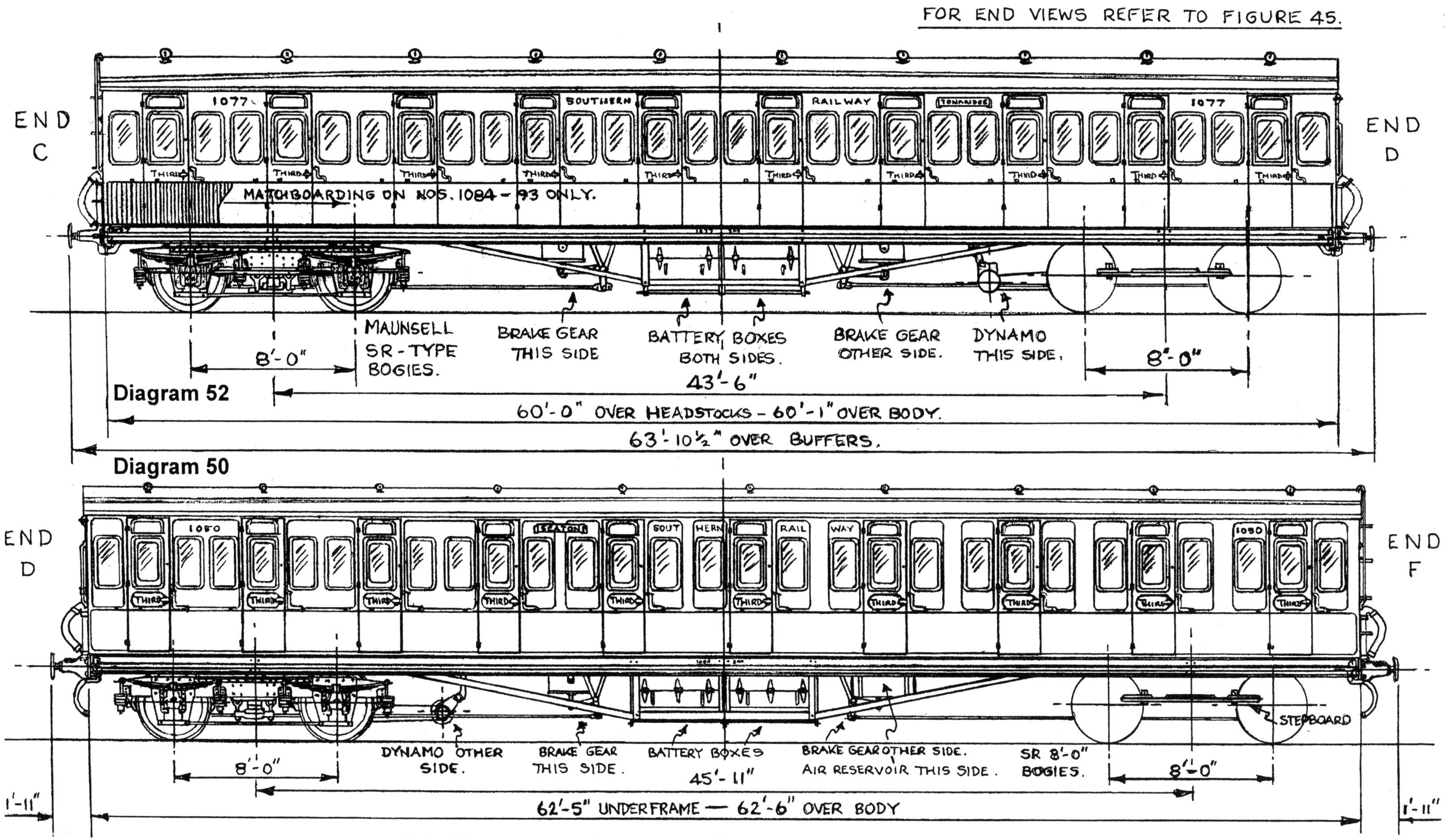

END
D

END
C

Diagram 52

8'-0"

MATCHBOARDING ON NOS.1084-93 ONLY.

MAUNSELL
SR-TYPE
BOGIES.

BRAKE GEAR
THIS SIDE.

BATTERY BOXES
BOTH SIDES.

43'-6"

BRAKE GEAR
OTHER SIDE.

DYNAMO
THIS SIDE.

8'-0"

60'-0" OVER HEADSTOCKS – 60'-1" OVER BODY.

63'-10½" OVER BUFFERS.

END
F

END
D

STEPBOARD

Diagram 50

8'-0"

8'-0"

SR 8'-0"
BOGIES.

BRAKE GEAR OTHER SIDE.

AIR RESERVOIR THIS SIDE.

DYNAMO OTHER
SIDE.

BRAKE GEAR
THIS SIDE.

BATTERY BOXES
THIS SIDE.

45'-11"

62'-5" UNDERFRAME – 62'-6" OVER BODY

1'-11"

1'-11"

Note: Diagram 52 coaches numbered between 968-74 & 1094-1112 had square-cornered window frames and steel-sheeted ends.
All other details as above.

Figure 46 The SECR ten-compartment strengthening thirds.

Chapter 13.

SR Maunsell Stock

By mid-1959 there were still 46 pull-push sets (28 of LSWR origin, eight LBSCR and ten SECR) in stock, but even allowing for the fact that some were on newer underframes, not one vehicle was less than 34 years old, while several were approaching their half-century. Since the Barnes accident of December 1955, concerns had been raised about the ability of all-timber bodied vehicles to withstand a rear-end collision, as well as the risk of fire due to electrical arcing should an accident occur within the electrified network. For those pull-push sets operating away from the third rail, this was less of a concern, but there were a surprising number of locations where the stock ran over electrified lines in the course of their daily duties. On top of this, the locomotives employed were also showing their age, but there was little prospect of replacement.

In the same year, the British Transport Commission issued its notorious 30-year rule – effectively consigning any carriage over that age to the scrap heap. Clearly, if interpreted literally, this would wipe out the entire pull-push stock at a stroke, so something had to be done. The Beeching Plan was still in the future and, even allowing for the completion of the Kent Coast electrification, some pull-push operation was expected to continue for a while yet. It was judged that the five LSWR

'Ironclad' sets and the steel-panelled SECR vehicles could last a little longer, but that the LBSCR and most of the LSWR vehicles should be replaced at the earliest opportunity.

Accordingly, orders L4634 and L4746 were placed in June 1959 and February 1960, each for the conversion of 20 Maunsell coaches into ten pull-push sets (Nos 600-19), and these appeared between October 1959 and February 1961. They comprised a driving brake composite, originally built in 1935 and an open saloon third (reclassified as second since June 1956), dating from 1933. The end gangways were removed and large electric-stock pattern buffers were fitted at the outer ends. However, to facilitate ticket issue and collection the gangways within each set were retained. Two small end windows were provided for the driver, as well as droplights in place of the pressed steel lookouts. All lavatories were sealed and the windows sheeted over, although the frosted windows on the opposite sides were retained. **Figures 47** and **48** illustrate these final conversions.

Initially, sets 600-7/16-19 were allocated to the Central section, 608/9/12-15 to the South Western and 610/11 to the South Eastern. However, quite a lot of movement took place subsequently, as sets 603/11 were noted at Seaton and Bournemouth respectively in 1960/61 and 608/9/14 were seen at

Plate 170 Maunsell pull-push set 602, showing the compartment side of the driving brake composite, at Tunbridge Wells West, circa 1962. *The Lens of Sutton Association*

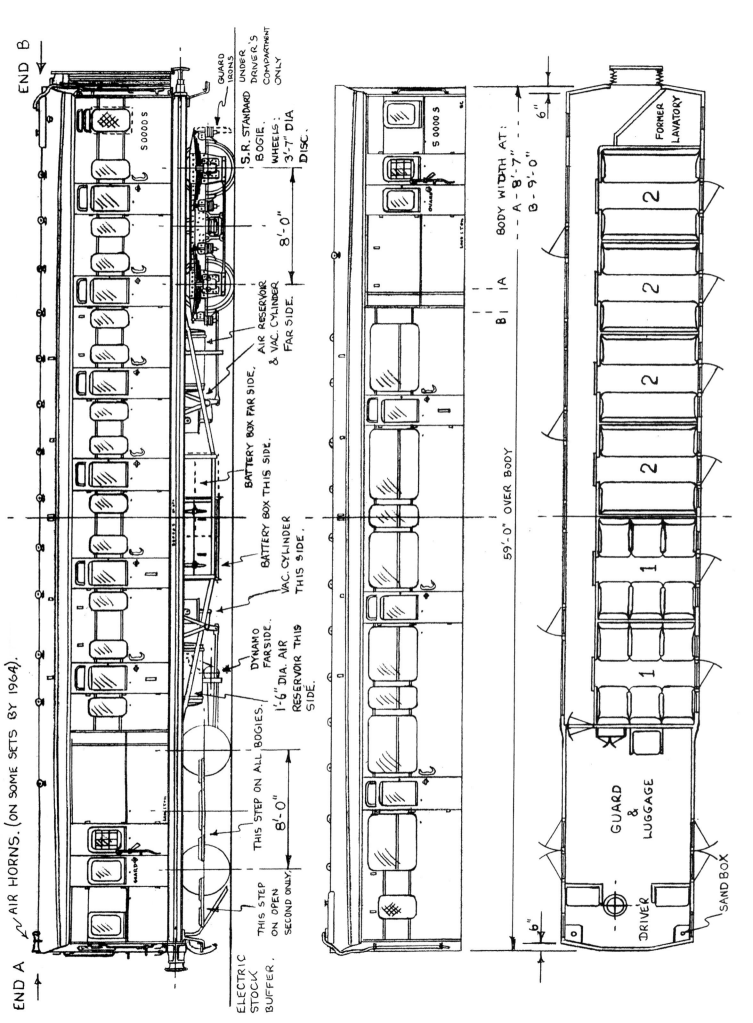

Figure 47 The Maunsell driving brake composite; SR diagram 2407.

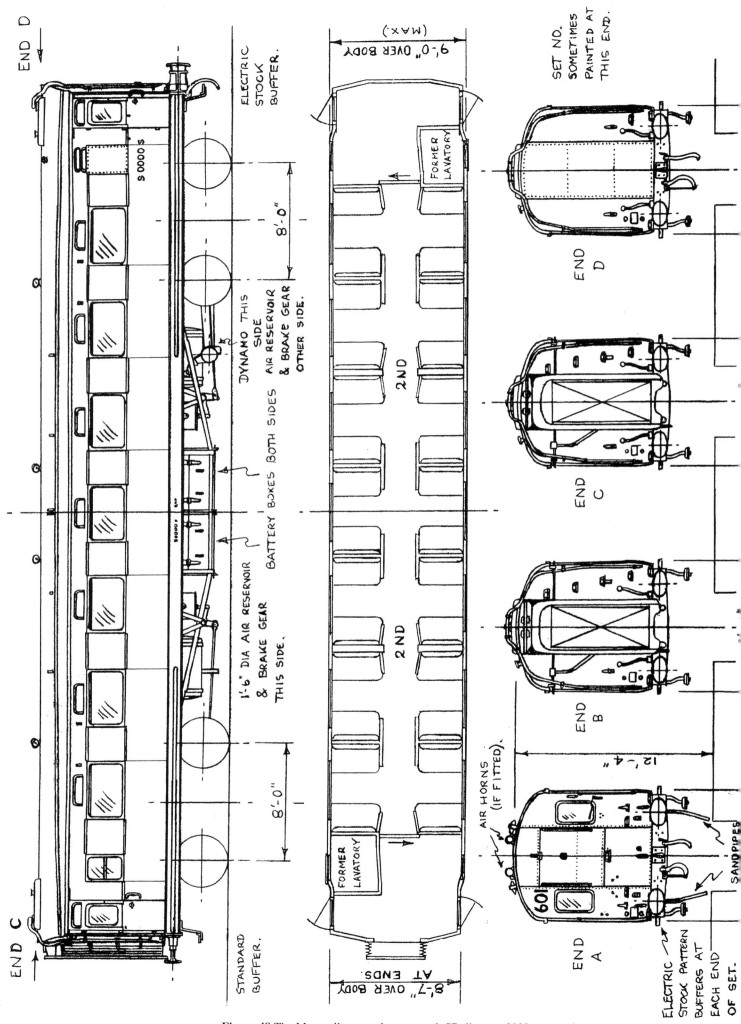

Figure 48 The Maunsell open saloon second; SR diagram 2023.

Plate 171 Set 616 at Seaton Junction on 19 April 1963, along with 'M7' No 30048. This shows the corridor side of the driving brake vehicle. Pull-push operation using Southern Region stock on the lines west of Salisbury ceased just 14 days later, with ex-GWR stock taking over. *A. E. West*

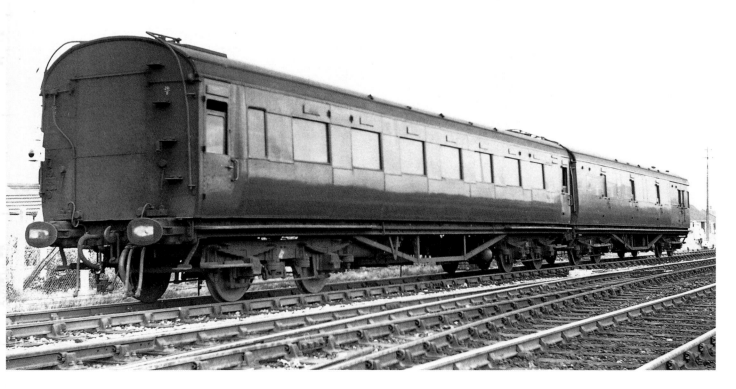

Plate 172 Set 616 again, but from the opposite end, at Wareham on 18 September 1964, now being used as conventional hauled stock since the withdrawal of the last 'M7s'. Open second No 1359 is nearest the camera, with brake composite 6695 beyond. This was one of very few Maunsell pull-push sets to receive the yellow first class cantrail markings. *A. E. West*

Tunbridge Wells West, Allhallows, Westerham, Maidstone West and Horsham during the same period and set 612 was recorded at Brighton in 1961. Sets 608-10 were at Yeovil, Seaton and Exeter on 1 January 1963 and became Western Region stock with the transfer of all lines west of Salisbury on that date. All returned to the Southern Region later in the year, once ex-GWR '5400' and '6400' pannier tanks, '1400' 0-4-2Ts and GWR auto-trailers had been drafted in as temporary replacements west of Salisbury — much, it has to be said, to the chagrin of the locomotive crews concerned!

The arrival of these sets resulted in the withdrawal of all eight LBSCR sets and most of the LSWR stock, while the decision to cease pull-push operation over the Cranleigh and Steyning lines took effect in March 1961, reducing the number of sets required still further. This left just sets 1, 381/3-5, 652/6/63 of the older stock remaining at either Bournemouth or Tunbridge Wells West to survive into 1962 — and all had been withdrawn before the year was out. The writing was clearly on the wall for pull-push operation and just the Maunsell sets, six 'H' class and 20 'M7s' remained in service at the start of 1963. Set 607 had already suffered accident damage at Eastbourne and was deleted from stock in September 1961. The open second was retained as a loose strengthening vehicle, while sets 618/9 were also disbanded early in 1963. Both open seconds became loose strengtheners, while the brake composites were employed on the Hayling Island branch as ordinary vehicles until closure in November 1963. Both vehicles were later sold to Chipman Weed Killing Company of Horsham and survive today on the Swanage Railway. Prior to the release of the open seconds, the only strengthening coaches remaining until late 1962 were some ex-SECR 100-seat vehicles.

Withdrawal of the remaining Maunsell sets commenced in December 1963, as the last Oxted and Three Bridges–Tunbridge Wells West services were given over to diesel operation, leaving Bournemouth-allocated sets 603/4/6/8-17 running into 1964 on Swanage, Lymington and Brockenhurst via Wimborne services. Withdrawal of the last motor-fitted 'M7s' took place at the end of May 1964, bringing to an end the traditional steam-operated pull-push era on the Southern Region, after 59 years. Set 609 was noted at Salisbury in July 1964, but for what duty is not known. Several of the sets remained in traffic until the following November, but not in pull-push mode and hauled by whatever motive power Bournemouth shed could muster. Driving brake composite No 6688 from set 613 was reinstated subsequently and was finally withdrawn in September 1966, but it is not known for what purpose it was used in the meantime. However, by then trials for a very different form of pull-push operation were being planned, culminating in the Bournemouth line electrification of July 1967, so it may have been retained for these tests.

Table 11 gives details of the last Southern Region pull-push sets.

Table 11
SR Maunsell Sets

SR Set No	Running dates	SR coach Nos BC	SO	Original allocation 1959/60/1	Remarks
600	10/59-12/63	6693	1338	Central Section	At Tunbridge Wells West in 1963
601	10/59-12/63	6687	1351	Central Section	At Tunbridge Wells West in 1963
602	11/59-12/63	6681	1318	Central Section	At Tunbridge Wells West in 1963
603	12/59-10/64	6675	1320	Central Section	At Seaton by August 1960, later Bournemouth
604	1/60-11/64	6676	1360	Central Section	At Swanage by 1964
605	1/60-12/63	6677	1349	Central Section	At Tunbridge Wells West in 1963
606	11/59-11/64	6678	1328	Central Section	At Bournemouth by 1964
607	1/60-9/61	6682	1343	Central Section	Accident damage at Eastbourne 15/9/61, 1343 to loose stock
608	1/60-10/64	6689	1330	South Western Section	Noted at Yeovil. To WR 1/63, later returned to SR
609	11/59-11/64	6694	1353	South Western Section	To WR 1/63, later returned to SR
610	7/60-10/64	6679	1317	South Eastern Section	To WR 1/63, later returned to SR
611	7/60-5/64	6680	1323	South Eastern Section	At Bournemouth by 1960
612	11/60-5/64	6683	1356	South Western Section	At Brighton in 1961
613	10/60-11/64	6688	1347	South Western Section	Noted at Bournemouth
614	2/61-10/64	6690	1354	South Western Section	At Westerham in 1961
615	11/60-11/64	6691	1341	South Western Section	
616	8/60-10/64	6695	1359	Central Section	At Seaton in 1963
617	7/60-11/64	6696	1361	Central Section	At Bournemouth in 1963
618	1/61-4/63	6697	1342	Central Section	6697 at Hayling 1963, 1342 to loose stock
619	9/60-4/63	6699	1331	Central Section	6699 at Hayling 1963, 1331 to loose stock

No changes in formation recorded

Table 11.2
Carriage Summary

SR Diagram	SR Nos	Date of Pull-Push Conversion	Dimensions L x W	Seats 1	2	Remarks
2023	Between 1317 & 1360	10/59-2/61	59ft x 9ft		56	Ex-diagram 2005, built in 1933
2407	Between 6675 & 6699 (20 vehicles in each case)	10/59-2/61	59ft x 9ft	12	32	Ex diagram 2403, built in 1935

All coaches were to SR route restriction 4

Chapter 14.

Air-control Vans

In 1923/24, when the 'Balloon' driving brake thirds and the 1909/11 arc-roofed driving brake composites were permanently formed into sets, it was soon found that the luggage accommodation was insufficient for the country area services then being operated. To overcome this, ten ex-LBSCR Billinton six-wheeled guard's vans were equipped with through air pipes, so that they could run with the pull-push sets, coupled between the locomotive and the set. In fact, they tended to run as often with the arc-roofed corridor sets as they did with the 'Balloons' and 1909/11 vehicles, all being allocated to specific Central section duties. They were rarely, if ever, seen on South Western or South Eastern section pull-push workings and here, if a van

were needed, it would have to trail either the engine or the train, depending on the direction of travel. This was likely to be unpopular with the crew, as the van would need to be run round at the end of each journey.

The July 1924 working notices list just eight vans: Nos 34, 782, 92, 810, 197, 479, 492 and 495, so at this date only two had been repainted and renumbered in SR livery. Workings were based on Brighton (one), Seaford (one), Littlehampton (two) and Horsham (three), with one van standing spare, each duty taking in a variety of destinations during the course of the day. By September 1928, all ten vans were available and all carried SR livery. Allocations at this time were as follows:

Van Nos	Allocation	Working	With set No
777/81/2	Horsham	One to Three Bridges, Redhill, Guildford and Brighton	993
		One to Three Bridges, Guildford and Bognor	987
		One to Guildford, Chichester, Midhurst and Three Bridges	756
779, 876,	Littlehampton	One to Ford, Arundel, Chichester and Three Bridges	988
903		One to Ford, Pulborough and Chichester	737
		One to Ford, Bognor and Arundel only	759
810	Cranleigh	To Guildford, Horsham and Billingshurst	981
816	Seaford	To Lewes, Brighton and Horsted Keynes	982
887	Bognor	To Barnham, Chichester, Midhurst and Horsham	736
890	Brighton	To Haywards Heath, Seaford and Horsted Keynes	738

Plate 173 LBSCR air-control van No 782, to diagram 901, seen at Horsham on 18 August 1935, coupled to a 'Balloon' set.
L. E. Brailsford

After 1927, the side lookouts were steadily removed (following a side-swipe in Lewes Tunnel), while in 1929/30 vacuum brakes were provided in lieu of Westinghouse — both these modifications being generally applied to all LBSCR vehicles, not just to the pull-push stock. Van No 779 was damaged in an accident at Lewes in May 1930 and withdrawn (so clearly was not on its 1928 booked working by then), van

No 889 being substituted in August 1930. However, the September 1931 carriage working notices still give the same allocations as 1928 — even if many of the pull-push sets themselves had been changed around. By January 1935 the position was as below (this also demonstrates how often the pull-push sets were swapped about):

Van Nos	Allocation	Working	With set No
777	Horsham	To Dorking North and Three Bridges	739
781	Horsham	To Three Bridges and Guildford	740
782	Horsham	To Three Bridges, Redhill, Brighton and Dorking North	752
810	Cranleigh	To Guildford, Horsham, Three Bridges and Dorking North	753
816	Bognor	To Barnham, Worthing and Emsworth	735
876	Littlehampton	To Chichester, Arundel, Pulborough and Midhurst	988
887	Littlehampton	To Worthing only	742
889	Littlehampton	To Worthing, Arundel and Ford	737
890	Bognor	To Portsmouth, Horsham, Three Bridges and Dorking North	734
903	Horsham	To Guildford, Three Bridges and Dorking North	749

Plate 174 A Bognor–Horsham motor train arrives at Ford behind 'D1' tank No 2221, early in 1938 (the conductor rails for the mid-Sussex electrification are already in position). The train is formed of a diagram 901 air-control van and a 'Balloon' pull-push set, with a 'Balloon' nine-compartment third to SR diagram 70 on the rear. Only two of these were air-piped (SR Nos 2179/80) and both were still officially formed in sets 733/8 at this time, so the identity of this coach remains a mystery. *D. H. Wakely*

Van No 903 was to SR diagram 902, the rest were to diagram 901 although this distinction was of no concern to the operating department. As may be seen, some allocations remained constant but many of the duties themselves had changed considerably since 1928; almost certainly brought about by the spread of electrification. Withdrawal began with vans Nos 782 and 876 during 1936 and was completed in mid-1940 when Nos 887/90 were taken out of service. The final survivors ran mostly on Guildford–Horsham–Brighton services.

In 1939 it was decided that just five more modern replacements were needed and ex-SECR 'utility' vans Nos 2001-5 were earmarked for fitting with air control pipe work. Unlike the LBSCR vehicles, these were plain luggage vans without any accommodation for the guard. Van No 2003 could not be traced in time for the work to be completed and no 1996 was substituted in August 1939. These five were originally allocated as follows:-

Van Nos	Allocation	Working
1996	South Eastern Section	Tonbridge–Paddock Wood–Maidstone West
2001	Central Section	Brighton–Horsham–Guildford
2002	Central Section	Cranleigh–Guildford–Horsham–Brighton*
2004	South Western Section	Bournemouth–Ringwood–Brockenhurst
2005	South Eastern Section	Sevenoaks–Paddock Wood–Maidstone West

*This duty later commenced and finished at Horsham instead of Cranleigh.

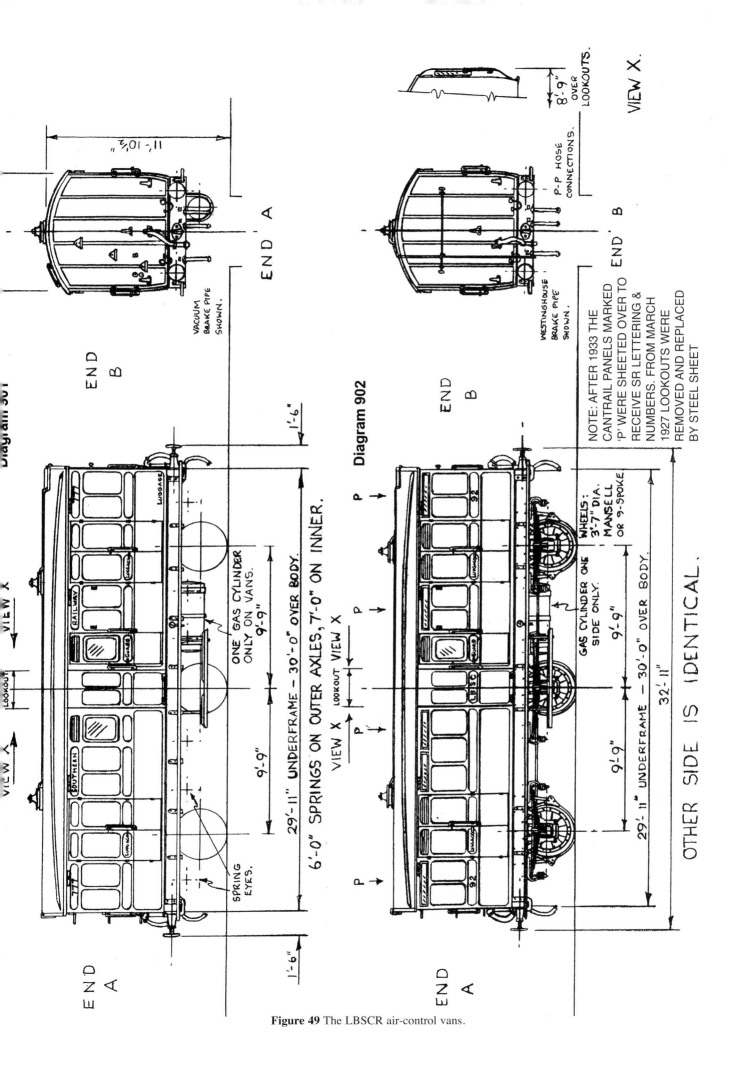

Figure 49 The LBSCR air-control vans.

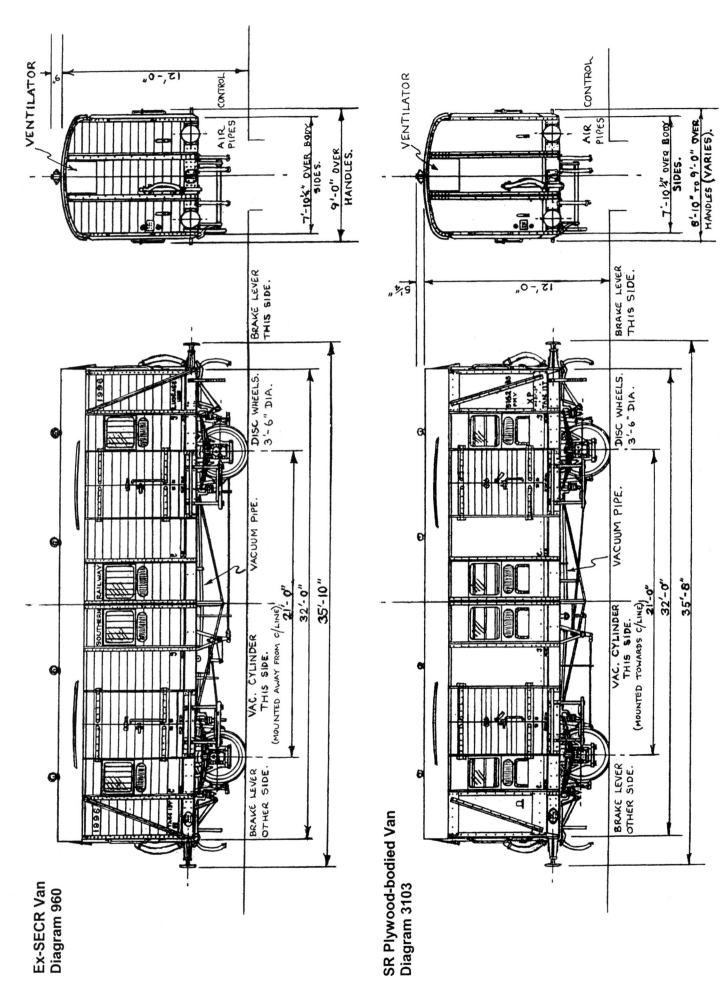

Figure 50 The SECR/SR air-control vans.

Plate 175 'D1' class tank No 2605 heads a Tunbridge Wells West–Eastbourne pull-push train near Rotherfield in 1939, formed of an SECR air-control van and a 'Balloon' set. *S. Oborne*

Plate 176 SECR air-control van No 2002 at Tonbridge on a Maidstone West service in September 1949, coupled between an 'H' class tank and LBSCR set 730, seen previously in Plate 112. *K. G. Carr*

Apart from van No 2004, which deserted the South Western section for South Eastern lines between 1946 and 1955, the duties remained remarkably constant, although individual vans were moved about. Withdrawal finally came between September and December 1962 — long after all the other former SECR vans had entered departmental service. The air-control equipment was refitted to five BR-built plywood-bodied vans

(Nos 1621-5) between November 1962 and March 1963, but by then only the Bournemouth–Brockenhurst services required the provision — mainly for the conveyance of prams — and it seems likely that not all five were actually used for the purpose. The pull-push gear was finally removed in late 1964 and the vans were returned to ordinary traffic.

Table 12 gives details of the 'air-control vans'.

Table 12
Air Control Vans

SR Diagram	SR Nos	Relevant LBSCR NOS	Date of P-P Conversion	Dimensions L x W	Remarks
901	777/9/81/2, 810/6/76/87/90	34/7, 48/9, 180/97, 479/92/5	1924	30ft x 8ft (8ft 9in over lookouts)	Van 779 damaged at Lewes 5/30, rest withdrawn between 1936 and 1940
901	889		8/30	30ft x 8ft	Replacement for van 779
902	903	92	1924	30ft x 8ft	
960	1996, 2001/2/4/5	Ex-SECR	8/39	32ft x 7ft 10in	Withdrawn 9-12/62
3103	1621-5	Built by BR	11/62-3/63	32ft x 7ft 10in	Plywood body. Air pipes removed 1964

All vans were to SR route restriction 0.

Appendix 1

Memorandum of Meeting held at Grosvenor Road On Thursday, 22 November 1928

Present:	Mr C. W. Pepper	Chief Mechanical Engineer's Department
	Mr England	Locomotive Running Department
	Mr Hall	Locomotive Running Department
	Mr H. Webber	Chief Operating Superintendent's Department

Pull and Push Arrangements

The question of working services on all sections of the railway with locomotives and coaching stock fitted with Central section control gear was considered and list 'A' attached shows the number of engines which will be required to be fitted with pull and push gear to cover the existing services and several services it is anticipated will be worked shortly as pull and push workings.

So far as the Central section is concerned the present number of engines fitted will cover both the Central and Eastern section workings. The whole of these locomotives will, with the exception of one, which has already been fitted, require to be fitted with vacuum ejectors and combination valves and 45 Western section engines will have to be fitted with Westinghouse pumps and Central section pull and push gear.

The Locomotive Running Department representatives wish to record the following observations:

(i) In compiling list 'A' it has been considered that the engines recommended to be fitted with pull and push gear is the minimum figure to avoid complaint from the Operating Department as in the majority of cases delay will be caused to the services for engines to run round in the event of a pull and push engine not being available. This applies particularly to the Eastern and Western sections.

(ii) So far as the engines on the Western section are concerned it should be noted that the T1 and O2 class engines, which now work pull and push services are fitted with steam brake on the engine.

(iii) There may be some difficulty with Eastern section water cranes but this can be settled as soon as the present fitted engine and stock has been tried for Eastern section pull and push routes.

(iv) It should be noted that engines fitted with pull and push apparatus often have to work in other services and this is one of the reasons the number to be fitted has to be kept at a safe margin.

List 'B' shows the present allocation of pull and push coaching stock, which would require to be dealt with as shown in the remarks column. It should not be lost sight of that, in a good number of cases, extra vehicles, in addition to the actual pull and push stock, have to be attached to pull and push sets.

In order to transfer Central section pull and push stock to the Eastern section, rearrangement of the sets will have to take place, as the high-roof Central section stock is not suitable for working on the Eastern section.

List 'A' – Engines required for pull and push services

Western section

Service	No of Engines
Wimbledon & Streatham/Clapham Junction & Kensington	2
Weybridge & Virginia Water	2
Local services, Guildford	4
Lymington & Bishops Waltham	2
Lee-on-the-Solent & Gosport	2
Local services, Bournemouth	6
Yeovil branch	1
Seaton branch	1
Turnchapel branch	2
Spares	23
Total	**45**

These engines to be fitted with Westinghouse pumps and Central section P & P gear.

Central section

Service	No of Engines
West Croydon	2
Tunbridge Wells West	3
Horsham	8
Littlehampton	4
Bognor	2
Brighton	5
Newhaven	1
Eastbourne	4
Fratton	1
Spares	20
Total	**50**

These engines to be fitted with vacuum ejectors and combination valves.

Eastern section

Service	No of Engines
Gillingham	3
Tonbridge	1
Reading	2
Spares	5
Total	**11**

Central section engines to be fitted with vacuum ejectors and combination valves.

List 'B' – Carriage stock required for pull and push services

Western section

Set Nos	Class of Stock	Workings	Remarks
23-30	Half bogie blocks	Bournemouth district (5)	See Note 1
351-360	"	Gosport, Fareham & Alton (2)	
376-377	"	Yeovil (1-set 351)	
		Guildford, Farnham & Ascot (2)	
		Chertsey (2)	
		Swanage & Lymington (2)	
		Wimbledon & Streatham/	
		Clapham Junction & Kensington (2)	
		Spare sets (4)	
375	Low-roof bogie stock (3 coaches)	Unallocated	See Note 2
361-363	Open compartment gangway stock	Spare sets	See Note 3
364	"	Callington	
365	"	Guildford & Farnham	
366	"	Bordon branch	
367-369	"	Plymouth area	
370-371	"	Portland (but to be transferred to Midhurst-Petersfield)	
372-374	"	Bishops Waltham, Seaton & Lee-on-the-Solent	

Open gangwayed thirds 740-2 will need to be piped for pull and push working.
A total of 71 vehicles to be fitted with Central section control apparatus or pipes (order L547, dated 20/5/30 refers).
Four vehicles to diagram 12 (Nos 188, 219, 292, 497) and one to diagram 109 (No 2631) will, along with set 375,
no longer be required for pull and push working and the existing gear may be stripped.

Note 1: These sets are formed of Western section bogie block vehicles and speed restrictions apply to the running of this stock.
To overcome this and to allow complete interchangeability between pull and push sets, the bogies will need to be altered to swing link
at the same time as the control alterations are made.

Note 2: These three vehicles (Nos 2626, 163, 6406) are now working as an ordinary train and the pull and push gear may be stripped.
This stock is old and will be withdrawn during the next year or two.

Note 3: These sets were specially built or converted for pull and push work and are still required for these services.

Eastern section

Set Nos	Class of Stock	Workings	Remarks
649, 650,	Six-wheeled stock	Otford & Sevenoaks,	See Note 4
651, 653,	"	Dartford & Gillingham/	
677	"	Swanley & Gravesend West St.	
732-733	Bogie compartment stock	Ash, Aldershot, Farnham/ Ash & Reading services	See Note 5
481-482	Open compartment gangwayed stock	Isle of Wight, returned to mainland to replace 6 & 4 wheeled stock at Hundred of Hoo	See Note 6

A total of eight vehicles will require modification for pull and push working.

Note 4: These six-wheeled sets, renovated for two years, are due for withdrawal at the end of 1929. After providing for four additional
P & P services in the Dorking-Horsham area and the necessary spares on the Central section, it is proposed that six 2-coach Central
section sets could be transferred to replace this stock. These vehicles will require the provision of vacuum brakes.
Note 5: These vehicles are still suitable for pull and push work and will require fitting with air-control pipe work (to be dealt with
along with Western section stock).
Note 6: This stock has already been fitted with air control, but requires fitting with vacuum brakes, for which purpose order L259
(issued 6/27) will be amended and reissued (done on 24/6/29).

Central section

Set Nos	Class of Stock	Workings	Remarks
736	Third brake-open	Bognor	See Note 7
737	compartment	Littlehampton	
738, 748	elliptical-roof stock.	Brighton	
739, 750	Composite or third-	Brighton (spare sets)	
740-7, 749	ordinary compartment	Spare sets	
979	low roof stock, non-	Brighton (all third)	
980	gangwayed.	Spare set (all third)	
751	Ordinary compartment	Polegate	See Note 8
752	stock, non-gangwayed,	Brighton (spare)	
753	low roof.	Brighton	
754	,,	Eastern Section, on trials.	
755	,,	Spare	
756, 757	,,	Horsham	
758	,,	Eastbourne (spare)	
759	,,	Littlehampton	
760	,,	Tunbridge Wells West	
981	Side corridor stock,	Cranleigh	See Note 8
982	gangwayed one end,	Seaford	
983, 990, 994	low roof.	Eastbourne	
985	,,	Bognor	
984, 986, 991	,,	Tunbridge Wells West	
987, 993	,,	Horsham	
988	,,	Littlehampton	
989, 995, 997	,,	Brighton	
992	,,	Hastings	
996, 998	,,	West Croydon	
999	,,	Portsmouth	
777, 781, 782	Six wheeled Guards' Vans	Horsham	See Note 9
779, 876, 903	,,	Littlehampton	
810	,,	Cranleigh	
816	,,	Seaford	
887	,,	Bognor	
890	,,	Brighton	

A total of 92 coaches (14 for the Eastern section, 78 for the Central section) to be fitted with vacuum brakes and vacuum release valves in the driving compartments (order L456, dated 8/5/29 refers).

Note 7: It will be necessary for the Traffic Department to change round a number of the spare sets in these workings to other workings on the Central section as they are not suitable for working on the Eastern section owing to the elliptical roofs. The coaches will require fitting with vacuum brake and vacuum release valves for operating the brakes in the driving compartment.

Note 8: Coaches will require fitting with vacuum brake and vacuum release valves for operating the brakes in the driving compartment.

Note 9: These 'air-control vans' will only require the provision of vacuum brakes. (Van no 779 was withdrawn following accident damage at Lewes in May 1930 and no 889 was substituted in August 1930).

Footnote

Subsequent meetings recorded progress between April 1929 and early 1931. The programme was varied somewhat from that originally proposed, as ex-LSWR open stock sets 361-66/70/71 were omitted and replaced by eight further bogie 'block' sets (Nos 22, 350/78-80, 731, 977/78), as the decision was taken to restrict the open stock to the South Western section. Several of the LSWR bogie 'block' sets were sent to the Eastern section in lieu of the planned transfer of LBSCR low-roof sets. A final memo, stating that all works had been completed and were proving entirely satisfactory in service, was issued and signed by R. E. L. Maunsell on 29 December 1931.

Source: H.O. File 52068 – Pull and Push Trains, courtesy R. C. Riley.

Appendix 2

Railmotor and Railcar Halts

All three main Southern pre-Grouping constituent companies opened small unstaffed halts coincident on the introduction of steam railmotors, petrol railcars and/or pull-push trains. Some of these had only a brief life while others were later rebuilt into something a little more substantial – some were later renamed. A few continue to serve the present railway network in the 21st century.

Name	Situated between	Date opened	Company
Albert Road Bridge	Fratton and East Southsea	1 July 1904	LSWR/LBSCR
Albert Road Halt	Ford and Devonport	1 Nov 1906	LSWR
Bandon Halt	Waddon and Wallington	11 June 1906	LBSCR
Bedhampton Halt	Havant and Fratton	1 April 1906	LBSCR
Beeches Halt	Wallington and Sutton	11 June 1906	LBSCR
Beltring & Branbridge Halt	Paddock Wood and Yalding	1 Sept 1909	SECR
Beluncle Halt	Sharnal St and Port Victoria	July 1906	SECR
Bingham Road	Woodside and Coombe Lane	1 Sept 1906	LBSCR/SECR
Brambledown Halt	Queenborough and Leysdown	March 1905	SECR
Bungalow Town Halt	Shoreham and Lancing	1 Oct 1910	LBSCR
Camel's Head Halt	St Budeaux and Ford	1 Nov 1906	LSWR
Cheriton Halt	Sandling Jcn and Shorncliffe	1 May 1908	SECR
Chevening Halt	Dunton Green and Brasted	16 April 1906	SECR
Clyst St Mary & Digby Halt	Exmouth Jcn and Topsham	31 May 1908	LSWR
Collington Wood Halt	Pevensey and Bexhill	3 Sept 1905	LBSCR
Cooden Halt	Pevensey and Bexhill	11 Sept 1905	LBSCR
Denton Halt	Gravesend Central and Hoo Jcn	July 1906	SECR
Doleham Halt	Ore and Winchelsea	1 July 1907	SECR
Dunmere Halt	Wadebridge and Bodmin	2 July 1906	LSWR
Durley Halt	Botley and Bishops Waltham	23 Dec 1909	LSWR
Dyke Junction Halt	Hove and Portslade	3 Sept 1905	LBSCR
East Malling Halt	Malling and Barming	cFeb 1913	SECR
Ebbsfleet & Cliffsend Halt	Ramsgate and Minster	1 May 1908	SECR
Elmore Halt	Fort Brockhurst and Lee-on-the-Solent	11 April 1910	LSWR
Farlington Halt	Havant and Fratton	9 July 1928	SR
Fishbourne Halt	Chichester and Bosham	1 April 1906	LBSCR
Fishersgate Halt	Portslade and Southwick	15 Sept 1905	LBSCR
Glyne Gap Halt	Bexhill and St Leonards	3 Sept 1905	LBSCR
Grain Crossing Halt	Sharnal St and Port Victoria	July 1906	SECR
Grogley Halt	Wadebridge and Bodmin	2 July 1906	LSWR
Guestling Halt±	Ore and Winchelsea	1 July 1907	SECR
Ham Bridge Halt	Lancing and Worthing	3 Sept 1905	LBSCR
Hartington Road Halt	Lewes Road and Kemp Town	1 Jan 1906	LBSCR
Harty Road Halt	Queenborough and Leysdown	March 1905	SECR
High Halstow Halt	Cliffe and Sharnal St	July 1906	SECR
High Rocks Halt	Tunbridge Wells and Groombridge	1 June 1907	LBSCR
Holland Road Halt	Brighton and Hove	3 Sept 1905	LBSCR
Hurst Green Halt	Oxted and Hurst Green Jcn	1 June 1907	LBSCR
Ifield Halt*	Crawley and Faygate	1 June 1907	LBSCR
Jesse Road Bridge	Fratton and East Southsea	1 July 1904	LSWR/LBSCR
Kingsley Halt	Bentley and Bordon	7 March 1906	LSWR
Leigh (Lyghe) Halt	Tonbridge and Penshurst	1 Sept 1911	SECR
Lions Holt Halt	Exeter and Exmouth Jcn	26 Jan 1906	LSWR
Lipson Vale Halt	Plymouth Nth Rd and Friary	1 June 1904	LSWR
Littlehaven Halt	Faygate and Horsham	1 June 1907	LBSCR
Longfield Halt	Farningham Rd and Southfleet	1 July 1913	SECR
Lucas Terrace Halt	Plymouth Friary and Plymstock	1 June 1905	LSWR

Lyminster Halt	Angmering and Ford Jcn	1 Aug 1907	LBSCR
Melcombe Regis	Weymouth and Portland	30 May 1909	LSWR/GWR
Meyrick Park Halt	Bournemouth Central and West	1 March 1906	LSWR
Middle Stoke Halt	Sharnal St and Port Victoria	July 1906	SECR
Milton Range Halt	Gravesend Central and Hoo Jcn	July 1906	SECR
Milton Road Halt	Gravesend Central and Hoo Jcn	July 1906	SECR
Monks Lane Halt	Hurst Green and Edenbridge Town	1 July 1907	LBSCR
Mount Pleasant Road Halt	Exeter and Exmouth Jcn	26 Jan 1906	LSWR
Nanstallon Halt	Wadebridge and Bodmin	2 July 1906	LSWR
Normans Bay Halt	Pevensey and Bexhill	11 Sept 1905	LBSCR
Nutbourne Halt	Bosham and Emsworth	1 April 1906	LBSCR
Pevensey Bay Halt	Pevensey and Bexhill	11 Sept 1905	LBSCR
Polsloe Bridge Halt	Exmouth Jcn and Topsham	31 May 1908	LSWR
Roffey Road Halt	Faygate and Horsham	1 June 1907	LBSCR
Roundball Halt	Honiton and Sidmouth Jcn	22 Sept 1906	LSWR
Rowan Halt	Hove and The Dyke	18 Dec 1933	SR
Salfords Halt	Earlswood and Horley	8 Oct 1915	LBSCR
Sandhurst Halt	Blackwater and Wokingham	May 1909	SECR
Sindlesham Halt	Wokingham and Earley	1 Jan 1910	SECR
Snailham Halt	Ore and Winchelsea	1 July 1907	SECR
Snowdown Halt	Shepherdswell and Adisham	1 Jan 1914	SECR
Southbourne Halt	Bosham and Emsworth	1 April 1906	LBSCR
Southease & Rodmell Halt	Lewes and Newhaven	1 Sept 1906	LBSCR
Spencer Road Halt	Coombe Lane and Selsdon Rd	1 Sept 1906	LBSCR/SECR
Stoke Crossing Halt	Sharnal St and Port Victoria	July 1906	SECR
Stone Cross Halt	Stone Cross Jcn and Pevensey	11 Sept 1905	LBSCR
Stone Crossing Halt	Dartford and Northfleet	2 Nov 1908	SECR
Stonehall & Lydden Halt	Shepherdswell and Kearsney	1 Nov 1914	SECR
Swanscombe Halt	Dartford and Northfleet	2 Nov 1908	SECR
Teston Crossing Halt	E Farleigh and Wateringbury	1 Sept 1909	SECR
Three Oaks Bridge Halt±	Ore and Winchlesea	1 July 1907	SECR
Uralite Halt#	Hoo Jcn and Cliffe	July 1906	SECR
Warblington Halt	Emsworth and Havant	1 Nov 1907	LBSCR
Warren Halt	Folkestone Jcn and Dover	1 June 1908	SECR
Westham Halt	Weymouth and Portland	1 July 1909	LSWR/GWR
Weston Mill Halt	St Budeaux and Ford	1 Nov 1906	LSWR
Whipton Bridge Halt	Pinhoe and Exmouth Jcn	26 Jan 1906	LSWR
Wyke Regis Halt	Weymouth and Portland	1 July 1909	LSWR/GWR

*Name changed to Lyons Holt Halt on 6 July 1907.

#Was a private station prior to this date.

±Opened as Three Oaks & Guestling Halt, one halt serving both locations.

Appendix 3

Summary of Southern Railway Pull-Push Sets

Set Nos	Vehicle Type	Dates	Remarks	Chapter
1-6	LSWR Non-Corridor	1937-1962	Inc some SECR stock later	6
22-30	LSWR Bogie Block	1926-1939		5
31-36	LSWR Non-Corridor	1939-1960	Inc one SECR coach later	6
37	SECR Non-Corridor	1941-1960	One LSWR, later LBSCR coach	12
350-360	LSWR Bogie Block	1915-1940	Inc LSWR sets 1P-10P	5
361-366	LSWR Ex-Railmotor	1919-1931	Ex-LSWR sets 11P-16P	4
363	LSWR Vestibule	1933-1958	Ex-set 372 in 1933	4
367-369	LSWR Vestibule (3rd)	1906-1940	Plymouth area sets	4
370-371	LSWR Vestibule	1909-1931	Portland area sets	4
372-374	LSWR Vestibule	1914-1960	Set 372 reno'd 363 in 1933	4
375	LSWR Non-Corridor	1914-1931	Arc-roofed set	6
376-380	LSWR Bogie Block	1927-1939		5
381-385	LSWR Corridor	1948-1962	Ironclad stock	7
481-482	SECR Ex-Railmotor	1930-1960	On IoW before 1930, not P-P	11
483-484	LCDR 4-Wheel	1924-1938	On IoW	10
503/505	LBSCR Arc-Roof	1938-1955	On IoW, ex-sets 731 & 728	9
504	LBSCR Arc-Roof	1937-1958	Ex-set 999/980	9
513-514	SECR Ex-Railmotor	1924-1959	Articulated, not P-P fitted	11
600-619	SR Maunsell	1959-1964		13
649-654/677	SER/LCDR 6-Wheel	1912-1930	Ex-SECR sets 267-270/3-5	10
649-651	LBSCR Arc-Roof	1931-1959	Sets 649/50 inc LSWR coach	9
652-655	LSWR Non-Corridor	1935-1962	Inc one SECR coach later	6
656-658	LSWR Non-Corridor	1937-1961	Inc one SECR coach per set	6
656	SECR Non-Corridor	1956-1962	Replacement set	12
659-663	SECR Non-Corridor	1938-1962	Sets 662/3 from 1950 onwards	12
714-731	LBSCR Arc-Roof	1937-1960	Ex sets 981-998	9
714-715	SECR Non-Corridor	1938-1961	Originally all LBSCR vehicles	12
731	LCDR 6-Wheel	1914-1926	Ex-SECR set 266, not P-P later	10
731	LSWR Bogie Block	1930-1939		5
731-739	LSWR Corridor	1943-1961	Ex-emigrant stock	7
732-733	LCDR Bogie	1912-1936	Ex-SECR sets 271/2	10
733	LBSCR Balloon (3rd)	1937-1942	Ex set 979	8
734-735	LBSCR Balloon	1934-1941	Compartment stock	8
736-750	LBSCR Balloon	1905-1943	In sets from 1923 only	8
751-760	LBSCR Arc-Roof	1909-1959	In sets from 1924 only	9
977-978	LSWR Bogie Block	1930-1938	Not close-coupled	5
979-980	LBSCR Balloon (3rd)	1905-1937	In sets from 1923 only	8
980	LBSCR Arc-Roof	1937	Ex set 999, later set 504	9
981-999	LBSCR Arc-Roof	1911-1937	Later sets 714-731 & 980	9
Air control Vans	LBSCR, SECR, SR	1924-1964		14

Total stock 170 sets, although maximum stock at any one time did not exceed 96 units.

Plate 177 'M7' No 30051 with the Railway Enthusiast Club's 'Compass Rose' rail tour at Farnborough on 5 October 1957. *R. C. Riley*